THE **SLOW FOOD** GUIDE TO
CHICAGO

ABOUT SLOW FOOD

Slow Food is an international movement, founded in Italy in 1986. Today it has some seventy thousand members in more than forty-five countries. Slow Food is dedicated to preserving regional cuisines and food traditions worldwide. In addition the organization advocates biodiversity, taste education, conviviality, and the pleasures of the table.

Participants in the Slow Food movement are committed to finding alternatives to the standardization of the world's tastes while promoting local, seasonal foods and "virtuous globalization." Through its publications, events, and Web site (www.slowfood.com) Slow Food provides the information members need to support its mission.

About Slow Food USA

Slow Food USA is a nonprofit organization that oversees the activities of its more than 12,500 members and 150 local chapters, or convivia. Each convivium advocates sustainability and biodiversity through educational events and public outreach that encourage the enjoyment of pure foods that are local, seasonal, and organically grown. Slow Food USA and its members also work to identify and promote artisans who grow, produce, market, prepare, and serve wholesome food.

About This Guide

The Slow Food Guide to Chicago is the second in a series of guidebooks focusing on major cities or regions of North America and celebrating traditional, typical, or innovative foods, producers, restaurants, or other businesses that exemplify Slow Food principles. We welcome any comments, corrections, or nominations from readers for future editions of this guide.

For more information about membership or the activities and programs of Slow Food USA, go to the national Web site (www.slowfoodusa.org).

THE **SLOW FOOD** GUIDE TO
CHICAGO
RESTAURANTS, MARKETS, BARS

KELLY GIBSON AND
PORTIA BELLOC LOWNDES
WITH SLOW FOOD CHICAGO

CONTRIBUTING EDITORS
Amy Cook
Melissa Graham
Janine MacLachlan
Joel Smith

SERIES EDITORS
Patrick Martins and Ben Watson

Chelsea Green Publishing
WHITE RIVER JUNCTION, VERMONT

Managing Editor: Collette Leonard
Project Editor: Marcy Brant
Copy Editor: Robin Catalano
Proofreader: Eric Raetz
Indexer: Sue DuBois

Photographs by Joe DeNatale.
Photographs copyright © 2003.

Book design by Peter Holm, Sterling Hill Productions.

Printed in Canada on recycled paper.

First printing, September 2004.

Library of Congress Cataloging-in-Publication Data
Gibson, Kelly.
The Slow Food guide to Chicago : restaurants, markets, bars / Kelly Gibson and
Portia Belloc Lowndes.
p. cm. —(Slow Food guides)
Includes index.
ISBN 1-931498-61-X (pbk.)
1. Restaurants—Illinois—Chicago—Guidebooks. 2. Grocery
trade—Illinois—Chicago—Guidebooks. I. Lowndes, Portia Belloc. II. Slow
Food Movement III. Title.
TX907.3.I32C454 2004
647.95773'11—dc22
                                    2004011130

Chelsea Green Publishing
P.O. Box 428
White River Junction, VT 05001
(800) 639-4099
www.chelseagreen.com

To all the people who have helped make Chicago more sustainable: farmers, chefs, and—most importantly—enlightened consumers.

THE SLOW FOOD GUIDE TO CHICAGO

Kelly Gibson and Portia Belloc Lowndes

Contributing Editors

Amy Cook	Janine MacLachlan
Melissa Graham	Joel Smith

Contributors

Elysabeth Alfano	Michael Graham	Julie Pallotta
Dana Altman	Kristine Greiber	Lynn Peemoeller
Corinne Aoyogi	Greg Hall	Alice Phillips
Shauna Babcock	Erik M. Hill	Will Phillpot
Paul Baker	Matthew Hohmann	Jennifer Quirke
Bret Beall	Fred Hunter	Diane Redding
Tracy Boutelle	Maggie Kast	Roger Rhodes
Nancy Burhop	Courtney Knapp	Sue Rhodes
Lew Check	Catherine Lambrecht	Grisela Rodriguez
Ann Cherek	Barbara LeBuhn	Maria Santonato
Chris Cherek	Marjorie Leventry	Gary Snyderman
Cari Cridler	Mark Linsner	Anna Sobor
Jessica Davis	Charlie Belloc	Leslie Swibes
Elizabeth Donovan	Lowndes	Emma Tassares
Peter Engler	Lydia Marchuk	China Tresemer
Renee Enna	Mel Markon	Josh Westlund
Eric Fidler	Maureen Moynihan	Marc Witham
Jameson Fink	Carol Muller	Gary Wiviott
Kelly Flynn	Dick Mulvihill	Joann Yocum Hutto
Kurt Friese	Gina Onesto	Laura Zimmerman
Rob Gardiner	Bob Pallotta	

Special thanks to Bays English Muffins

CONTENTS

SLOW FOOD PROGRAMS

Slow Food's local chapters, in the United States and internationally, are working to support a number of important initiatives, including the following programs.

The Ark of Taste and Presidia
The Slow Food Ark of Taste aims to rediscover, catalog, describe, and publicize foods that are threatened and in danger of disappearing due to industrial agriculture and large-scale distribution systems, environmental damage, loss of genetic diversity, overzealous hygiene laws, and the standardization of taste.

The Ark provides a specific, case-by-case study of why these traditional foods matter. Information on products included in the Ark of Taste is provided to researchers and the media, and promoted through Slow Food publications and Web sites. Internationally, the Ark currently contains more than 750 products, while in the United States the American Ark has "boarded" around 50 rare foods—ranging from the New Hampshire chicken to the Olympia oyster of Puget Sound.

Presidia are active projects coordinated by Slow Food to increase the visibility of marginalized small-scale producers. Most Presidia products are selected from among Ark products based on their taste quality, risk of extinction, and potential for development. With the formation of a presidium, Slow Food works with producers to stabilize production techniques, establish stringent production standards, and promote local consumption. The Presidia raise the profile of these ancient crafts and have created a model for making traditional food production economically viable in this age of globalization.

There are now more than 250 Presidia projects worldwide, ranging from Canadian Red Fife wheat to American raw-milk cheeses and Criollo corn from the highlands of Chiapas, Mexico.

For more information on the Ark and Presidia, visit the site of the Slow Food Foundation for Biodiversity at www.slowfoodfoundation.com.

—Anya Fernald
Program Director
Slow Food Foundation for Biodiversity

The Slow Food USA Ark/Presidia Committee (APC) was created to fight for biological and cultural diversity in our nation's farm and food sectors. We are committed to the viability of America's small farms and support food producers who stand in opposition to the industrial agriculture that has consumed our countryside. Since 1900 the United States has lost 93 percent of its genetic diversity in terms of crop varieties, and only 30 crop plants currently provide 95 percent of human nutrition worldwide. In the year 2000, 85 percent of America's cropland was devoted to only four crops: corn, soybeans, wheat, and hay. Only wheat is remotely close to what we would call food; all the rest go to feed livestock largely raised in containment facilities, or are shipped to food factories, only to reappear in soft drinks and highly processed foodstuffs.

None of this is inevitable, and the APC aims to prevent these tragic and unnecessary losses, which make our world a poorer place—less sustainable and certainly less interesting. Over the next few years, the APC intends to "board" a minimum of five hundred products on the American Ark of Taste and start a minimum of twenty Presidia projects across the United States. For more information on American Ark products and on how you can help identify them, go to the Slow Food USA Web site (www.slowfoodusa.org).

—Todd Wickstrom
Chair
Slow Food USA Ark/Presidia Committee (APC)

The Slow Food in Schools Project
Slow Food in Schools (SFIS) is a project designed to teach children about the importance of traceability in the food supply. Through the creation of more than thirty school gardens and a curriculum for teachers, Slow Food supports the education of our youngest generation on the value of eating locally and seasonally.

Following our mission as an eco-gastronomic organization, we believe that the school lunch program needs to be recognized as a vehicle for revolutionizing the way children eat and live. If every school were to adopt a healthier means of engaging the way food is prepared and served, children would be able to develop a lifelong appreciation for fresh, wholesome meals and the sustainable ways in which they are grown or produced.

Slow Food International's Vice President, Alice Waters, states, "A Slow School education is an opportunity that should be universally available—the more so because kids aren't eating at home with their families anymore. Our most democratic institution, the public school system, now has an obligation to feed our children in a civilized way around a table.

And students should be asked to participate—not just as a practical life exercise, but as a way of putting beauty and meaning into their lives."

Slow Food USA, through its Education Committee, has worked toward this goal in many ways, from developing gardens in schools and communities across the country to sponsoring SFIS each year and developing food-centered curricula to implement in schools. Local convivia are laying the groundwork for a national movement that will reshape a child's relationship to food and to the land. From Arizona to New York, leaders throughout the country have established innovative projects that inspire schools to see the transforming influence a lesson can have on, say, tasting a tomato in season or preparing a simple meal.

In 2004 Slow Food USA sponsored two fully integrated garden-to-table projects at schools in Waimea, Hawaii, and Ojai, California, that will change the way children come to the table and share in conviviality. By building on these projects and creating strong models, we can begin to make a powerful statement that will work toward our goal of establishing lunch as an academic course. Through our grassroots efforts, we are laying the foundation for a national-level policy shift to make all public school students become involved in the food they eat.

—Cerise Mayo
Slow Food USA

INTRODUCTION

Chicago is widely known as America's "Second City," and that name suits it, to a degree. With only 3 million people, its population is much smaller than that of New York City (though if you add in all 262 of its suburbs, both the greater Chicagoland area and the Big Apple's five boroughs have roughly 8 million residents). Yet in many important respects Chicago takes a back seat to no one. It is the home of both the Blues and of the busiest airport in the world (O'Hare International). The first skyscraper was built here back in 1885, an engineering feat that changed the face of urban architecture. Chicago somehow manages to be both quintessentially modern and yet deeply anchored in tradition. In many ways it's the most American of cities.

Chicago's uniquely central location—the gateway between East and West, at the southern tip of the Great Lakes—has always made it the physical and cultural crossroads of our nation. And this is more than a mere rhetorical flourish. Chicago's first "European" settler was actually an African-American named Jean Baptiste Point du Sable, who came from Haiti, married a Native American woman, and in 1779 built his home just east of the present-day Michigan Avenue bridge. Cultural diversity? It's old hat to us in Chicago. Poles, Irish, Greeks, Germans, Chinese, Italians, Ukrainians, Swedes, Vietnamese, Indians, Thais, and Spanish-speaking peoples of all nations have come here over the years, along with many other immigrants. Some passed through, while others stayed and put down roots, weaving their cultures (and especially their food traditions) into the fabric of the city. And although neighborhoods, here as everywhere, have changed and evolved over the years, there remains a strong sense of community pride and cultural identity within many of the city's ethnic enclaves. There are still restaurants and shops with artisans who practice their craft in much the same way their parents and grandparents did, both here and in the old country. Walking down certain blocks in the city, it's easy to imagine yourself traveling in a foreign land.

Food is one thing we all have in common. It connects us to our past, to the land, and to a community—even if it isn't one's own community. The making and sharing of food can help to break down linguistic and cultural barriers and create new and complex relationships. In the course of researching and writing this book, we met chefs, proprietors, and even counter staff who were eager to talk about the food they were preparing and serving. From Chicago's finest restaurants to the humblest taquerias and lunch trucks, people who really care about food took pride and pleasure in sharing something more profound than a mere financial transaction. These people embody important aspects of the Slow Food philosophy—through their everyday work they celebrate and defend culture, common pleasure, and conviviality.

Once extolled by poet Carl Sandburg as "Hog Butcher for the World" and "Stacker of Wheat," Chicago has its origins in agriculture, and was famous both for its stockyards and as a major grain-shipping port. Even today, in the canyons created by decades of architectural one-upmanship, and in residential neighborhoods throughout the city, there is a renewed appreciation for organic and sustainably grown regional produce. From the many new farmers' markets sprouting up everywhere to the menus of the city's top-end restaurants, this trend toward fresh, seasonal, and local food involves far more than mere nostalgia for our agricultural roots. It offers city-dwellers a sense of excitement, discovery, and community, and a way to re-engage with the food they buy and eat on a very personal level—something that is sadly lacking when we shop only at the supermarket.

The publication of this book is only the latest effort in Slow Food's ongoing mission, to identify and promote our world's food traditions and the honest pleasures of the table. With 150 convivia (chapters) in the United States alone, Slow Food remains steadfastly committed to bringing the concept of eco-gastronomy to food lovers everywhere. While this guide does not claim to be perfect (none is), we hope that it will prove a helpful resource for locals and visitors alike, and that readers will send in their comments and suggestions for consideration and possible use in future editions.

The Slow Food Guide to Chicago is the work of many Slow Food members and like-minded food lovers, who were eager not only to share their knowledge and experiences, but also to shine a spotlight on the places in our city that best exemplify Slow Food's ideals. It was truly a labor of love, and we wish to thank them all for their energetic, thorough, and dedicated approach to the assignment. The next time you enjoy an excellent meal in Chicago, raise a glass in their honor. Or better yet, invite them along.

—Kelly Gibson and Portia Belloc Lowndes

KEY TO SYMBOLS USED IN THIS BOOK

Prices

$ = average entrée or main course costs less than $10
$$ = average entrée or main course costs between $10 and $20
$$$ = average entrée or main course costs between $20 and $30
$$$$ = average entrée or main course costs more than $30

All price symbols are approximations made for comparison's sake only.

Neighborhoods and Suburbs

Neighborhoods within the city limits of Chicago appear in **boldface** type, above the street address at the head of each listing. Names of suburbs are set in ***boldface italics*** and appear below the street adress.

In this book we have designated with the icon of the snail (the Slow Food mascot) those establishments that go above and beyond in their support of the concepts of sustainability and biodiversity, from the producers they buy from through the foods they prepare and sell.

When appropriate, we have also included any special or unusual information in the entries (for instance, "Cash only," "BYOB," or "Closed Monday").

Finally, we have added a "Notable" section of brief listings at the end of most sections. Think of these places as honorable mentions—definitely worthy of inclusion, but perhaps not yet "slow" enough or familiar enough to our reviewers to warrant a full-length entry.

THE **SLOW FOOD** GUIDE TO
CHICAGO

PART ONE

CUISINES

AFRICAN

Banadir Restaurant *(Somali)*
Edgewater
6221 North Clark Street
(773) 274-2778
$ (Cash only)

Located in a quaint space furnished with leftover furniture and paneling from the previous occupants (an Italian sandwich shop), this Somali restaurant is a real find. The people are some of the nicest you will encounter, and service is uniformly friendly, encouraging, and generous. Daily specials, plus a bargain Friday afternoon buffet, are offered.

Somali food is related to, yet different from, Ethiopian cuisine. The Somali flatbread *anjera* is thicker, denser, and less sour than the Ethiopian *injera*; at Banadir, unpuffed pita is substituted. Somali meats (chicken, beef, and goat) tend to be marinated, then grilled or roasted, and sometimes only lightly stewed. The presence of pasta dishes harks back to Italy's occupation of part of Somalia starting in 1889. The cuisine also has a strong Arabic influence, indicated by the *suqar* (stewed or sautéed beef or chicken dishes resembling Indian curries). A pitcher of homemade, all-natural (and bright orange) mixed fruit juice (mangoes, papayas, and others) is brought to each table. A variety of breakfast dishes are also available, including liver and onions.

Less-than-ideal aspects (aside from the aforementioned decor) include a corner television set (where more time is spent changing channels than actually viewing) and the use of Styrofoam plates during the buffet (though stoneware plates are used with the regular menu). However, one can usually find a number of Somali cab drivers patronizing this establishment, which is always an endorsement of the cooking.

Queen of Sheba Café *(Ethiopian)*
Edgewater
5403 North Broadway
(773) 878-2352
Closed Monday; BYOB
$-$$

Relatively new, Queen of Sheba Café features some of the most flavorful Ethiopian cuisine in the city. Each dish is meticulously prepared to order with top-quality, mostly fresh ingredients. The lamb *fit fit* is delicate, with bits of the slightly sour Ethiopian flatbread *injera* sautéed with lamb stew that is lightly spiced with cardamom, ginger, and garlic. The *siga tibs* is more robust—an abundance of beef tenderloin, onions, and fresh chiles sautéed in *nit'ir qibe* (Ethiopian spiced butter with basil, fenugreek, white cumin, and other herbs and spices); lamb and chicken *tibs* are available as well. A variety of *wats* (stews flavored with spicy *berbere* sauce) are offered, and taste "alive" rather than long-stewed, as at some other venues.

Vegetarian options are abundant and flavorful, from the *yekik alicha* (lentils simmered with green pepper, ginger, and garlic) to the *fosolia* (green beans and carrots spiced with ginger and garlic) and *ye abesha gromen* (hearty collards flavored by onion, garlic, cardamom, and ginger). The accompanying rolled *injera* pancakes are torn to serve as dining utensils, adding both extra texture and a slightly sour element to each bite.

The decor includes African baskets, wall hangings, and an unusual ceiling drape above the bar area. The colorfully embroidered white tablecloths add a touch of homeyness and elegance. Potential downsides include the television in the corner and a smoking section in the rather small restaurant (though the ventilation system is excellent). The service is exceptional.

From start to finish, Queen of Sheba is a winning Ethiopian dining experience.

NOTABLE

Addis Abeba   (*Ethiopian*)
Wrigleyville
3521 North Clark Street
(773) 929-9383
$-$$

Formerly Moulibet, this Ethiopian restaurant offers delicious food in a simply decorated environment. Flavors are robust, from the various vegetarian selections to the meat, poultry, and fish *wats* and *tibs*. The *injera* are warm, unlike at most other Ethiopian restaurants, and that warmth adds to the sensory experience of dipping into the various stews and sautéed dishes.

Parking in this busy neighborhood is difficult, so consider taking public transportation or a cab to get there.

Mama Desta's Red Sea Restaurant   (*Ethiopian*)
Lakeview
3216 North Clark Street
(773) 935-7561
$-$$

A full range of Ethiopian and Eritrean delights have been served at this Lakeview location for twenty years (a Washington, D.C., location served embassy staff for years). The decor is uninspired, with dark wood paneling

AFRICAN LUNCH TRUCKS

Chicago does not have the plethora of street vendors, carts, stands, and so forth found in other cities, but we do have lunch trucks. It's true that the vast majority ply the Loop (downtown) with such treats as Burritos as Big as Your Head and turkey sandwiches that are more of a testament to modern packaging than culinary goodness, but there are a number of gems, not the least of which are lunch trucks offering African food, mainly West African.

Although most vendors offer a slightly wider range of foods, Nigerian offerings are the most popular. *Egusi* stew, often referred to as the national dish of Nigeria, is finely chopped spinach blended with ground melon seed, dried stockfish, hot pepper, and cooked tomato over mixed—and I do mean mixed—meat. *Egusi* stew often contains bits of bone-in fish, cow's foot, cow skin, flavorful stewed goat ribs, tripe, cartilage, and small pieces of stew beef. *Fufu* (mashed cassava root) is the traditional starch accompaniment and is delicious dipped in the spicy juices. Another popular dish is *jollof* rice, which slightly resembles Louisiana jambalaya. The basic ingredients are rice cooked with stock, tomatoes, and spices, with various meats added in.

There are three areas where you are more than likely to find the African lunch trucks, as they are, obviously, mobile and travel from location to location during the course of the lunch hour. My personal favorite, Vee-Vee's, can often be found around noon on upper Columbus Drive at South Water. This is directly across from the Fairmont Hotel.

TBS's lunch truck, along with others, often stops around noon in the 800 block of North Clark Street. East of Michigan Avenue in front of Prentice Hospital in Streeterville is a hotbed of lunch truck activity, with the occasional African lunch truck sighting.

The African lunch trucks generate quite a bit of friendly interplay between the driver and the customers, who are mainly West African cabbies; it's almost as if an impromptu social club springs up wherever the drivers stop.

—*Gary Wiviott*

Bolat African Cuisine
3346 North Clark Street
(773) 665-1100

TBS African Restaurant
4507 North Sheridan Road
(773) 567-3407
8910 South Commercial Street
(773) 933-9520

Toham African Restaurant
1422 West Devon Avenue
(773) 973-4602

Vee-Vee's
6232 North Broadway
(773) 465-2424 or 465-3692

and aging tables, but you come here for the food, not the ambience. An unusual (and excellent) way to start the meal is with Mama Desta's *kitfo* (spicy Ethiopian beef tartare, rather than the lightly cooked *lub lub* style), perhaps the best in the city.

Smoking is allowed in part of the restaurant, and that could also have an impact on the overall dining experience. Parking is difficult in this neighborhood, so opt for public transportation or a cab.

Ras Dashen Ethiopian Restaurant   *(Ethiopian)*
Edgewater
5846 North Broadway
(773) 506-9601
Closed Tuesday
$-$$

Ras Dashen is one of the few Ethiopian restaurants in Chicago where the round platter of *injera* covered with various stews and vegetables is served on a round central table surrounded by comfortable wicker chairs (though more traditional tables and chairs are also available). The decor is simple but appropriate, and the service is exceptional. The family that owns and operates this restaurant goes out of its way to make your experience truly rewarding. One unique touch is the slight browning/caramelization of the onions, peppers, and meats presented in the *tibs*, contributing a deeper, more complex flavor profile than is found elsewhere. The *berbere* sauce used to flavor the *wats* is unusually complex and spicy without being overwhelming.

Service may be a bit slow here, but that's primarily because most of the food is being prepared to order.

Tizi Melloul   *(Moroccan, Mediterranean)*
River North
531 North Wells Street
(312) 670-7610 or 670-4338
$$$

Spectacular decor welcomes diners to this Mediterranean restaurant with a focus on Moroccan cuisine. The Moroccan-inspired (and round) Crescent Room is reserved for those ordering the prix fixe menu (a bargain at $30 for several courses). The main dining room is well appointed, featuring the colors of northern Africa. The chef, Ryan McCaskey, has adapted his French training to what the restaurant has termed "Mediterranean Rim" cooking; he utilizes a high proportion of organic produce, and is working to include more organic and locally grown produce in the future.

Specifically Moroccan foods are represented by lamb-based *merguez*

sausage, *harissa*-enhanced vegetables, *tagines*, and *b'steeya*. Among the Mediterranean offerings, the pan-roasted mussels are uniformly praised (deservedly so), and the roasted meats and fish are usually very well prepared.

Service varies from attentive and polite to virtually nonexistent. A variety of entertainment is offered on various evenings, from live music to belly dancing. For those interested in an introduction to Moroccan cuisine in an upscale setting, Tizi Melloul is located within easy access of Loop and downtown offices and hotels.

AMERICAN

 Blackbird
West Loop Gate
619 West Randolph Street
(312) 715-0708
Closed Sunday
$$$

"Local, seasonal, and organic have become buzzwords, but really, very few chefs are living that ideal," says Blackbird chef/partner Paul Kahan. "It's not easy. The winter menu gives me sleepless nights." But Kahan's sleeplessness is the Slow diner's dream.

Blackbird's minimalist white decor contrasts with the riot of flavors, colors, and textures that pop off the plate. Kahan not only cooks masterfully, he also approaches cooking with a flavor-focused, holistic, waste-nothing philosophy. He seeks out organically produced beef; not an easy task since organic beef is more difficult to produce than chicken or pork, and thus is harder to find and more expensive. But Kahan now has a relationship with a Minnesota co-op, and can offer organic sweetbreads on his constantly changing menu.

Soups are often puréed vegetables—parsnips when seasonally sweet, and, on one occasion, celeriac spiked with smoked salmon and brioche croutons. An appetizer *vol-au-vent*, a puff pastry cup filled with a perfect balance of earthy mushrooms, black truffles, and heirloom apple salad, made one diner wish for a full-size entrée portion. Of course, it's the details that set the best chefs apart, and Kahan is a master with the extra touch. He has an affinity for quail eggs, which he uses to punctuate an heirloom lettuce salad in a potato nest or to top wild striped bass with farro (an ancient cereal grain with a mellow, nutty flavor) and black trumpet mushrooms.

Kahan's commitment to the full cycle of meal preparation makes one want to spend time in his kitchen, picking up flavor-boosting tips. Leftover wine from unfinished bottles is poured into the vinegar vat. Meat trimmings are used in the house-made charcuterie. Throughout the seasons staff can be spotted preserving sour cherries or pickling beets, kohlrabi, shallots, and garlic. With all the preserving and pickling that goes on at Blackbird, the kitchen resembles a grandparents' farmhouse more than a stainless steel commercial space.

Elissa Narrow's desserts have impressed even the legendary Julia Child, who is said to have been delighted with Narrow's Meyer lemon cake. Others are partial to her apple charlotte made with toasted brioche, served with maple ice cream and cider-caramel sauce. A summer visit was topped off with buttermilk cake with fresh cherries and cherry sorbet drizzled with cabernet syrup.

 Charlie Trotter's
Lincoln Park
816 West Armitage Avenue
(773) 248-6228
Closed Sunday–Monday
$$$$

Charlie Trotter's legendary restaurant continues to offer innovative food with great integrity, all in an elegant and serene yet very comfortable atmosphere.

Trotter's emphasis on using the freshest and highest-quality ingredients available allows him to improvise with intricate culinary creations that change daily. He offers three degustation menus per day. Vegetables are mostly organic and are often featured rather than sidelined. Fish is line-caught. Vegetable juices, herb infusions, emulsified stocks, purées, and broths provide healthful complexity; Trotter does not rely on heavier liquids like cream.

After sixteen years in business, Trotter still aims for perfection with each dish. The menus themselves reflect his intricate attention to the customer's taste buds. From the impressive vegetable menu, an acorn squash soufflé in a pumpkinseed vinaigrette vies with the equally alluring dishes from the kitchen table menu, like Téte de Moine with Black Truffle and Savory Fruitcake. Seafood offerings from the grand menu again showcase fruits and vegetables. Here, South African langoustines with red curry partner with such diverse flavors as sunchoke, young coconut, and pomelo. I love the simplicity of buttermilk *panna cotta* contrasting with the exotic addition of carambola and preserved ginger.

Also of note are Trotter's books, which feature the exceptional photography of Tim Turner. Such titles in the series as *Charlie Trotter's Vegetables* or *The Kitchen Sessions with Charlie Trotter* celebrate the food in lush detail, complete with complementary wine suggestions and Trotter's thoughts on the sources and seasons of certain foods. Like casting a play with complex characters and many acts or assembling an orchestra capable of the finest jazz improvisation, Trotter brings all his resources to bear when it comes to filling his market basket.

 ## The Dining Room at the Ritz-Carlton
Streeterville
160 East Pearson Street
(312) 573-5223
Closed Monday–Tuesday
$$$$

The soaring ceilings of the wood-paneled Dining Room at the Ritz-Carlton are set off by crystal chandeliers with lampshades that mimic a chef's toque. Pale blue banquettes offer the perfect level of comfort for settling into the tasting menu of your choice. The staff pulls off a seamless performance, never rushing and never going too slow. But once the food arrives the atmosphere fades into the background.

The restaurant sets a high standard in the use of seasonal and local foods and emphasizes fresh Midwestern ingredients. A recent winter menu included roasted venison loin (set off with poached pears, chestnuts, and fresh pears with red currant sauce ivoire) and a memorable goose-filled ravioli in a bacon cream sauce. Vegetarians will be delighted with the tasting menu, which includes sheep's-milk ricotta gnocchi with brown butter sauce and spaghetti squash. If you're going to splurge on a dinner at the Dining Room, go all the way and let them pair the wines for each course—the wines will be approachable and chosen from an extensive list.

Even the serving staff is excited about the ingredients. During one summer visit, the server presented a platter of heirloom tomatoes "from 70th Street Farm, picked this afternoon and kissed by the sun." And while the staff answered constant questions from an enthusiastic table, a member of the Rolling Stones, in town for their latest tour, dined quietly in the opposite corner, in complete privacy.

The restaurant's famous cheese cart features twenty or so excellent cheeses from around the world, served tableside with considerable flair. Notably, there are award-winning Midwestern cheeses like Capriole goat cheese from southern Indiana, as well as Uplands Cheese Company's Pleasant Ridge Reserve and Trader Lake Cedar sheep's-milk cheese, both from Wisconsin.

Pastry chef En-Ming Hsu offers the perfect topper for the meal, serving up desserts that are wonderfully balanced and not overly sweet. The orange-lemongrass soup surrounding a coconut savarin explodes in the mouth, and a Saigon cinnamon ice cream complements a warm toffee cake topped with banana slices so thin you can practically see through them.

 **Lula Café**
Logan Square
2537 North Kedzie Avenue
(773) 489-9554
Closed Tuesday
$-$$

Ira Glass, the social anthropologist who hosts National Public Radio's *This American Life*, calls Lula Café "the kind of restaurant everyone wants in the neighborhood."

He's so right. This slower-than-Slow gem of a restaurant masquerades as a hip café in the still-gentrifying Logan Square neighborhood. The young staff sports the requisite tattoos and eyebrow piercings, and boasts about the sustainably raised meat and cinnamon-rind sheep's-milk cheese.

One unsung highlight of Lula Café is that you enjoy the same premium ingredients, many of them organic, that you'd find on the tables of Blackbird, North Pond, and the Ritz-Carlton, but at prices that won't challenge the budget. Most dinner entrées hover just below $10, with specials never over $22. Chefs/partners Amalea Tshilds and Jason

Hammel regularly shop Chicago's Green City Market, buy organic bacon and chicken from Gunthorp Farm, and give diners the option to upgrade to organic eggs. During one visit Hammel was looking forward to experimenting with fresh organic polenta, a cornmeal that's not degerminated and needs to be stored in the freezer to avoid fermentation.

Hammel and Tshilds use these well-raised ingredients as the basis for a multiethnic odyssey of a menu, which visits Asia and circles the Mediterranean from Spain all the way to North Africa. Options include a Moroccan chickpea sweet potato *tagine* with couscous, punctuated by hot Saigon cinnamon and drizzled with house-made *harissa*; a leek and goat cheese tart with watercress-anchovy salad; or a Niman Ranch pork chop with fennel gratin, Future Fruit Farm's Luscious Pear sauce, and sage. Even straightforward sandwiches like organic bacon, lettuce, and tomato or roast turkey with avocado get a flavor boost from condiments like chile aioli and delicious bread from Red Hen.

Be sure to commit to dessert, even if you haven't saved room. One seasonal favorite is an almond spice cake served with dates on a languid pool of guajillo chile chocolate ganache. Hammel says the ganache is inspired by a classic Mexican *mole*, and it has a nice gentle kick at the finish—perfectly balanced and not at all overpowering.

Breakfast is just as popular, particularly in warm weather when the outdoor café is open. Brunch specials might include custard-stuffed brioche French toast with Bing cherries and vanilla crème anglaise, or Rushing Waters rainbow trout with Yukon Gold mashed potatoes, sunny-side-up eggs, and caper rémoulade.

Naha
River North

500 North Clark Street
(312) 321-6242
Closed Sunday
$$$-$$$$

Chef/owner Carrie Nahabedian had tall boots to fill when she opened Naha in 2000 in the former location of Gordon, the legendary Gordon Sinclair's venerable eatery. Yet despite overhauling the formerly dramatic, almost over-the-top interior with clean, open spaces and minimal yet comfortable fittings, Nahabedian has honored the site's tradition of innovative and assertive food.

Nahabedian takes a very personal approach to what she puts on her menus. Reflecting her family's Armenian roots and the time she spent in California, her inspirations are seasonal produce, the weather, and her heritage. One of the most platonically perfect items on the menu is

Mother's Own Feta Cheese Filo Triangles, served on a Mediterranean Greek salad. The direct simplicity inherent in this dish is reflected in other, exquisitely executed dishes, albeit with a more sophisticated approach. Hudson Valley Foie Gras with Roasted Heirloom Apple and Quince Tarte Tatin, Green Peppercorns, and Banyuls; and Pacific Coast Halibut and Warm Organic Heirloom Potato Salad with Leeks, Crème Fraîche, and Chives, are just two of the stunners on a recent menu. A stellar list of wines by the glass or bottle yields a few enchanting surprises, as well as more familiar favorites from around the globe.

Nahabedian looks at the weather to get a feel for what her diners will be in the mood for. During a recent cold snap as only Chicago can deliver, the menu featured a cornucopia of substantial winter vegetables, including beets, braised cabbage, squash, and turnips, all paired with game or hearty meats. Organics are a preference.

Nahabedian also takes particular pleasure in sourcing exotic or unusual ingredients, such as argan and pine nut oils from a store in Paris that specializes solely in oils. The argan oil made an appearance recently with Roast Bobwhite Quail with Organic Carnaroli Risotto, Smoked Duck, and Crimson Pearl Onions. Argan oil production is supported by a Slow Food International Presidium (see p. ix). Four all-female cooperatives in Morocco husk the argan seeds and press the oil, which is deep golden yellow in color and has notes of hazelnuts and a deeply toasted flavor. The new industry provides an important income for women who often have few opportunities to work outside the home. The Presidium sustains the work of the cooperatives by seeking new markets.

In partnership with her cousin, Michael, Nahabedian has created an airy and amiable dining room that reflects her easygoing nature. Whether you come here to impress an important client, celebrate a special occasion, or just to enjoy great food and relax with friends, Naha never fails to deliver.

 **North Pond**
Lincoln Park
2610 North Cannon Drive
(773) 477-5845
Closed Monday
$$$-$$$$

While the food is the main reason to visit North Pond, the setting offers an excuse to linger. The circa-1912 building was originally a warming house for skaters on the Lincoln Park lagoon, and now the restaurant is decorated in an Arts and Crafts style that pays homage to Chicago's rich architectural heritage. The best views of the park and the downtown skyline are in the room that was formerly the outdoor patio, now enclosed in a 2002 expansion to provide all-weather seating, but sporting nine-foot windows that open to catch a late spring breeze.

Chef/partner Bruce Sherman passed the Slow Food litmus test when he was frequently spotted at Chicago's Green City Market, physically loading a truck with fresh produce destined for North Pond's kitchen. For instance, when visitors stop by for dinner during summer, they can enjoy a tartlet featuring Len Klug Farm blueberries picked the day before and purchased only that morning.

Sherman came to the stove via a circuitous route. He studied at the London School of Economics, worked in restaurant management and catering, lived in India for three years, and studied cooking in Paris. In 1999 he arrived at North Pond and has wowed Chicagoans ever since.

The five-course tasting menu is a delightful way to experience Sherman's range. Courses might include Roasted Sea Scallops with Melted Leeks, Cauliflower *Mousseline*, and Apple Emulsion, followed by Lamb with Caramelized Onion Ravioli, Broccoli Flan, and Wine Syrup. For those in the mood for more casual fare, lunchtime visitors can enjoy one of the best upscale grilled cheese sandwiches in the city, served with a baby beet salad.

A three-course brunch offers many choices, and might begin with Wild Salmon served with a Goat Cheese Terrine, followed by Smoked Pork Tenderloin with Roasted Squash, Brussels Sprouts, and Balsamic Vinegar Reduction, topped off with pumpkin and ginger ice creams, or three other tempting desserts.

Sherman is another example of chefs who consider their impact on the world outside the kitchen. He tacks a dollar charge onto each bottle of wine, which the North Pond then matches and donates to food-related nonprofit organizations (including Slow Food). He composts and recycles 90 percent of the restaurant's trash, and is active in Chefs Collaborative, a professional group dedicated to local growers, artisanal producers, and sustainable growing practices. He's currently planning to open a second restaurant focused on sustainable seafood. Sherman was named one of the best new chefs for 2003 by *Food & Wine* magazine, although Chicago cognoscenti have enjoyed his cooking for some time.

302 West
302 West State Street
Geneva
(630) 232-9302
Closed Sunday–Monday
$$$

An old bank building has been given new life by this elegant yet comfortable restaurant. The menu changes daily—a reflection of owner Catherine Findlay's commitment to using only the best available seasonal foodstuffs. They use only wild fish, and are careful to tell the diner where the fish hailed from—Atlantic halibut with Horseradish Crust, Arctic char glazed with Vermont Sharp Cheddar and Scallions, or Caribbean blue marlin in a jerk broth. But seafood is only half the story. Meat, poultry, and game lovers will be satisfied as well. Pheasant breast is stuffed with herbed sausage and served with braised Belgian endive. A fruit-and-nut wild rice cake and a lamb-and-apricot syrup reduction accompany Australian lamb loin. Venison is served with a pear-parsnip purée and a zinfandel–black pepper sauce. Chicken is Amish free-range, pork comes from Niman Ranch, and other meats are also naturally raised. Salad greens come from an organic farm in Ohio, which produces year-round in a greenhouse. During the growing season other produce comes from the Geneva Community Farm just outside of town.

The exclusively American wine list is carefully chosen. It too changes frequently, so there's always something new to try. A number of smaller, lesser-known wineries are represented, and the restaurateurs' excitement in sharing their finds shines through.

The dessert list is as long as the regular menu, and everything is made in-house from scratch. In fact, some sweets lovers have been known to come here just for dessert.

Thyme
West Town

464 North Halsted Street
(312) 226-4300
Closed Monday
$$$

To chef/owner John Bubala, the Slow Food season officially begins in April, when he goes foraging for morel mushrooms for an annual dinner he hosts with Slow Food Chicago. Bubala is clearly a chef who knows his ingredients, and he's happy to hunt them himself if necessary. In addition to his springtime morel adventures, he travels to Cape Cod in October to harvest bay scallops alongside a team of fishermen, and frequently takes his young children on farm visits to educate them about where food comes from.

Over the years Bubala has tasted countless foods and honed the skills of his palate. His signature appetizer, Giant Shrimp and Vanilla Bean *Nage* with Red Wine Syrup and Chives, features Grana Padano, an Italian cow's-milk cheese similar in style to Parmigiano-Reggiano. Once, when the cheese order arrived with a different brand, a regular customer noticed the change immediately. "When I was first starting out, I was always challenging the other chefs to come up with something different," says Bubala. "Now I know the value of honing a dish until it's just right, and then sticking with it."

Bubala also works through the seasons with his menu to take advantage of delicious ingredients as they become available. Then he prepares them simply, but with a dedication to quality. His roasted beet salad begins with several varieties of beets, roasted at 300°F in a *mirepoix* with garlic and thyme for about two hours, yielding beets that are much more flavorful than those cooked less slowly. And Bubala is just as careful with his meat. Legs of lamb hang on the premises for twenty-one days, resulting in a more earthy and aromatic flavor. Rabbit is rotisserie-roasted on a spit in a wood-burning oven—again, a simple preparation, but with the attention that makes all the difference in flavor. Bubala frequently describes his cooking as peasant food, prepared just as people have been doing for hundreds of years.

And while patrons relish the food, they also appreciate dining alfresco while listening to live jazz on the expansive 150-seat terrace surrounded by mature trees and a view of downtown. Inside the comfortable main

dining room, diners get a view of the open kitchen. And, for a grand finish, Bubala's desserts are paired with suggestions for cordials or ports, but another favorite is the French farmhouse cheeses with brioche.

 Tru
Streeterville
676 North St. Clair Street
(312) 202-0001
Closed Sunday
$$$$

"Think outside the box" is the motto at Tru, where Chef Rick Tramonto and restaurant savant Rich Melman transport the diner into an experience like an exotic fairy tale, surprising and seamless to the very end. From the synchronized service, where pouring water and clearing plates take on the elements of a well-choreographed dance, to the little velvet step stools next to each seat that keep one's evening bag close to hand, Tru does not miss a beat.

The sparse dining room is dotted with square cutouts that showcase seasonal produce, a subtle reminder of the restaurant's mission. In fact, everything at Tru is subtle, including the hushed tones and the dim lighting—everything, that is, except the food and the magnificent place settings. Unusual and delicious soups, for instance, arrive in cups that look as if they belong in a museum. At Tru food is literally elevated to

an art form. Consider the Iranian osetra caviar staircase: a glass staircase that winds its way through the colorful roe of whitefish and sturgeon, served with perfect toast points and other traditional accompaniments. Or the marinated tuna and salmon that perch upon a fishbowl with a live fighting fish swimming inside.

Yet the food at Tru is not just about presentation. There are few chefs in Chicago as devilishly innovative as Tramonto. Each emulsion, gelée, purée, sauce, and *jus* showcases the absolute essence of its perfectly fresh components. Tramonto blows convention out of the water with dishes like Chocolate Foie Gras served on Brioche French Toast with a Caramelized Banana-Chocolate sauce, yet somehow manages to remain faithful to the idea of seasonal, fresh, local, and sustainably grown ingredients. Complex vegetable combinations, ragouts, and meats are all so fantastically imagined that it is impossible to label any one a signature dish or a menu standard. There's not much repetition at Tru, except in the constant quality of the creations.

A three-course prix fixe menu is de rigueur; however, almost any combination is possible, from two- to five-course dinners to a special degustation dinner. Regardless, you will be treated as if you were the only patron in the restaurant. The wine list has something for everyone and includes half-bottles. Be prepared to spend as much time with your experience here at Tru as you would in your favorite grand restaurant in France.

Pastry chef Gale Gand excels at her end of the meal as well, with desserts as simple as Strawberry-Rhubarb Crisp and as sophisticated as Cherry Charlotte with Lemon Confit and brown sugar ice cream. She takes as much time with her ingredients and her own vision of perfection as Tramonto does with his dinner courses. And patrons never leave the restaurant empty-handed: Gand sends them off with a selection of her homemade truffles to enjoy the next morning as they relive their experience over a personalized, signed copy of the previous night's menu.

NOTABLE

Allen's—The New American Café
River North
217 West Huron Street
(312) 587-9600
Closed Sunday
$$$

Chef Allen Sternweiler's seasonally changing menu utilizes the freshest seafood, local produce, and meats, especially wild game (you'll always find venison, pheasant, or rabbit on the menu). The space is designed in a minimalist prairie style, with a wood-paneled dining room that is separated from the bar by glass doors that allow diners to see—but not hear—the scene at the bar. In the spring the outdoor dining area is exposed to a beautiful tree-lined street.

Burgundy Inn
Lincoln Park
2706 North Ashland Avenue
(773) 327-0303
$-$$

The Burgundy Inn is an Old Chicago institution holding out in a rapidly gentrifying neighborhood, where it is now sandwiched on all sides by new three-hundred-thousand-dollar cinderblock condominiums. Owner/chef Frank Scoglio and Jenny, the personable and efficient bartender, run a great bar, but an even better restaurant. The food is served in two small, 1950s-style knotty pine rooms. It's so warm and inviting that you might as well be in your grandfather's hunting cabin in the North Woods.

The soups may be reason enough to dine at the Burgundy; he makes them from scratch every day, and each one is pure, rich comfort. Prime rib is the special on Friday and Saturday nights.

Scoglio has been cooking at the Burgundy Inn for more than forty years, through all the restaurant's moves and incarnations. When asked how he learned to cook so well, Frank—now age seventy—answers, "I'm still learning how to cook."

Crofton on Wells
River North
535 North Wells Street
(312) 755-1790
Closed Sunday
$$$

Suzy Crofton has been a longtime proponent of artisanal ingredients and is well known in Chicago for her stints at a number of local restaurants. The care she takes with the menu at her serene and elegant namesake restaurant is evident. It changes seasonally, with nine entrées and about twelve appetizers, soups, and salads. The entrées showcase a variety of game, seafood, and vegan choices. The daily specials are all paired with one of nearly 150 wines Crofton personally selects for the restaurant. Desserts are matched with an appropriate wine as well.

erwin: an american café and bar
Lakeview
2925 North Halsted Street
(773) 528-7200
$$-$$$

At erwin: an american café and bar, Chef Erwin Drechsler just might greet you at the door. This hands-on chef/owner can be seen working the small but inviting dining room, showing customers to their tables, and even taking their coats. He applies the same attention to detail to his seasonal menus that feature fresh, local ingredients. The menu features old favorites with contemporary twists, a combination he calls "urban heartland cuisine." The wood-grilled hamburger with horseradish slaw and homemade pickles (one of their regulars' favorites) is a perfect example. Overall, erwin is very much a Midwestern neighborhood joint that happens to serve very inventive and thoughtful food.

Green Zebra
West Town
1460 West Chicago Avenue
(312) 243-7100
Closed Monday
$$-$$$

After making his name at Trio, then following up with his masterful focus on seafood at Spring, Green Zebra's chef-owner Shawn McClain has turned his culinary gaze to vegetables.

Green Zebra is a small modern space, decorated in leaf and soil colors that make it feel tranquil and relaxed. Small plates in tasting portions progress from light and cool dishes to warmer, fuller dishes, and range from $7 to $14 apiece; four or five of these dishes make a satisfying meal.

Preparations span the globe from Italy to India. Recent offerings have featured asparagus-avocado *panna cotta* with tomato gelée and crème fraîche foam; spicy scallion pancakes with *kim chee* and chili-garlic sauce, and a fennel risotto cake with preserved lemon and a Syrah wine reduction. Those in need of a flesh fix might try the tangerine-honey-drizzled chicken or Alaskan halibut with sunchokes and white asparagus on a bed of tandoori-spice-scented Israeli couscous. Dessert, with a tempting array of homemade ice creams, is not to be missed.

The wine list is up to the kitchen's challenge and offers crisp, refreshing whites, along with lighter reds from the United States, France, Australia, Italy, and New Zealand, including some half bottles and a dozen by-the-glass choices.

Lovitt
See Vegetarian, p. 180.

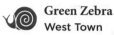 **mk Downtown**
River North
868 North Franklin Street
(312) 482-9179
$$-$$$

Many Chicagoans treasure mk as a special treat for a night out on the town. The experience starts when you enter an old brick building that sits on a quiet block just north of the gallery-filled River North neighborhood. The celebrated chef and restaurateur Michael Kornick opened mk in November 1998, with a commitment to using seasonal and regional produce whenever it's available. In some cases farmers who supplied the product are even featured on the menu.

Pastry Chef Mindy Segal aims to please with her cheeky American-themed desserts like Cake and Shake and One Banana, Two Banana. Don't expect just any old thing for Cookies; instead you'll get a plate that will satisfy both the adult and the kid in you. The dessert menu also changes with the seasons, so fruit desserts shine during the summer months.

Other Location
mk North, with a different menu, is located at
305 South Happ Road in Northfield; (847) 716-6500.

Mod
Wicker Park
1520 North Damen Avenue
(773) 252-1500
$$$

Mod is just that—futuristically modern—but also something of a paradox. Walk into the *Jetsons*-inspired space of hard, shiny, brightly hued plastic surfaces and the last thing you would expect to dine on is some of the region's best organic and seasonal ingredients prepared in an earthy, soul-satisfying manner, with a huge nod to Alice Waters. Fiddlehead ferns, morel mushrooms, and fava beans were just some of the representative items featured on the menu on a recent spring visit.

Mod offers an eclectic selection of wines by the glass, and also prepares its own fruit-infused vodkas.

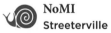
NoMI
Streeterville
Park Hyatt Chicago Hotel
800 North Michigan Avenue
(312) 239-4030
$$$$

The whole vibe at NoMI suggests ease, warmth, and refinement. The backdrop to your dining experience is a view of Michigan Avenue and the reverently lit Water Tower.

Chef Sandro Gamba's commitment has always been to buy local and seasonal ingredients. He has established strong ties to a cooperative of farmers in Wisconsin who grow specifically with him in mind. Like many chefs working under corporate-owned dictates, he fights a bureaucratic uphill battle to buy products that match his standards, but the food coming from the kitchen reflects his hard-won victories.

The menu at NoMI changes every two weeks and its offerings blend earthiness with elegance. The staff is extremely knowledgeable, yet rather formal and impersonal. The wine service is exceptional, though, with a well-tended cellar of more than fourteen thousand wines to choose from.

The Outpost
Wrigleyville
3438 North Clark Street
(773) 244-1166
$$

The Outpost is just what its name suggests—an outpost of authentic, thoughtful cuisine in a neighborhood chockablock with sports bars, fast-food chains, and otherwise mostly mediocre offerings. Owner Kevin O'Donnell sustains more discerning diners near Wrigley Field with contemporary American cuisine laced with Asian flavors and a commitment to organic, local, and seasonal ingredients.

Flavors from the trade routes of the South Seas subtly wend their way through American classics. For instance, the Illinois Pork Chop features locally grown pork served with white cheddar grits, bacon, mizuna greens, and apple cream gravy. On the lighter side, the menu offers a bluefin tuna in saffron broth with goat cheese, fresh corn, and a chile reduction.

With an emphasis on Australia, New Zealand, and the Americas, The Outpost's wines match the cuisine with modesty and eclecticism.

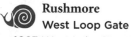 ## Rushmore
West Loop Gate
1023 West Lake Street
(312) 421-8845
Closed Sunday
$$–$$$

This unassuming spot is tucked underneath the El tracks on Lake Street among many of the packinghouses in the West Loop and only a stone's throw from Randolph Street's "Restaurant Row." Rushmore's location affords it the luxury of this proximity without all of the fluff and high concept of Randolph Street. Its loftlike atmosphere is entirely urban, with exposed brick walls, wood floors, and an open kitchen. The food is all-American comfort, featuring nightly blue plate specials like buttermilk fried chicken and beer-battered fish-and-chips. Chef Gilbert Langlois is passionately dedicated to featuring the freshest seasonal and sustainable ingredients on his inventive menu. In fact, the menu states that Rushmore only serves seafood that comes from environmentally conscious fishing practices.

Seasons at the Four Seasons
Streeterville
120 East Delaware Place, 7th Floor
(312) 649-2349
$$$-$$$$

Opulence is the buzzword for this classic Chicago restaurant, just off the Four Seasons lobby. From the luxurious decor to the extensive, attentive service only a hotel restaurant can provide, to the consideration put into its menus, Seasons promises the ultimate pampering of the senses. Special services like afternoon tea, traditional Japanese breakfast (think fish, miso, brightly colored pickles), and a three-course lunch served within an hour to accommodate business-oriented diners (sometimes "business" means shopping along Michigan Avenue, which is adjacent to the hotel) do nothing to diminish the attention put on the central issue: the food.

Chef Robert Sulatycky keeps French tradition at the heart of his cuisine but innovates with influences from Asia and New England. *Opulent* could certainly describe the foie gras served with rhubarb crème brûlée and tiny discs of black pepper brittle. Kobe beef sirloin, with a medley of matsutake, black, and trumpet mushrooms is unusual and demonstrates the chef's versatility and his nod to authentic cuisines from around the world.

Brunch at Seasons is an affair to remember, with six tables of intricate and sumptuous offerings. Along with omelet and juice stations, Midwestern and Asian dishes sit side by side with classic breakfast items. On a recent visit, heirloom tomato salad vied with Spice-Steamed Snapper on Banana Leaf with Sizzling Chile Oil, and Pepper-Crusted Ahi Tuna with Vodka-Caviar Cream.

Tomboy
Andersonville
5402 North Clark Street
(773) 907-0636
Closed Tuesday
$$

Tomboy has long been one of the top restaurants in hip Andersonville. Casual by any standard (on our last visit we were seated next to someone who was knitting), their menu focuses on both traditional and New American items. Start with their signature Porcupine Shrimp, or the Tomato Chipotle Crêpe. Entrée anchors include roasted duck, filet mignon with a Gorgonzola cream sauce, and stuffed chicken breast with a chipotle-chèvre sauce. Finish with crème brûlée served in a parasol glass, or go for warm chocolate anything. Regulars have mixed feelings

about the new liquor license at this longtime BYO favorite, but the recent acquisition of the restaurant by longtime and popular chefs Linda Raydl and Stacey Malow (not to mention a fabulous martini menu) should go a long way toward assuaging the brown-bag base.

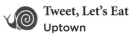

Tweet, Let's Eat
Uptown

5020 North Sheridan Road
(773) 728-5576
Closed Monday–Tuesday; BYOB
$–$$ (Cash only)

Tweet, the quaint creature nestled in the wing of the Uptown bar, Big Chicks, is a new bistro with a sweet resonance. As Chef Janice Martin explains, having worked at high-end restaurants, including a stint at the tony Charlie Trotter's, she wanted a restaurant where her friends and family could join together at the table. Her success in realizing that wish comes without sacrificing high-quality ingredients. Since Tweet's inception, Martin has sought out local growers and farmers' markets for her ingredients, and pledges to serve these with love.

Tweet proprietress Michelle Fire, also the owner of Big Chicks, brings conviviality and brio to the warm setting. Art from her personal collection decorates the restaurant walls and lends a pleasant complement to the warmly designed, asymmetrical dining area.

 West Town Tavern
West Town
1329 West Chicago Avenue
(312) 666-6175
Closed Sunday
$$

In 1999, Drew and Susan Goss, the owners of the successful Zinfandel Restaurant in River North, began to look for a space to open a small neighborhood restaurant. After a two-year search, they found it—in their own West Town neighborhood. The Gosses opened West Town Tavern in 2001, intending to create an eatery embodying the spirit of an early American tavern—where the community could gather for food, drink, news, and gossip.

For the past few years, the Gosses' dream has been a reality for residents of West Town and others looking for great food or a nice glass of wine. Starters include mussels roasted with garlic and chile peppers, and tavern beer cheese served with crunchy toasts. The main dishes provide many choices, from zinfandel-braised pot roast to pan-seared sea scallops with mushroom risotto and duck confit to a fresh herb-stuffed trout.

Zealous
River North
419 West Superior Street
(312) 475-9112
Closed Sunday–Monday
$$$

In his spacious warehouse renovated with cool, clean colors, bamboo groves, and a glass-enclosed wine cellar, Michael Taus carries on the tradition of his mentor, Charlie Trotter. While local sourcing of ingredients does not seem to be as much of a priority, an exuberant celebration of the intersection of exotic foods from all over the world does. Phil Vettel of the *Chicago Tribune* claims this synthesis on Taus's part is "seamless." Taus ably combines disparate ingredients, textures, and flavors. One exhilarating example marries frogs' legs, kohlrabi, and tomato-mint jam; another maple syrup/soy-glazed cod, Maine lobster wontons, and yuzu-ginger sauce.

Duke of Perth
Lakeview
2913 North Clark Street
(773) 477-1741
$-$$

The Duke of Perth is as authentic a Scottish pub as you'll find in Chicago, complete with almost ninety brands of single-malt whisky—the largest selection in the city—and hard-to-find British beers on tap. They have a complete restaurant menu featuring such Scottish specialties as Hebridean leek pie, Scotch eggs, curried strips of lamb, and shepherd's pie. Every Wednesday and Friday the Duke fills to the rafters for the $8.95 all-you-can-eat fish-and-chips special.

There's no television in this handsome, antique-filled pub, which is a refreshing change. So, just like at a real pub, you can actually talk to someone without them looking over your shoulder!

The Grafton
Lincoln Square
4530 North Lincoln Avenue
(773) 271-9000
Open to 2:00 A.M., Saturday to 3:00 A.M.
$

Too many Irish pubs look more like the Disneyland version, with every inch covered with maps, stout posters, and walking sticks. If you need a kitschy map to tell you which county your Irish forebears came from, you won't find it at The Grafton. Instead you'll find a warm and welcoming staff, led by partners Billy Lawless, Jr. and Malcolm Malloy.

When you enter you'll see a long, classic bar to your right and a stable of high-backed booths on the left. Farther back a fireplace, couches, and more tables provide a family-room atmosphere in the early evening, and a comfortable snug for musicians from the nearby Old Town School of Folk Music later on.

Even if it had average pub food, The Grafton's atmosphere would still merit a mention in this guide. But, in fact, the food is much better than average. Start with smoked salmon, diced and served with the usual trimmings. Potato skins usually deserve their bad rap, but are worthy here when topped with leeks, smoky bacon, and rich Cheddar cheese. There are several tasty sandwiches. The Grafton's burger is better than most to start with, but top it with a fried egg and it becomes even more indulgent than usual. Fish-and-chips are another good choice, with moist and tasty cod encased in a crisp batter. End with terrific homemade apple pie and

you've got yourself a full belly. Just make sure to leave some room for a pint or three.

The Pepper Canister
River North
509 North Wells Street
(312) 467-3300
Open to 2:00 A.M., Saturday to 3:00 A.M.
$

The Pepper Canister is a relative newcomer to the endless line of Irish-inspired pubs in Chicago, but it has quickly become one of the best. Named for the distinctively shaped St. Stephen's Church in hip Temple Bar, Dublin, The Pepper Canister gives the "Saints" (nonsmokers) preferred seating by the window on busy Wells Street. "Sinners" (smokers) sit toward the back, with a nice big booth called the Confessional. The bar is clean and stocked with eight well-chosen draft beers.

Though not extensive or flashy, the menu lists both inventive and traditional choices. Appetizers include terrific Bantry Bay Chowder, with big chunks of carrots, potatoes, and fish, many bits of smoky bacon, and a dash of curry seasoning. If you have yet to experience Scotch eggs, you are in for an ultra-cholesterol-laden treat! Imagine: hard-boiled eggs encased in pork sausage and deep-fried. Speaking of eggs, The Pepper Canister serves perhaps the best Irish breakfast in the city, complete with traditional Irish bacon, white and black sausage, eggs, and more. Mini Reuben sandwiches are much better than expected, come three per order, and make a nice starter. Martyr's Dip is a cheesy, satisfying version of artichoke dip, served with hot baguettes. Devil's Calamari is spiced with some red pepper flakes.

Among the lunch choices, The Pepper Canister offers two burgers. The Garret Ripley (named for a sister pub) is the standard version, cooked to order on a nice sesame-seed bun. The brandy cream sauce on the house Pepper Canister burger is a much tastier dressing than the usual. For the herbivores out there, the Veggie Steeples—sautéed mixed vegetables tossed in balsamic vinegar, with goat cheese in a tortilla roll—are a nice option.

Many items carry the religious theme, but unlike most Irish pubs, it's the food, not just the draft Guinness and the black-and-tans, that keeps folks coming back.

NOTABLE

The Irish Oak
Wrigleyville
3511 North Clark Street
(773) 935-0666
Open to 2:00 A.M., Saturday to 3:00 A.M.
$-$$

Four connected first-floor rooms in an old Wrigleyville building are decorated with genuine, if faded, artifacts from Ireland, including a photograph of the slain patriot Michael Collins.

The first thing set down on the table is a firm-textured, brown Irish bread that is baked on the premises from a recipe belonging to the owners, the Lawless family. The menu features mostly standard pub grub—burgers, sandwiches, and salads—but there are a number of Irish favorites as well. An Irish breakfast is served all day and consists of two eggs, two rashers of bacon, two bangers (sausage links), baked beans, grilled tomatoes, toast, and a slice of black pudding. Galway Bay oak-smoked salmon with Irish soda bread and Annie's Seafood Cocktail (salmon and shrimp with a homemade sauce) are excellent. There are

some Irish beers to help wash down the traditional Irish stew, chock-full of lamb and potatoes. An Irish version of potato skins done with onions, leeks, and Irish bacon is worth trying. Live entertainment gets underway at 7:00 P.M. Thursday and 8:30 P.M. on Friday and Saturday.

Red Lion Pub
Lincoln Park
2446 North Lincoln Avenue
(773) 348-2695
Closed Sunday
$

The Red Lion Pub happens to be directly across the street from the old Biograph Theatre, where John Dillinger met his end when ambushed by federal agents in 1934. So when you hear ghost stories of sightings in the bar, you have to wonder who the ghost might be! Built in 1882, the building has had many uses, including as a gambling hall, apartments, and a laundry house, and it has a certain nostalgic feel. Having a pint at the Red Lion Pub almost makes you feel like you're in Merry Old England—complete with an old red standup English phone booth.

Part country pub and part London city bar, the Red Lion offers a laidback, cozy environment that is very conducive to having a good conversation and sampling the fine English fare. The Red Lion offers a lot of English favorites such as shepherd's pie, sausage rolls, steak and kidney pie, burgers, Welsh rarebit, and ploughman's sandwiches. An excellent variety of British beers and weekly entertainment featuring literary readings and an open-mic night make this place a popular favorite.

CARIBBEAN

Borinquen Restaurant   *(Puerto Rican)*
Humboldt Park
1720 North California Avenue
(773) 227-6038
$

Simplicity is often the hallmark of great regional or ethnic cooking. Yet simple ingredients can result in a complexity of flavors that defines a culture's cooking.

Such is the case at Chicago's Borinquen Restaurant. The Humboldt Park eatery is a simple building, simply decorated, with an added cinderblock dining room behind its cafeteria-like front room.

The food at Borinquen is the soul food of working-class Puerto Rico. It heavily emphasizes the foods that are available to those who live in less wealthy communities outside of the cosmopolitan city of San Juan.

At Borinquen one will find tasty, fatty, slow-roasted pork redolent of garlic and *sazon*, a prepackaged seasoning mix of coriander and annatto. Other Puerto Rican specialties on the menu include *mofongo*, a deep-fried ball of green plantain surrounding a hidden treat of pork or chicken in the middle, and *pastele*, a luscious steamed dumpling of mashed plantain. One will also find excellent seasoned greens and pigeon peas lovingly and slowly simmered with *morcilla*, a spicy blood sausage.

However, the star of Borinquen's menu is an untraditional Puerto Rican dish, the *jibarito* (literally translated, "little hillbilly") sandwich. The *jibarito* consists of two flattened, deep-fried plantains filled with a choice of roast beef, roast pork, chicken, or ham along with garlicky mayonnaise, tomatoes, and cheese.

The beauty of the *jibarito* lies in the complexity and contrasts among otherwise simple ingredients: crispy and moist, savory and sweet, cold and hot. The *jibarito* has become the food symbol of working-class Puerto Ricans in Chicago, just as the rest of Borinquen's menu represents the comfort food of the working class on the island of Puerto Rico.

El Rinconcito Cubano   *(Cuban)*
Logan Square
3238 West Fullerton Avenue
(773) 489-4440
$-$$

If you have ever been to Cuba, a visit to El Rinconcito Cubano is a must. Once you walk into the small storefront restaurant, which has been on West Fullerton for more than thirty years, you're transported to a typical neighborhood restaurant in Havana or Santa Cruz: from the smell of the Caribbean food wafting from the kitchen and the prominent Boing/Boing Con Fruta soda machine to the friendly chatter of the Saturday-night crowd of exuberant Cubano *hombres*.

The authentic Matanzeras regional cuisine is realized by owner Roy Quintanas, who shops every morning at the local markets to select the freshest ingredients, and his sister, Rosetta, who cooks every meal from scratch.

Start out with the *croquetas*, a breaded spiced ham appetizer that melts in your mouth. Don't be fooled by the iridescent yellow dip that comes with the *croquetas*; it is a superb mayonnaise-based sauce that is the perfect taste accompaniment. Other starters include traditional beef *picadillo*, stewed in a slightly sweet tomato sauce, or *tasajo*, marinated dried beef.

From the exceptional *bacalao*, dried cod cooked in a tomato-based criollo sauce, to the superb *pescado a la Matanzera*, a regional Matanzas-style fish dish made with whatever fish is fresh that day, everything is full of flavor. The hands-down favorite may be the *bistec de pollo*, a flattened breast of chicken marinated and cooked to perfection. All entrées on the menu are, of course, served with classic black beans and rice and first-rate buttery garlic bread.

As one of the regular patrons explained to us, "Every night is Saturday night" at El Rinconcito Cubano.

La Bruquena   *(Puerto Rican)*
Humboldt Park
2726 West Division Street
(773) 276-2915
$-$$

Walking into La Bruquena from the cold night air, the lacquered pine floors and egg yolk–yellow walls hung with art for purchase from local artists pleasantly greet you. On warm nights, the floor-to-ceiling front windows slide open, with tables and chairs set on the sidewalk for people watching while you dine alfresco.

La Bruquena offers food *con sabor a patria,* or "with the taste of the home country." The same menu is used for breakfast, lunch, and dinner. Seeing no specific breakfast dishes on the menu, we learned that early arrivals order soups such as *caldo de pollo* (chicken broth) with either a sandwich *de lechón* (of roast pork) or *arroz, habichuelas, y carne guisada* (rice, beans, and beef stew) for their breakfasts.

The menu opens with interesting appetizers such as *tostones rellenos de pulpo* (small plantain cups stuffed with octopus). Just as exotic and flavorful are *carne frita, guineitos verdes, y morcillas* (fried pork, green banana, and blood sausage) served together in bite-sized pieces.

The main courses reflect the diversity of Puerto Rico's geography and economy. Coastal seafood specialties are varied and expensive compared to other menu offerings: conch meat salad; red snapper stuffed with shrimp in tomato sauce; *mariscada* (lobster, shrimp, octopus, and conch meat cooked to your taste); and shrimp or lobster prepared with tomato sauce, with garlic and butter sauce, with rice and tomato soup, or on tender yellow rice.

La Bruquena offers hearty and moderately priced Puerto Rican dishes such as *mofongo con caldo* (green plantains mashed with pork rinds and garlic), *pasteles con ensalada* (green plantain and banana dough stuffed with pork, then boiled) and *cuchifrito con guineas* (pork innards cooked in Creole sauce, served with green bananas). Roasted meats and chicken dishes are served with your choice of rice and beans, fried plantains, or *mofongo.*

Children are welcomed with chicken fingers, grilled cheese sandwiches, and hamburgers, though most kids will be just as happy with an order of rice and beans or a pork chop with fried plantains.

Papa's Cache Sabroso Restaurant   *(Puerto Rican)*
Humboldt Park
2517 West Division Street
(773) 862-8313
Closed Monday
$–$$

Papa's Cache Sabroso is a warm, cozy restaurant and take-out place featuring a limited menu executed very well. The co-owners are a husband-and-wife team from Puerto Rico and Ecuador, respectively.

Papa's specialty is *pollo chon*. *Chon* is shorthand for *lechon*-style chicken, because the chicken is prepared, seasoned, and cooked similarly to *lechon* (roast suckling pig). Papa's *pollo chon* is marinated overnight, then, prior to cooking, is slathered with a *mojo de ajo* (garlic sauce). The chicken cooks for ninety minutes on a rotisserie over an open gas flame, until it is mahogany brown. The chicken is juicy and flavorful and has the occasional crisp, spicy bit of skin. Accompanying the sectioned chicken on the platter is freshly cooked, soft, and succulent yuca, which is nicely positioned to absorb all the chicken juices; this variation gives one insight into why yuca is such a popular starch. Alternatively, you can order crisp *tostones* (fried flattened ovals of plantain), which have been anointed with *mojo de ajo* before serving.

Papa's also makes a very good rendition of that Chicago-invented Puerto Rican community favorite, the *jibarito* sandwich. Papa's secret is that everything is made fresh, from slicing, pressing, and frying the plantains to the freshly grilled rib eye steak. This is quite important, as the starchy plantains become rubbery if they linger under a heat lamp. Rice and pigeon peas or rice and beans accompany your sandwich.

On weekends Papa's offers *lechon asado* (roast pig) as well as *ensalada de camarones con tostones* (shrimp salad with plantains) and *camarones en salsa con tostones* (shrimp in pesto sauce with plantains).

The flan is very good here and sells out quickly. If you want to try some, ask for it with your initial order. It can easily disappear before you have had time to finish your meal and consider dessert.

NOTABLE

Café Marianao   (*Cuban*)
Logan Square
2246 North Milwaukee Avenue
(773) 278-4533
$ (Cash only)

Café Marianao serves up some of the best authentic Cuban coffee in town. There is a method to ordering the coffee at this tiny white-and-yellow brick shop on Milwaukee Avenue, so if you're a first timer, follow these instructions. Start by ordering your food at the bar from one of the guys on the right side. Steak sandwiches cost about $3.50, and the Cuban toast (Cuban bread pressed with butter and garlic) is also a good bet.

Then go to your left to order your coffee. They have an amazing traditional *cafe con leche*. Good Cuban coffee, including *cafe con leche*, is rarer in this city than good Cuban food. Café Marianao uses whole milk,

generous amounts of sugar, a good proportion of coffee, and a little but-ter and/or salt—which is what makes it authentic.

Pay at the end of your meal, telling the order taker which coffee you purchased. A huge *cafe con leche* costs a dollar, and a good-sized Cuban coffee is half that. A *colada* is *cafe con leche* with chocolate; a *cortadito* is a shot of Cuban coffee with a little milk.

Ibis   *(Puerto Rican)*
Humboldt Park
2509 West North Avenue
(773) 278-4433
Closed Sunday; BYOB
$-$$

At Ibis, instead of plated meals, side orders can be selected for a family-style dinner: Meat platters of *lechon* (roast pork), *morcilla* (blood sausage), and *carne frita* (fried pork meat) come by the pound. Homemade stews are also available: *cuchi guisado* (pork ear stew), *cabrito* (goat stew), *pollo guisado* (chicken stew), or *carne guisada* (beef stew).

Mofongo, mashed green plantain with fried pork, is served loosely mounded in a wooden cup. Unlike *mofongos* served elsewhere in round fried balls, which require soup for moisture and edibility, Ibis's *mofongo* is much less dense and can be eaten alone. Our waitress explained the secret to the lighter *mofongo*: It is made fresh to order.

Puerto Rican food is not usually considered spicy, but Ibis offers condi-ments of hot peppers or their homemade *sofrito*—a mixture of onion, garlic, peppers, and cilantro sautéed in oil.

Desserts offered are flan, *budin* (bread pudding), and a sublime *tem-bleque* (coconut custard).

Ed's Potsticker House

Bridgeport

3139 South Halsted Street

(312) 326-6898

BYOB

$

Ed's Potsticker House is a dual-personality Chinese restaurant in Chicago's Bridgeport neighborhood, which is home to both the Daley family (famous for two mayors—Richard J. and Richard M.) and Comiskey Park, where the Chicago White Sox play their home games. On the one hand Ed's is an eggroll/fried rice/egg fuyong emporium catering to neighborhood families. Yet just below the surface lurks a wonderful array of Northern Chinese specialties.

Northern Chinese cuisine can be quite hearty, with an emphasis on wheat flour; dumplings, noodles, and buns, as opposed to rice; and braised, roasted, and smoked meats. Northern cuisine, in a fashion similar to Szechuan, also has a tendency to be slightly oily to the American palate, and spicy with chiles.

Of particular interest is the smoked pork, consisting of thick scallion pancakes with thinly sliced, slightly fatty smoked pork served with hoisin sauce and shredded scallions. A drizzle of chile oil elevates this rich dish to an almost obscenely delicious level.

Ed's has a number of dumpling starters, including its namesake, a long, loosely rolled "cigar" of a potsticker. It also offers quite good *shao long bao* (soup dumplings) and any number of noodle dishes, all of which make an excellent first course.

Soups include tofu with spinach, and pork meatball and beef noodle. Other notable menu offerings include lamb with cumin, jellyfish, drunk duck, pork belly with garlic flavor, pan-fried seafood noodles, and sea cucumber with tendon.

Ed's also has a number of flavorful vegetable dishes, including baby bok choy with shiitake mushrooms, and an amazing garlic-eggplant dish that with a less adept hand might taste cloyingly sweet. Potatoes with Vinegar Flavor are a study in simplicity, as is Fried Tofu in Beijing Sauce, which contains large pieces of star anise.

From the clean, bright interior, with lovely wall murals, to the friendly waitstaff, some of whom speak English, to the moderate prices and large, flavorful portions of Northern Chinese food, Ed's Potsticker House is a Chicago favorite.

Lao Sze Chuan
Chinatown
2172 South Archer Avenue
(312) 326-5040
$$

Lao Sze Chuan's courteously efficient waitstaff is always ready to refill your water glass, which is especially important given the restaurant's spicy Szechuan dishes. Your meal starts off nicely with a small complimentary plate of sliced cabbage in chile oil—simple yet well prepared, and a good omen of what's to come.

Excellent starters are the Spicy Rabbit (on the bone) or the Sliced Beef and Maw Szechuan-style, served in spicy chile oil, as well as the Chengdu Dumplings. For the less adventuresome, there are also the ubiquitous American/Cantonese egg rolls and potstickers.

In the strictly Szechuan camp, Chicken with Chilies looks lethal, with what appears to be a hundred small dried red chiles, but it is surprisingly mild—as long as one avoids eating the dried chiles themselves. There's a similar dish made with rabbit, which is also quite good.

Lao Sze Chuan has a number of interesting, wildly diverse, and delicious menu items, from Tea-Smoked Duck to wonderfully rich Braised Pork Elbow. The kitchen does seafood—both shellfish and fin fish—well, and whole fish are a house specialty. Salt and Pepper Three Delights (scallop, squid, shrimp) is highly recommended.

Vegetable entries include Potherb with Dried Chiles, Long Beans Dry-Fried with Dried Shrimp, and Green Beans Fried with Spices, which is a deceptively hot and spicy dish. Chili Potato is an odd-sounding dish for a Chinese restaurant, since one does not normally associate potatoes and Chinese food, but the still-firm potato slivers, bathed in oil that the dried chiles had been fried in, is a delicious, though starchy, treat.

Lao Sze Chuan offers a small number of Chinese desserts. Rice Pudding for Two is a warm pancake of sticky rice with lotus seeds, watermelon seeds, peanuts, and sweet red-bean paste. The Chengdu Dumplings in Wine Sauce is a sweet rice-wine soup with small chewy rice-flour dumplings filled with sugar and ground black sesame seeds.

Other Location
500 East Ogden Avenue, Westmont; (630) 455-4488

The Phoenix
Chinatown
2131 South Archer Avenue
(312) 328-0848
$-$$

The Phoenix is an attractive, well-appointed, white-tablecloth restaurant with a second-floor view of the Chicago skyline. During the day The Phoenix is a bustling dim sum house, complete with rolling steam carts and a full range of offerings. By evening the pace slows, and they offer a wide-ranging menu of excellent Cantonese dishes, including several banquet menus.

The dinner menu at The Phoenix has any number of delicious recipes, including abalone, Peking duck, and whole fish prepared a variety of ways. A favorite starter at The Phoenix is squab: the legs are marinated and then dry-fried with a Szechuan pepper-salt mixture, and the breast is served in a stir-fry with the crispy, savory legs around the dish—a lovely presentation. Also on the poultry front is a starter of Roast Duck with Jellyfish. On a platter they ring the jellyfish with roast duck and dot the outside with very intense mustard paste, which adds to the overall flavor.

The Phoenix has the largest variety of dim sum available in Chicago, and from the standpoint of both taste and presentation it is outstanding. Offerings run the gamut from delicious steamed shrimp dumplings with delicate translucent wrappers, to heartier barbecued meats and fried items, to the traditional taro cake and congee. While everything is quite good, the differing types tend to come in waves; for example, a number of fried items, followed by pan-fried, followed by steamed. Given this, resist the tendency to fill up on one type of item; patience is a virtue if one is to experience the full range of foods.

There are a few other tips to enhance your Phoenix dim sum experience. If you want any barbecued duck, rib, pork, or the like, ask for it as you sit down and the staff will bring it when ready. (The barbecue is ready about every twenty minutes and goes fast.) Sunday is the busiest day for dim sum, with waits up to an hour at peak times. The best day to go is Saturday, when they are not as busy and have almost as many dim sum items as on Sunday.

On the first floor The Phoenix also has a late-night café serving Shanghai snack items and bubble tea until midnight. Of special interest are *shao long bao* (soup dumplings), which are served with slivered ginger and are quite exceptional. In addition to a small number of dim sum items, Phoenix Café has wonderful soups (the spicy brisket noodle has amazing depth of flavor), and dumpling and rice dishes. Service is brisk, and the open kitchen, which we wish was visible from more of the room, is a treat to observe.

Shui Wah Chinese Cuisine
Chinatown
2162 South Archer Avenue
(312) 225-8811
BYOB
$$

Shui Wah is located in the "New" Chinatown Square—an interesting set of restaurants, groceries, and shops. One could easily patronize the restaurant a number of times a week without ever getting weary of the food. It's a diverse place—not in its modest yet spotlessly clean physical space, but in its menu. During the day Shui Wah has arguably the best dim sum in the area. At dinner and in the early evening a number of Cantonese favorites are offered alongside the light and tasty Chiu Chow specialties. Chiu Chow dishes feature lots of vegetables served over fowl and other meats, often in a sweet or piquant sauce. Finally, there's a late-night menu of both Chiu Chow specialties and snacks. This is in addition to a full-on Chinese banquet menu for six to sixty people.

Luckily, the food is excellent regardless of which menu you order from. During the day you order dim sum from a paper menu, as opposed to selecting from the more typical rolling carts. The steamed dishes are uniformly light, flavorful, fresh, and hot; the fried items are crisp and greaseless; and the braised foods come loaded with deep, rich flavor. Shui Wah also has congee (rice porridge) available in the morning, including delicious preserved egg congee.

The evening and Chiu Chow menus contain such notables as whole fish, roasted poultry, and braised meats. The oxtail is excellent, as are the noodle dishes and various stir-fried vegetables, my favorite being pea shoots with fermented tofu. The late-night menu is accented with lighter fare; I particularly enjoy the spiced salt-fried tofu; the tofu—light, almost ethereal—is served with a salt/five-spice dredging dip. Jellyfish, poached chicken, and braised eel are specialties of the house as well.

Silver Seafood
Uptown
4829 North Broadway Street
(773) 784-0668
$-$$

Silver Seafood, located in Chicago's "New Chinatown" neighborhood, is a pleasantly appointed Cantonese restaurant specializing in seafood. It stands kitty-corner across the street from the famous Green Mill, a landmark Chicago tavern that is home to jazz, poetry slams, and a slightly Bohemian atmosphere (see p. 200).

The majority of Silver Seafood's customers are Asian. However, the servers are bilingual, and both menus—American-style Cantonese and Cantonese (Guangzhou)—are printed in English.

As befits a restaurant with seafood in its name, Silver Seafood does seafood very well, with a fin fish and lobster tank kept spotlessly clean and in full view of diners. Recommended dishes include oysters in the shell with black beans or ginger and scallion, clams in black bean sauce, head-on shrimp stir-fried dry with salt and spices, and whole fish, typically tilapia or red snapper, either steamed or fried and served with a variety of sauces.

In addition to whole fish Silver Seafood has fish fillet with stir-fried vegetables, as well as cuttlefish, lobster, abalone, and several wonderful soups. Silver Seafood is also known for its delicious roasted birds, including duck, pigeon, and squab. Silver Seafood also has many of the Cantonese standards like steamed chicken with a wonderful ginger-scallion dip, and many types of tofu preparations and stir-fries. For those with a slight sweet tooth, sweet glazed shrimp ringed with candied walnuts is a winning dish.

In addition to a full range of well-prepared Cantonese specialties, Silver Seafood has fresh fruit and milk-based bubble teas, and there is a raised platform area where there is occasional musical entertainment on the weekends. Silver Seafood has wine and beer available, though the wine selection is limited; corkage for BYOB is a reasonable $5 per bottle.

Spring World
Chinatown
2109 South China Place
(773) 326-9966
BYOB
$

Beneath a deceptively mild-mannered decor lies a powerhouse of a Chinese restaurant, with many interesting and delicious items well beyond typical Cantonese-American fare. Spring World is certainly not your parent's Chinese-American restaurant.

Szechuan-style starters include the wonderful beef and maw or sliced beef tendon with a sweat-inducing chile sauce, or a wonderful julienne of cold jellyfish with scallion paste. Accompany this with the crisp, lightly pan-fried scallion cakes—the perfect accompaniment to chile-based heat—and you are off to a great start.

Yunan Ham with Leeks (preserved pork with leeks) will taste surprisingly familiar to those who have tried salt-cured country ham, but it has been given a wonderfully Yunan spin. Another familiar yet unusual offer-

ing is Yunan Beef with Mushroom in a flavorful, dark, rich sauce. A few other delicious Yunan specialties are Yunan Rice Noodle or Lamb Stew with fish and sour pickle casserole.

Spring World has excellent vegetable dishes, from the delicious Eggplant with Garlic Sauce to the spicy Szechuan String Beans and a refreshing Stir-Fried Watercress.

In addition, Spring World has one of the best lunch specials in Chicago: $3.95 for soup, main course, rice, and tea. Kung Pao Chicken, Twice-Cooked Pork, or even the ubiquitous General Chen's Chicken for just a little more than $5.00 with tax and gratuity is hard to pass up.

It's difficult to go wrong here, and it would take many, many visits to explore all of the Yunan, Szechuan, and Shanghai offerings.

("Little") Three Happiness
Chinatown
209 West Cermak Road
(312) 842-1964
$

In Chicago's Chinatown there are two restaurants bearing the name Three Happiness: a large second-floor restaurant on South Wentworth, which is not very good, and "Little" Three Happiness on West Cermak. Different owners, different menus, different philosophies.

"Little" Three Happiness is a modest-looking Chinese restaurant, short on decor but long on wonderful food—a perfect example of Calvin Trillin's "Inverse Ambience Theory of Chinese Restaurants." The restaurant does many things well, from Cantonese/American (their Shrimp Toast is excellent) to Hong Kong–style seafood (Stir-Fried Crab with Ginger and Scallion is a perennial favorite), to vegetable dishes such as a simple stir-fry of watercress or *ong choi* (water vegetable).

Noodle dishes, both thin wheat-flour noodles and fresh rice noodles stir-fried crisp with a variety of ingredients, are particularly good at Three Happiness. Highly recommended are the Pan-Fried Thin (flour) Noodles with Mixed Seafood. In the Pan-Fried Rice Noodles with Roast Duck, the subtle five-spice seasoning perfectly complements the rich duck and its crispy skin.

Three Happiness really excels in the seafood category. The Dry Stir-Fried Crab with Ginger and Scallion is wonderful, though the Clams with Black Bean sauce are equally delicious; light saucing and an even hand with spicing allow the flavor of the pristinely fresh clams to shine though. Fresh fish fillets and/or lobster prepared a variety of ways are also available and quite tasty. The mixed seafood consists of standards like shrimp and squid, quickly delving into more exotic items, such as fish lung and sea cucumber (a.k.a. sea slug).

Salt and Pepper Shrimp—shell-on shrimp quickly cooked in a dry wok with salt, five-spice powder, and Szechuan pepper—are spicy, juicy, and delicious. Three Happiness also has shell-off salt-and-pepper shrimp with the same spicing, but coated with a light batter and fried. In fact, the kitchen prepares shrimp many different ways, including shell-on boiled.

Any of the sour green dishes, chicken, tripe, or squid make a nice counterpoint to the crisp noodle dishes, as do the bitter melon offerings. Sautéed Snails with Black Bean and Garlic are difficult to eat but quite delicious, and Pike Fillets Steamed with Ginger and Scallion will offer the less adventurous a delicious alternative to sea cucumber or snail.

Crispy-Skin Chicken, served with cilantro, lemon wedges, and a Szechuan pepper-salt mix for dredging, is a wonder of a dish. Crisp, succulent skin and moist, tender meat are perfectly complemented by the lemon's acidity and the flavor of the dredging mixture.

After a meal at "Little" Three Happiness, you'll agree that good things do come in smaller packages.

NOTABLE

Seven Treasures
Chinatown
2312 South Wentworth Avenue
(312) 225-2668
Open to 2:00 A.M.; BYOB
$

Seven Treasures is a large, modestly appointed Hong Kong barbecue and noodle specialist in the heart of Chicago's Chinatown. While the restaurant offers a full range of menu options, Noodles in Soup with Won Ton and Fresh Shrimp Dumpling is, along with barbecue, the specialty of the house. An excellent way to experience both is to order house-made noodles in soup with fresh shrimp dumplings and one or more barbecued meats in the soup. Five types of noodles are available, including house-made *e-fu* (long, flat egg noodles that have been deep-fried, then drained), thick and thin rice noodles, and two types of dumplings. The menu also contains a full spectrum of other options, from Hong Kong steak to whole fish and several vegetable and vegetarian entrées.

The restaurant has recently undergone remodeling and is bright, cheery, and very clean. There's an open kitchen where you can watch the staff preparing dumplings, noodles, and soup, and an open barbecue area with the visually appealing meats stimulating the appetite. Seven Treasures has bubble tea, as well as one of the best hot chile oil table sauces in Chicago.

══ A WALK AROUND ARGYLE STREET ══

From the late 1800s through the Jazz Age of the Roaring '20s, the Argyle Street area of Chicago's Uptown community, with a mix of Jews and Italians, was an affluent and fashionable residential district and a shopping and entertainment destination second only to Chicago's downtown. After World War II, Uptown went into decline, and with it went Argyle Street, its stores and markets eventually closing down and boarding up.

The area suffered years of urban blight and neglect, and as rents declined many new immigrants and the less fortunate moved into Uptown. In the 1960s and 1970s businessmen Jimmy Wong and Charlie Soo envisioned and promoted the revitalization of the Argyle Street area as a "New Chinatown." Following the Vietnam War, numerous Vietnamese, Thai, and Laotians, many of them ethnic Chinese, settled in the area and opened shops, restaurants, and markets. Today the area is undergoing rapid gentrification.

The three blocks of Argyle Street (5000 North) between Sheridan Road on the east and Broadway on the west, plus the area around it, is once again a vibrant and lively shopping, dining, and entertainment district. On the weekend you'll find Argyle in full swing, with cars bumper to bumper as Asians from all over the Midwest vie for parking spaces and pack the local markets, gift shops, jewelry stores, and restaurants. Plan on at least half a day if you want to slowly take in the sights and smells and sample some of the best Asian food in the city.

Start your tour of the area at **Ba Le** (1) (5018 North Broadway). Originally from Saigon, the bakery shows that city's French influence in the freshly baked baguettes and croissants and freshly made Vietnamese pâtés.

If you are looking for plenty of room to spread out and want something more extensive to get your day started, head south a block to **Furama** (2) (4936 North Broadway) for very good and lightning-fast Chinese dim sum. Cart service is offered every day from 9:30 A.M. to 2:30 P.M. The fruit smoothies are particularly good and very filling. Order one to go for the walk.

In between Ba Le and Furama is **Thai Grocery** (3) (5014 North Broadway). The affable owner, Eddie Lin, has run this well-stocked Thai market, deli, and take-out since 1974. He imports excellent jasmine rice, and if you are looking for an authentic Thai mortar for making curry paste, this is the place to buy one.

Cross Broadway and head east on the north side of Argyle. **Sun Wah Bar-B-Q** (4) (1134 West Argyle) proudly displays its pressed and roasted ducks in the window. Not surprisingly, the restaurant features its duck, chicken, and pork in soups, with noodles, and over rice.

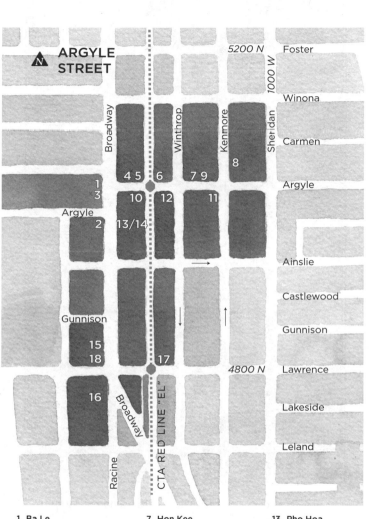

ARGYLE STREET

1. **Ba Le**
   5018 N. Broadway
2. **Furama**
   4936 N. Broadway
3. **Thai Grocery**
   5014 N. Broadway
4. **Sun Wah Bar-B-Q**
   1134 W. Argyle
5. **Sea World Food Market**
   1130 W. Argyle
6. **Vinh Tho**
   1112 W. Argyle
7. **Hon Kee**
   1062–64 W. Argyle
8. **Agudas Achim North Shore Congregation**
   5029 N. Kenmore
9. **New Hong Kong Bakery**
   1050–52 W. Argyle
10. **Chiu Quon Bakery**
    1127 W. Argyle
11. **Viet Hoa Plaza**
    1051 W. Argyle
12. **Hoa Nam Grocery**
    1101 W. Argyle
13. **Pho Hoa**
    4925–G N. Broadway
14. **Tai Nam Market**
    4925–J N. Broadway
15. **Uptown Theater**
    4816 N. Broadway
16. **Riviera Theater**
    4746 N. Racine
17. **Aragon Ballroom**
    1106 W. Lawrence
18. **Green Mill Lounge**
    4802 N. Broadway

If you are looking to do some cooking with seafood, the gentlemen at **Sea World Food Market** (5) (1130 West Argyle) will scoop live lobster, crab, frog, carp, or other fish from tanks and will dispatch and clean it for you while you wait.

If that experience leaves you a bit queasy, stop at **Vinh Tho** (6) (1112 West Argyle), a Chinese herbal specialist. The staff will be happy to fill an herbal prescription or recommend a special mixture or tea to settle your stomach and your nerves. It also stocks an incredible variety of ginseng products.

Hon Kee (7) (1062–64 West Argyle) is an excellent spot to pick up pre-pared duck, chicken, and especially suckling pig. A glimpse of the area's ethnic past can be found a half a block north on Kenmore. **Agudas Achim North Shore Congregation** (8) (5029 North Kenmore), dedicated in 1923, is the city's last remaining congregation built in the cathedral style and operating as a Jewish house of worship. Today it serves immigrant Jews from the former Soviet Union.

Return to Argyle to continue your tour. The area hosts several very good Chinese bakeries. **New Hong Kong Bakery** (9) (1050–52 West Argyle) prepares excellent ham-and-cheese, curry, and pork buns, as well as an assortment of tea cakes, pastries, and cookies. **Chiu Quon Bakery** (10) (1127 West Argyle) is also very popular and serves a limited dim sum menu. On the south side of Argyle is the incredibly busy **Viet Hoa Plaza** (11) (1051 West Argyle). This grocery and vegetable market offers a large selection of fresh meat, poultry, and fish. If you prefer a less frantic shopping experience, try the smaller but pleasant **Hoa Nam Grocery** (12) (1101 West Argyle), a short distance to the west.

As you continue west back to Broadway, be sure the browse the multitude of gift shops selling everything from children's toys and clothes to bamboo plants and Chinese pottery. Turn left at Broadway and proceed south to the narrow mall of shops and restaurants at 4925 North Broadway. Here you'll find **Pho Hoa** (13), which serves one the best bowls of *pho* in the area—and it serves only *pho*. The classic beef-and-noodle soup can be ordered in a great variety of combinations (except vegetarian, of course) and comes to the table piping hot, accompanied by the traditional plate of bean sprouts, cilantro, sliced peppers, and lime wedges. Next door you'll find the excellent **Tai Nam Market** (14). As with all of the Asian markets in the area prices are very reasonable.

Across the street from Silver Seafood is what remains of the once glorious Uptown Theater District. The now-shuttered **Uptown Theater** (15) (4816 North Broadway), constructed in 1925, is the largest theater building in the country, based on square footage. Preservationists are trying to save this landmark, with its ornate interior, from the wrecking ball. The **Riviera Theater** (16) (4746 North Racine) and the **Aragon Ballroom** (17) (1106 West Lawrence Avenue) once hosted the likes of Benny Goodman and Duke Ellington. Today the theaters still function as venues for entertainment revues, featuring an eclectic mix of traditional and of-the-moment bands. A fitting end to your tour of the historic Argyle Street area is to catch a drink and the live jazz at the **Green Mill Lounge** (18) (4802 North Broadway). Established in 1908, it is the oldest continuously operated nightclub in the country. The interior hasn't changed much since the days when it was frequented by Charlie Chaplin, Gloria Swanson, and Al Capone. The club features world-renowned jazz bands and vocalists. It offers a popular poetry slam on Sunday nights.

EASTERN EUROPEAN

(*See also Polish*)

Healthy Food   *(Lithuanian)*
Bridgeport
3236 South Halsted Street
(312) 326-2724
BYOB
$ (Cash only)

If you're a hard-body, Atkins-diet protégé, you aren't likely to consider the food at Healthy Food to be, well, healthy. However, if you're in the mood for comfort food—the kind loaded with carbs and seasoned with pork, Healthy Food is the place for you.

In this melting pot of a neighborhood just south of Chicago's Chinatown, Healthy Food is a delight on many levels. Ask anyone in Chicago where to go for good Lithuanian food and you'll be directed to this simple diner, reminiscent of a 1950s coffee shop, complete with a Formica lunch counter and Naugahyde-covered barstools. However, the religious artifacts displayed on the walls, the owner's collection of amber, and the friendly waitresses dressed in full skirts and peasant blouses signal that you're in for a flashback, Lithuanian style.

When Lithuanians first immigrated to the United States, seeking religious freedom and an escape from economic uncertainty, they worked in Chicago's slaughterhouses, at the steel mills, and on the railroads. It was basic manual labor—the kind that called for hearty, filling, and sustaining foods. Such a meal at Healthy Food begins with a bowl of steaming sauerkraut soup with just enough sourness to make it interesting. This is accompanied by pumpernickel rye bread—darker and nuttier than typical rye—from the nearby Baltic Bakery.

While the menu offers a well-prepared variety of "American" entrées, the Lithuanian dishes—"made from scratch"—shine brightest. Try a *varskeciai*, a dumpling filled with slightly sweetened cheese curds. If it's meat you're hungry for, *koldunai*, dumplings filled with beef and a bit of pork for moisture and flavor, are served with a sprinkling of crumbled bacon. If you're looking for a heartier entrée, try the smoked sausages.

Lithuanian traditional cuisine took shape over many centuries and was greatly influenced by cultural contact with neighboring nations. A good example is *kugelis* (potato cake), which Lithuanians adapted from the German kitchen. This has since become a favorite dish throughout Lithuania and is now a staple of the Lithuanian diet. Mashed potatoes, eggs, onions, bacon, and a little bit of butter are baked in the oven for a long time, then sliced and sautéed. It is served at Healthy Food with sides of sour cream and homemade applesauce.

Always known for their hospitality, Lithuanians go all out to prepare food and drink for guests, for they want their guests to comment afterward, "There was an abundance of everything; the only food missing was bird's milk." At Healthy Food, you may not find everything, but you will certainly find an abundance of delicious and typical Lithuanian food.

Old L'Viv   *(Ukrainian)*
Ukrainian Village
2228 West Chicago Avenue
(773) 772-7250
Closed Monday
$ (Cash only)

Irena Lakonechnaya, proprietor of Old L'Viv, explains that Ukrainians *must* have soup with their meals. One spoonful of her ruby-red borscht, earthy and thick and laden with beets, carrots, and potatoes, is all it takes to see why.

Lakonechnaya came to the United States and Chicago's Ukrainian Village in the 1980s from the city of L'Viv in Ukraine. For the past ten years in this tidy, church-filled neighborhood, she has fed both longtime Ukrainian immigrants hungry for a taste of home and a recent influx of young professionals. A tall, sturdy blonde who exudes matronly warmth and a bashful good nature, Lakonechnaya is eager to talk about her homeland and the food she prepares and serves in her tiny six-table restaurant.

For those not familiar with Ukrainian food, Old L'Viv is a great place to start, and not least because everything is offered from a self-serve buffet. Lakonechnaya prepares all the food herself and offers her diners what amounts to a top-ten list of traditional Ukrainian favorites. As she puts it, the food she makes is "a little mix of Polish, Lithuanian, and Ukrainian." Potatoes are a staple of the Ukrainian diet, so their presence in a dish is often what sets it apart from its Russian or Lithuanian counterparts.

The meal starts with a big bowl of soup that Lakonechnaya brings to the table. Four different kinds—Ukrainian borscht, traditional cabbage soup, meatball, and chicken noodle—were offered on a recent visit. At the buffet, the selection includes a variety of meats, chicken, side dishes, salads, and simple desserts. Meat can include schnitzel, which is made from a mixture of ground pork, veal, and beef, breaded and fried and eaten with mushroom gravy. The goulash was not a particularly strong entry, but the sautéed pork loin cutlets luxuriating on a bed of lightly caramelized sweet onions were delicious. Perhaps the most remarkable item on the buffet was the cabbage rolls. Leaves of cabbage, wrapped around a nicely balanced filling of rice, carrots, pork, and beef, were so silky and expertly prepared that eating them was a rare, sensuous experience. These perfect little packages were covered in a light tomato sauce made rich and slightly creamy with the addition of sour cream.

Other traditional Ukrainian offerings include small, buttery potato dumplings, reminiscent of gnocchi, and blintzes, which are filled with a slightly sweet blend of farmer's and cream cheeses, raisins, and hints of vanilla and cinnamon. An array of simple, colorful salads round out the buffet. Sauerkraut that isn't sour at all but more savory (think German braised cabbage) stands out, as do grated beets with fresh horseradish, and grated carrots with garlic. One surrenders, at last, to Lakonechnaya's crunchy homemade salt pickles—and all this for only $7.

Old L'Viv usually gets busy around noon on Sundays, when Ukrainians flood in from church, reluctant to lose the sensation of being in another place and time. Other times it is a quiet, if modest, place for a hearty, satisfying meal. A small bar serves beer, wine, brandy, and a variety of vodkas without fancy names or labels dreamed up by marketers.

Russian Tea Time   *(Russian)*
Loop
77 East Adams Street
(312) 360-0000
$-$$

More than just a tea room (although full tea service is offered), Russian Tea Time is a gustatory trip across time and Russia and the former Soviet republics, from Tashkent to Moscow. Mother-and-son owners Klara and Vadim Muchnik have created an oasis of calm just off a bustling strip of Michigan Avenue and Chicago's arts district, designed to fit a variety of appetites and budgets. The Chicago Symphony Orchestra's music director, Daniel Barenboim, is said to be a regular.

The menu is so large as to be almost overwhelming. You might start with one of the hearty, homemade soups (mushroom-barley or borscht). Other first courses range from stuffed mushroom caps Azerbaijani style to pumpkin *vareniky* (dumplings) to *samsa* (cumin-seasoned lamb pastries).

To get a taste of the vast geography and cultures that Russia and the former Soviet republics span, Russian Tea Time's list of entrées is a great place to begin. The Muchniks have managed to create a compelling menu of Russian, Slavic, and Jewish classics with an infusion of Central Asian flavors. Traditional dishes from Ukraine, Uzbekistan, Kyrgyzstan, Czarist Russia, and Moldavia, just to name a few, are all represented here. If you can't decide, a listing of special combination platters allows you to sample a variety of specialties. Side dishes are equally varied: Tashkent Carrot Salad, Kirghiz Cracked Wheat and Parsley Salad, Eggplant or Beet Caviar, and Chickpea Spread. Both meat eaters and vegetarians will find plenty of options to choose from.

Russian Tea Time is the perfect stop for a pre- or post-theater supper. The warm and inviting space, punctuated by the brass samovars on display, creates an intimate Old World environment. Finally, for those whose tastes for the Russian extends to spirits, Russian Tea Time has a stellar vodka portfolio, with offerings from around the world as well as their own house-flavored vodkas.

FRENCH

FINE DINING

 Everest
Loop

440 South LaSalle Street, 40th Floor
(312) 663-8920
Closed Sunday–Monday
$$$$

Forty floors above the chaos that is Chicago's financial district, with a spectacular overlook of the city, is Everest restaurant. Besides being gorgeous in an architectural sense, it is also tops in romantic inspiration and, more importantly, great dining.

In the mid-1980s, Chef Jean Joho was lured out of his native Alsace to help establish Maxim's restaurant here in Chicago. Sometime later he joined the Lettuce Entertain You group and gained almost immediate success in the form of this Loop enterprise. Somehow he also finds the time to oversee his other dining venues, the more casual Brasserie Jo (Chicago and Boston) and the Eiffel Tower restaurant in the Paris Hotel, Las Vegas.

The simple black-and-light-tan decor with soft lighting belies the creativity just steps away in the kitchen. Diners have a hard time avoiding out-the-window-gazing in order to peruse the menu and enjoy the award-winning service.

The very first Slow Food member in Chicago, Chef Joho bases his success on finding the best local, seasonal products that look good as well as taste good. He has a way of taking otherwise overlooked or forgotten ingredients and making a dish that has the "Cinderella" touch, turning rice into risotto with edible gold leaf, for example. Many of the humble ingredients are from his native land, and so you will find turnips and cabbages among menu items as well as foie gras and pheasant. Common items are raised to a level not usually seen in daily fare—for instance, few people other than Chef Joho consider the parsnip a dessert ingredient.

Patrons have the flexibility of choosing between à la carte, a seven-course menu, and a pre-theater four-course meal. Although the menu changes often, one can always be assured of inspired combinations such as Cold Garden Vegetable Soup with Maine Lobster and Alsace Gewürztraminer, Cream of Chestnut with Duck Confit, and *Suere Rueva* and Roasted Filet of Line-Caught Striped Bass with a Tomato Crust and Yellow Tomato Coulis. The enjoyment goes past the selection of small American farmer's cheeses and lasts as you dive into the Caramel Cranberry Tart with Sautéed Apples and Cranberry Jelly.

The wine list also reflects Joho's homeland. Amid the many varied international selections is the largest collection of Alsatian wines outside of Alsace. Valet parking is complimentary, jackets and reservations are required, and smoking is *interdite*.

In 1995, Joho opened **Brasserie Jo**, a more casual bistro where he shines the spotlight on common ingredients, mostly derived from his native Alsace, and produces consistently delicious items full of flavor and texture. Quiche, *choucroute*, and *escargots à l'Alsacienne* are just a few of the offerings you will find there.

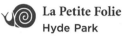

La Petite Folie
Hyde Park
1504 East 55th Street
(773) 493-1394
Closed Monday
$$$

Hyde Park proper is anchored by two mammoth institutions—the University of Chicago and the Museum of Science and Industry—both of which give home, comfort, and employment to thousands of citizens who rightfully ought to care about real food. So it's inexplicable why, culinarily speaking, the neighborhood has long been a dark sea on the far side of the moon, a land that time forgot.

To be sure, there are a couple of decent student hangouts, one of the city's best bakeries, some colorful old bars, and perhaps the city's best barbecue a few miles south, but for the most part Hyde Park has always been considered a culinary wasteland. So it's a small miracle that a restaurant here is now serving conscientious and well-prepared French food, and has managed to hang on doing so, for at least five years.

La Petite Folie is owned by Michael and Mary Mastricola, both longtime Hyde Park residents who met at the university more than twenty years ago. In 1995, in a not-so-small folly of culinary passion, they moved to Paris, where Mary earned the *grand diplome* of Le Cordon Bleu Paris, finishing first in her class. She and Michael were painfully aware of the dearth of high-level cooking in their old neighborhood and decided to try to bring fine dining back to their community. Their vision never wavered from what they had come to know and love in France—the warm, comfortable atmosphere of family-owned restaurants, in which diners felt as if they were in someone's home. And in spite of its nearly unnoticeable location in the back corner of a large shopping center, the interior of La Petite Folie is a quiet oasis. The white walls, nearly bare, are elegant and soothing, and the wide spacing between tables gives diners a luxurious amount of privacy.

The menu rotates seasonally around the French countryside. The summer features Provençal dishes; the winter Alsatian and Basque. Spring might sprout up from the Loire Valley, and autumn gives Michael the opportunity to pair Burgundy's wines with its harvest dishes.

If you're looking for a slow and leisurely, special-occasion meal, La Petite Folie is definitely a destination spot, and maybe the only one, in Hyde Park.

Le Titi de Paris
1015 West Dundee Road
Arlington Heights
(847) 506-0222
Closed Sunday–Monday
$$$

If you have the time, a trip to this suburban gem approximately thirty miles from the intersection of State and Madison is in order. Vastly popular for more than three decades, Le Titi de Paris is notable for providing authentic French cuisine outside of the city. Its warm and pleasing decor enhances the elegant, traditional meals made from global ingredients.

Chef Pierre Pollin joined the restaurant in its second year of operation, eventually purchasing it. Only recently, in the 1990s, has Chef Pollin delegated some of his menu duties to chef de cuisine Michael Maddox, who is also his partner. Sommelier and maître d'hôtel Marcel Flori oversees the seventy-four-page wine list of bottle, half-bottle, and by-the-glass offerings.

Diners may revel in dishes from the à la carte menu or enjoy the multi-course gourmand tasting menu. The appetizers are deceptively simple in appearance yet unmistakably tasty. Offerings include Mille-feuille of Home-Smoked Salmon and Scallion with Mascarpone Cream, Warm Tartlet of Braised Lamb, Brique Phyllo Surprise of Arizona Petit Gris Snails, and Maddox's seasonal classic, Frog's Legs Provençale with White Wine, Tomato, and Garlic.

Main dishes range from fragile-looking fish in a pillowy potato crust to robust, rib-sticking comfort foods. Mushroom-Crusted Veal Loin and the Seared Texas Venison Loin are two popular choices. Chef Maddox even provides a Vegetarian Cornucopia, the chef's selection of the day's market ingredients prepared to your specifications.

Desserts are, as you would expect, creative and delicious. Figures made of chocolate, ganache, cake, mousse, and other delectables bring a smooth finish to one of the best meals outside of the Chicago city limits.

Reservations are encouraged at this nonsmoking establishment.

Les Nomades
Streeterville
222 East Ontario Street
(312) 649-9010
Closed Sunday–Monday
$$$$

Originally a private club, this little hideaway offers an unbelievable refuge from the hustle and bustle of the frantic commercial area just a couple of streets away.

At first it is as if you are visiting a friend in one of Chicago's classic brownstones. The cluster of trees out front and the older neighborhood feel of the building help to start the relaxation process. Inside, on the first level, is a bright, civilized dining area replete with white-clothed tables and an eager staff. Upstairs is a warmer and more restful room complete with fireplace and dark woodwork. Attention to detail is the key to both the physical presence and the personal service encountered in this refreshingly subdued venue.

Beth and Roland Liccioni have held the reins here since 1994 and have brought their combined artistry from outstanding performances at stellar restaurants Carlos' and Le Français. Beth sees to the orderly flow of customers, and Chef Roland inspires awe from the kitchen with classic and contemporary flair.

The prix fixe menu is a traditional four-course offering of hors d'oeuvres, soups and salads, fish or meat and fowl, then cheese and desserts. A higher-level, five-course dinner is also available. The dazzling array of dishes, including terrines, foie gras, confits, and pâtés, are made with every ingredient imaginable. Here are inventive meat pairings, succulent fish, and outstanding soups. Main-component flavors are distinct and exciting, aided by complex sauces and emulsions. Product origins are often listed on the menu or can be provided by the serving staff. Choose carefully during the main portion of the meal and leave room for the artisanal cheeses and tempting mille-feuilles, sorbets, and tarts.

Jackets are required and patrons are asked to respect the hushed noise level. Reservations are essential, valet parking is available, and smoking is allowed in the bar area. For those planning an excursion to the Magnificent Mile, Les Nomades is a must.

Pili Pili
River North
230 West Kinzie Street
(312) 464-9988
$$

Pili Pili is a sunny oasis in an otherwise stark neighborhood. It may take you a while to find the place, but it's well worth the effort. Taking its name from a hot North African chile pepper, the French Provençal–inspired restaurant spices up the dining competition in the River North neighborhood near the Merchandise Mart complex. Jack Weiss, of Coco Pazzo fame, is at the helm of this restaurant, which opened in 2003. The spacious, well-lit dining room serves dinner nightly, while the more casual café area is open for lunch and serves throughout the day. A quick read of the menu highlights the spices, preparation methods, and ingredients of the Mediterranean so colorfully that, in your mind's eye, you are sitting in Provence.

The menu features a great balance of seafood, game, and vegetarian-friendly pasta entrées that branches out to include other Mediterranean-inspired choices: classics like *salade Niçoise*, onion soup gratinée, and friture of calamari; entrées from *vol-au-vent*, a classic French fricassee of chicken and vegetables in a cream sauce and served in a puff pastry, to *musaqqa'a*, the Greek lamb and eggplant dish. For lunch, sandwich options include the classic *croque monsieur*, or you can select from one of several individually portioned pizzas sporting not-so-classic toppings like pancetta, caramelized onions, or lamb sausage. Wonderfully crusty rustic breads are baked on the premises. Meats are slow-roasted in a rotisserie, while other entrées are prepared in a brick oven.

There are two standouts on the dinner menu: Tagine of Spit-Roasted Chicken, with lemon confit, herbs, and baby artichokes, and the spicy and comforting *mechoui*. This slow-roasted lamb shoulder is served with a mixture of couscous, dried fruits, and chickpeas.

Pili Pili prides itself on its hundred-bottle international wine list. Wines are available by the glass, in flights, or by the bottle. The Lemon Custard Tart is a refreshing, palate-cleansing must-have dessert after a heavily spiced entrée. The tart comes with *suprêmed* grapefruit sections in a light sauce, and the lemon shortbread's tart base is crisp and subtly flavored.

BISTROS AND BRASSERIES

Bistro Campagne
Lincoln Square
4518 North Lincoln Avenue
(773) 271-6100
$$

It would be hard to find a restaurant in this town that is more homey and comfortable than Bistro Campagne, even without the great food. Dark wood trimmings and little dining nooks add to the coziness and, unfortunately, the noise level. Bistro Campagne also has one of the most inviting outdoor sections in the city—a lawn with trees, flowers, and sitting spaces.

Chef Michael Altenberg relies on his sous chef, Arnie Shapiro, to keep patrons happy by providing excellently simple bistro fare for a reasonable price. Classics like steak *frites*, crème brûlée, and *brandade* demonstrate their rustic approach.

During Chef Altenberg's tenure at many of the other fine local restaurants, including Avanzare and Le Français, he developed an appreciation for quality-based cooking. It is easy to be swept up in his passionate explanations about his search for the ultimate fresh and organic ingredients that enhance his creations and the dining experience.

The mussels steamed in Belgian beer and the chicken shrouded in thinly sliced and fried onions and mushrooms are a couple of the hearty standards to be found here. Roasted meats and delicately sautéed fishes abide on the menu along with vegetarian choices and that French bistro standard, *croque monsieur.*

Desserts and cheeses are not overlooked. Chocolate dominates the sweet end of the menu with mousse cake, chocolate soufflés, and chocolate sauce for whatever the chef decides on that day. The cheeses, handcrafted and mostly from France, are one of the restaurant's bargains.

Chef Altenberg has changed the format and even the name of his restaurant Campagnola in Evanston to mirror this newer location in terms of concept and menu.

Other Location
815 Chicago Avenue, Evanston; (847) 475-6100

Le Vichyssois
220 West Route 120
Lakemoor
(815) 385-8221
Closed Monday–Tuesday
$$–$$$

In 1976 Bernard Cretier opened the restaurant bearing the name that signifies his origin. A native of Vichy, France, he has worked for French heads of state and has apprenticed with Paul Bocuse and at Maxim's in Paris and Chicago. His style is simple, direct, and flavorful. He brings new meaning to the phrase *cabbage salad.*

The menu is simple. Offerings such as onion tart *Niçoise*, cassoulet, warm cabbage salad, and vichyssoise stand cheek by jowl with lobster *à la nage*, *tournedos Bordelaise*, and braised lamb shanks. Specialty items like

Vidalia onion flan and potatoes *dauphinois* with fiddlehead ferns punctuate the list.

Chef Cretier's intent was to create a restaurant with a typical country-French "roadhouse" feel. Lace curtains and unusual art by French artist Gerard Purvis add to the atmosphere.

The wine list is impressive, but that's not the prize. Perhaps the best dining bargain in the area is Cretier's four-course prix fixe bistro menu, offering one appetizer, salad, entrée, and dessert for a very small outlay. This is one fantastic roadhouse, well worth the drive fifty miles from downtown Chicago.

Tournesol
Lincoln Square
4343 North Lincoln Avenue
(773) 477-8820
$$

In recent years, Chicago has experienced a renaissance of the small neighborhood French bistro. A leader in this movement, Tournesol was opened in June 2002 by Eric Aubriot, then owner of the upscale and eponymous Aubriot, and employee Michael Smith. Their goal was to provide the classic French bistro experience: good food with good value. They chose a simple yet urbane space in the burgeoning Lincoln Square neighborhood and modeled the menu after that of a typical Parisian bistro, tweaked for the American palate.

Tournesol offers a perfect French bistro experience—with all preparations adhering to the classic style. The kitchen is led by Chef Bob Zrenner, who has trained at such highly respected institutions as Al Forno, Tru, and North Pond. Zrenner insists that all dishes be prepared almost entirely from scratch, and emphasizes the use of organic produce and meats from local farms. Only the ice cream and breads are made off-site.

The menu includes several standard bistro appetizers. The *mussels mariniere* with parsley butter and cream broth puts the Red Hen baguettes to good use. The *escargot fricassé*—poached snails glazed with sautéed crimini mushrooms and finished with parsley and garlic-herb butter—is equally enjoyable. Main courses include the buttery pan-seared Idaho trout topped with classic caper brown butter and served with tournéed new potatoes and glazed Brussels sprouts on the side. The braised lamb shank is tender and filling, served with French green lentils and a rosemary *jus.*

Tournesol's 130-bottle wine list is intended to expose the customer to many small French regions and appellations that make marvelous wines at great values. Wine prices are kept low to encourage wine sales. Tournesol provides a little of everything—great food, good value, topnotch service, and neighborhood atmosphere.

Yoshi's Cafe
Lakeview
3257 North Halsted Street
(773) 248-6160
Closed Monday
$$

Yoshi's Cafe is an eclectic restaurant with a multicultural menu, friendly informal atmosphere, convivial bar, and patrons in all manner of dress, from casual to jacket and tie. Though the mix seems to suggest a neigh-borhood watering hole with good bar food, this is not the case. While Yoshi's does have the occasional special of Wagu Beef Burgers with hand-cut French fries, their specialty is not bar food but upscale, imaginative offerings that are quite reasonably priced, especially given the quality of ingredients and the skill of the chef.

In a past life Yoshi's was an upscale restaurant serving intricate Asian-influenced French cuisine, and Yoshi Katsumara, the owner/chef, was con-sumed 24/7 with the thought of degustation perfection. One day, as the story goes, Yoshi, who at the time had young children, said "Enough is enough" and changed the format of his restaurant to the urban oasis it is today.

Yoshi's formal training and imagination still shine through with such interesting offerings as Matsutake Mushrooms with Sautéed Prawns on Wasabi Mashed Potatoes, or Wagu Beef Steak with a red wine reduction, freshly grated wasabi root, and chanterelles.

Yoshi has an amazing hand with fish, be it sushi as an appetizer, sautéed fillet for an entrée, or beautiful presentations of whole-fin fish. Poultry is a strong suit as well: roast chicken is a perennial favorite, as is the duck breast, medium-rare on the inside, crisp skin on the outside.

Wonderful desserts and imaginative cocktails like the Blood Orange Martinis are not to be missed. A well-considered wine list and spot-on service round out the complete Yoshi's package.

NOTABLE

FINE DINING

Ambria
Lincoln Park
Belden-Stratford Hotel
2300 North Lincoln Park West
(773) 472-5959
Closed Sunday
$$$

A restaurant of fine decor, full of leather, dark wood, and white linens, Ambria provides both à la carte and tasting menus and a world-class wine list. Chef Gabino Sotelino creates the contemporary French cuisine that has kept this classy establishment in step with its trendy neighborhood. The perfect spot for a special evening out, many Chicago nuptials begin with a proposal at Ambria.

Carlos'

429 Temple Avenue
Highland Park
(847) 432-0770
Closed Tuesday
$$$$

Newly redecorated, Carlos' continues to garner an informed, appreciative following even though it is a thirty-minute drive (twenty-eight miles) from downtown Chicago. Proprietors Carlos and Debbie Nieto have been providing spectacular dishes in this North Shore destination for more than twenty years. Along with Ramiro Velasquez, chef de cuisine since 1999, the Nietos have amassed an impressive list of awards honoring their contemporary recipes made from ingredients of worldwide origin.

Selecting from an à la carte menu or a tasting menu of seven courses, diners in the wood-and-marble dining room can feast on myriad quiches, soups, salads, and main dishes. Of particular note is Carlos' *salade Niçoise*, perhaps the best found west of Provence. Three private rooms are available for special groups. The wine list is one of the best in the Chicago area and has been honored by *Wine Spectator*.

The Nietos also operate a more casual storefront destination in the center of Highland Park. Their **Cafe Central** is replete with salads, sandwiches, *tartines*, quiches, and delightful seafood dishes.

BISTROS AND BRASSERIES

Bistrot Margot

Old Town
1437 North Wells Street
(312) 587-3660
$$

In 1999 chef/owner Joe Doppes opened Bistrot Margot in the old but greatly reinvigorated neighborhood of Old Town. Chef Doppes, who learned part of his craft studying under Chef Jean Banchet, provides classic French comfort food at very affordable prices. An unusual Art Nouveau dining room is part of Chef Doppes's mission to give his establishment the ambiance and energy of early 1900s Paris.

Café Bernard

Lincoln Park
2100 North Halsted Street
(773) 871-2100
$$

Bernard Le Coq opened this Halsted Street standby in the 1970s and has been making full-flavored country-style French food ever since. A blackboard announces everything you need to know about the specials, and lots of artwork keeps one company in the relaxing atmosphere. Conveniently located in the theater district, fair-weather customers may find seating on the sidewalk for people watching. The companion **Red Rooster Wine Bar** is located next door and offers darkly satisfying, slow service.

Chez Joël
Little Italy
1119 West Taylor Street
(312) 226-6479
$$-$$$

A young and eager half-aproned staff, many from the nearby university, help provide diners with terrific meals and attentive service. Chef/owner Joël Kazouini serves traditional dishes indoors and alfresco. Valet service is available; parking in the area is problematic.

Cyrano's Bistro & Wine Bar
River North
546 North Wells Street
(312) 467-0546
Closed Sunday
$$

Bergerac native Didier Durand is the chef/owner of this very popular authentic bistro featuring the cuisine of the Bergerac region in southern France. Amid the French posters and gilt mirrors, patrons are served hearty fare—a result of Durand's experiences (since 1986) at such culinary greats as Carlos', La Forêt, Gordon, Le Perroquet, and La Bohème. Every Sunday, Durand can be spotted at the farmers' market at the Cooking and Hospitality Institute of Chicago (CHIC), selling his home-made pâtés and soups, ratatouille, and cassoulet, frozen and packaged in individual portions—truly Slow convenience foods.

Froggy's
306 Green Bay Road
Highwood
(847) 433-7080
Closed Sunday
$$

Fine dining in a casual café atmosphere best describes Froggy's. Chef/owner Thierry Lefeuvre provides regional and country-style cuisine inside this ivy-covered hideaway. Not unexpectedly, frog images play a part in the menu design and the interior decorations. This is one restaurant where you can see up close the size of a Balthazar of champagne.

Jacky's Bistro
2545 Prairie Avenue
Evanston
(847) 733-0899
$$–$$$

With the casual elegance of a French country bistro, Jacky's Bistro features skillfully prepared traditional and also contemporary French classics tinged with American influences, which are found in chef/owner Jacky Pluton's use of seasonal, locally sourced ingredients. Consistently good food, a warm, service-oriented staff, and the laid-back atmosphere have earned Jacky's Bistro an enthusiastic and loyal following. One can easily imagine whiling away the hours here, watching a Sunday afternoon turn into evening, comfortably ensconced in one of the inviting banquettes. Specialties run the gamut from roasted chicken, bouillabaisse, lamb shanks, fresh fish specials, and a selection of traditional steak preparations. An extensive wine list offers both familiar and more obscure pairings at all price ranges.

Kiki's Bistro
River North
900 North Franklin Street
(312) 335-5454
Closed Sunday
$$

Kiki's is an authentic standard of French bistro food, wine, and atmosphere, and one of the great local standbys. The warm and cozy interior, complete with lace curtains and plank flooring, recalls countryside restaurants.

In 1990 Georges "Kiki" Cuisance closed the venerable Le Bordeaux, causing much weeping and gnashing of teeth. He has made up for that loss by providing stick-to-your-ribs meals in this delightful River North bistro.

Former sous chef Javier Guzman now produces the classic fare. Many consider his French onion soup to be the best in the city. In fact, Kiki's may be the best place to have soups and stews in the city—just watch for the menu to feature the cream of asparagus with crabmeat.

There is plenty of parking on the usually uncrowded street, and valet parking is available. The specials list is printed daily.

La Crêperie
Lakeview
2845 North Clark Street
(733) 528-9050
Closed Monday
$

One of the *grand-pères* of French food in Chicago, La Crêperie opened its doors in the early 1970s to a bell-bottomed crowd looking for something different, simple, and inexpensive. Germain Roignant and his wife served up delicious seafood crêpes, hazelnut crêpes, and all combinations in between. Son Jeremy is now in charge, and the space is larger, including a patio in back. Even if the restaurant is showing its age a bit, it's worth a visit just for the history.

Le Bouchon
Bucktown
1958 North Damen Avenue
(773) 862-6600
Closed Sunday
$$

Le Bouchon, created in 1993, is a place where you can enjoy excellent comfort food in a relaxed, personable space. Chef/owner Jean Claude

Poilevey has spent thirty years educating Chicago-area diners in the art of food preparation and enjoyment. Burgundy native Poilevey will sate you with his traditional bistro fare—delicious morsels such as his signature *tarte a l'oignon Alsacienne*, a generous *pot-au-feu*, and his fabulous sautéed rabbit with shallots and mushrooms.

Mon Amí Gabi
Lincoln Park
Belden-Stratford Hotel
2300 Lincoln Park West
(773) 348-8886
$$–$$$

The wood-and-glass room dividers and chalkboard of daily specials at this bistro, ensconced in the Belden-Stratford Hotel, recall images of the venerable La Coupole in Paris. Chef/partner Gabino Sotelino (see Ambria, p. 63) gives his name and energy to this modern *auberge* offering straightforward standard fare and numerous specialties like their steak *frites* and *moules*, which are widely considered to be among the best anywhere.

GERMAN & AUSTRIAN

Chicago's North Side was once home to scores of German restaurants, taverns, and breweries. As with many ethnic groups, but particularly for immigrants from German-speaking countries, these establishments provided social cohesion, cultural continuity, and camaraderie for their clientele. Prohibition hit these institutions particularly hard, and while immigrants from Bavaria to Pomerania continued to arrive in Chicago throughout most of the last century, their children moved to the suburbs and have mostly assimilated. Most German restaurants followed suit. Miraculously, there remain several German social clubs in Chicago, and even a small part of town where German is still spoken (see sidebar, p. 72). Moreover, the oldest restaurant in Chicago is German; the Berghoff in the Loop was the first to receive a liquor license in Chicago after Prohibition, and remains popular among locals and tourists alike, not least for its annual open-air Oktoberfest celebration.

At present, however, most German/Austrian establishments in town primarily target two groups. The first is the aging immigrant population that the owners seem to regard as a captive audience, as reflected in the institutional nature of their fare. The second consists of beer-guzzling Teutonophiles who marvel at double-digit tap selections, a phenomenon alien to the Old World establishments they're trying to mimic (it's challenging enough to keep just one or two draught selections as fresh- and crisp-tasting as in Germany or Austria). In addition, many of these *Gaststätten* charge a hefty amount for what tastes like nuked frozen food covered with canned gravy. Some places are charming, some are popular; few are good, let alone Slow. Here are those few.

Julius Meinl
Lakeview
3601 North Southport Avenue
(773) 868-1857
$

If you can believe their Web site, a young Viennese boy named Julius Meinl was actually the first to come up with the "ingenious idea of selling roasted coffee." Now a major distributor of roasted coffee in Europe, the company is still run by the Meinl family and has a retail outlet in Vienna. Their second (and only other) retail location opened in November 2003 in Chicago's Lakeview neighborhood. Here they offer top-notch strudel, tortes, and pastries, as well as a few breakfast and lunch items. Similar to Starbucks, customers encounter a take-out area upon entry. This may be misleading, since during peak hours customers need to wait to be seated; in fact, it's advisable to make reservations if you're planning an evening visit.

This is the closest you'll get to a Viennese café experience in Chicago, though the genuine article would have a larger selection, a larger space, and a bit more bustle. It would also be less expensive, though Meinl's pricing isn't terribly out of line for this well-heeled and foodie-infested neighborhood, and they're ultimately not much pricier than Starbucks. They score well on authenticity: The coffee is roasted at the flagship store in Vienna, and European butter is used in their baked goods. The waitress on my last visit had spent several years in Austria, was well versed in the company's history, and was quite professional, even earnest—just as one would expect in an Austrian establishment. Overall, this is a fine fix for the Europhile suffering from café withdrawal.

Laschet's Inn
North Center
2119 West Irving Park Road
(773) 478-7915
$$

German taverns in Chicago can harbor insular cliques and shopworn regulars, and Laschet's is no exception—although they've upgraded their operation considerably by redecorating (though the old map of imperial Germany still haunts the front wall) and, more importantly, by introducing a full menu of traditional German food. They've immediately jumped to the front of the class: This is hands-down the best German food in Chicago. All dishes rank high in terms of authenticity and quality. The conviviality quotient is high as well: The lower-level bar area still draws the old-timers, and though high-profile business and political types regularly frequent the new dining area, the overall atmosphere remains quite casual.

Resi's Bierstube
North Center
2034 West Irving Park Road
(773) 271-3935
$$

Resi's Bierstube offers very reasonably priced German food in a setting you'll find kitschy, cute, or cozy, depending on whether you order your beer in a stein, boot, or glass. The intimate beer garden on the back patio is justifiably popular during the summer months. Regulars rave about Resi's sauerkraut: It tastes like it's been cooked in chicken broth, which isn't very traditional, but it is indeed the tastiest kraut I've had anywhere. In winter, they serve an authentically fatty and delicious goulash. The

GERMAN FESTIVALS

The Lincoln Square neighborhood puts on several German-themed events each year, but the biggest is the German-American Fest held each September. Celebrating General Baron Friedrich Wilhelm von Steuben, a hero of the American Revolution, the day starts with a parade down Western Avenue. Large beer tents are set up in Lincoln Square, and local German heritage clubs set up stands to sell homemade strudel, bratwurst, and *Brezele*. Commemorative liter-sized steins are sold, refilled, then refilled again over the course of the weekend-long fest. Not surprisingly, the crowd becomes more boisterous as day turns into evening, and there always seems to be a core faction that never really leaves. It's one of the best neighborhood festivals in Chicago.

The other major German festival is the *Christkindlmarkt*. More than sixty-five traditional timber booths are set up in the Daley Center Plaza (and in recent years also in the adjoining and infamously vacant Block 37 across from Marshall Field's). Considering that the event takes place in the middle of the Loop, it's a surprisingly authentic German Christmas market. As in Germany, the main draw is *Glühwein*, hot mulled wine served in ceramic cups. Given the average temperature of a Chicago December night, this shouldn't be hard to understand. When the *Christkindlmarkt* started eight years ago, most of the vendors were from the Plauen area, the southernmost part of old East Germany. Over the years other regions became represented as well, and 2003 saw the first appearance of non-German vendors. Some of the veteran vendors are even starting to substitute cheaper local ingredients in their traditional offerings (for instance, making *Soljanka* from salsa, which is a bit cheeky). Still, if you want a real *Frikadelle* (quaintly dubbed "German Burgers") or a hot slab of *Leberkäse* off the grill, this is the place to be.

wurst plate of brats, kraut, and potato salad is very tasty, though they mislabel the smoked sausage "Thuringer" (as do most German places in Chicago). The quality and authenticity here isn't quite as high as Laschet's Inn, across the street, but this is a fun place and well worth a visit.

NOTABLE

The Berghoff
See Bars, Pubs & Taverns, p. 195.

LINCOLN SQUARE:
A WALK DOWN LINCOLN AVENUE

Germans were once the dominant ethnic group on much of Chicago's North Side; in fact, major east-west thoroughfares bore the names of Kaisers and German cities before anti-German sentiment after World War I led to their being renamed and Anglicized as, for example, Shakespeare Street and Dickens Street.

The sole remaining contiguous stretch of German shops is in the Lincoln Square neighborhood along Lincoln Avenue. While most of the ethnic Germans in Lincoln Square have long since moved west to the suburbs, many still make regular trips to the old neighborhood to shop. Many of these shops are now staffed and/or managed by various Central and Eastern European immigrants. But most of these "new" shopkeepers, some of whom have been in the neighborhood for twenty or more years, also speak German—kept in practice by a stream of regular customers that wouldn't have it any other way.

In terms of food, Lincoln Square ranks among the best Chicago has to offer. The crown jewel is **Delicatessen Meyer** (1) — see the entry on p. 290. Also on the short list for cured-meat enthusiasts is **Lincoln Quality Meat Market, Inc.** (2). The hand-lettered *Fraktur* list of classic German cuts of meat and sausages that adorns their storefront is a charming atavism, since their current specialties are inspired by places a touch to the east. They make their own Bulgarian and Hungarian sausages, and it's quite impossible to keep enough of either on hand.

Just down the street, **Café Selmarie** (3) sounds like the token French establishment in this tiny Teutonic town (it's actually just an amalgam of the owners' middle names), but the fine tortes, cakes, and strudel in their take-out section strike a more Austrian chord. The other half of their space is dedicated to a restaurant with an eclectic menu focusing on new American and European comfort food. In summer, they take over a good part of the *Platz* (which sports a modest fountain), and this becomes a fine place to get a salad, a brioche, and a glass of *Hefeweizen*.

The most visually prominent establishment on the street is the **Chicago Brauhaus** (4). The food here is best described as adequate. The atmosphere, with live *Blasmusik* on weekends and a main dining area of beer-hall proportions, caters to the, um, mature crowd (did someone say *polka set?*). But nothing can keep the regulars from kicking up their heels once the oompah gets cranking, and after a few steins of Stiegl it's hard not to get swept up in the action. If the focus is on entertainment, you're probably better off here than at the other beer outlets on the block, which run the gamut from borderline dive to dank and scary.

1. **Delicatessen Meyer**
   4750 N. Lincoln
2. **Lincoln Quality Meat Market, Inc.**
   4661 N. Lincoln
3. **Café Selmarie**
   4729 N. Lincoln
4. **Chicago Brauhaus**
   4732 N. Lincoln
5. **Chopping Block Cooking School**
   4747 N. Lincoln
6. **Barba Yianni Grecian Taverna**
   4761 N. Lincoln

The latest addition to the street is **The Chopping Block Cooking School** (5). The Lincoln Square location opened just as this book went to press. Judging from the wares on sale in their storefront, this establishment looks to be targeting the higher-octane set that has been starting to shop (and live) here over the past five years. The staff is ambitious and polished; this will be an interesting place to watch.

The Greek restaurant **Barba Yianni** (6) anchors the north end of the block. It's not entirely out of place here, as Greek restaurants are as ubiquitous in Germany as Mexican ones are in the United States.

Delicatessen Meyer
4750 North Lincoln Avenue
(773) 561-3377

Lincoln Quality Meat Market, Inc.
4661 North Lincoln Avenue
(773) 561-4570

Café Selmarie
4729 North Lincoln Avenue
(773) 989-5595

Chicago Brauhaus
4732 North Lincoln Avenue
(773) 784-4444

The Chopping Block Cooking School
4747 North Lincoln Avenue
(773) 472-6700

Barba Yianni Grecian Taverna
4761 North Lincoln Avenue
(773) 878-6400

GREEK

Artopolis Bakery Cafe and Agora
Greektown
306 South Halsted Street
(312) 559-9000
$$

In the heart of Greektown on Halsted Street stands Artopolis. *Artos*, which means "bread," and *polis*, which means "city" in Greek, is the perfect name for this family-owned bakery and café that features homemade artisanal breads ranging from kalamata olive baguettes to sea-salt and poppy-seed sourdough loaves.

But homemade bread is not the only food you will find at Artopolis. A cafeteria line featuring traditional Greek specialties offers regular items and daily specials prepared on the spot. *Artopitas* made with homemade puff pastry filled with feta and kasseri cheeses, spinach and feta, or chicken and artichokes are just one of the Mediterranean entrées you can enjoy here or take out. Platters with hummus, eggplant spread, *taramasalata* (fish roe spread), and *tzatziki* (yogurt, garlic, and cucumber spread) are fresh and rich with flavor. Salads range from a traditional Greek style, replete with large chunks of feta cheese and *pepperoncini*, to seafood—chewy, flavorful calamari marinated in vinaigrette and scooped over a bed of lettuce. Artopolis also offers sandwiches made on their delicious homemade bread, fresh homemade soups (*avgolemono* and bulgur wheat with spinach, to name just two), and traditional Greek entrées such as *moussaka* and *pastitsio*. A wood-fired oven turns out personal-size pizzas with a variety of toppings.

If you're still hungry for dessert, try the *loukoumades*—deep-fried dumplings soaked in Greek honey and topped with walnuts, cinnamon, and sesame seeds that have inspired many health club memberships. Other Greek traditional desserts include baklava (walnuts, brown sugar, and cinnamon in phyllo dough), *galactoboureko* (custard in phyllo dough soaked in honey syrup), *bougatsa* (custard in phyllo dough with powdered sugar), and many types of Greek cookies.

Modern Greek music and a friendly staff contribute to the amiable surroundings. The restaurant is usually packed from lunch to late dinner. Fridays and Saturdays draw a sizable bar crowd, in particular wine lovers who go to enjoy a large variety of Greek wines. Finally, for those looking for a unique gift, Artopolis has a large section of its floor dedicated to a great variety of serving pieces, novelties, and Greek delicacies. Gift baskets with Mediterranean-inspired china, wine, and sweets are also available.

Santorini
Greektown
800 West Adams Street
(312) 829-8820
$$

The Kontos family represents the American dream in many ways. Greek immigrant James Kontos worked hard and opened his own eatery, the popular Tempo, which is just west of the John Hancock Building. The elder Kontos put his children to work—his two sons cooked, and his four daughters waited tables. Tempo's success paved the way for Kontos to realize his vision of bringing Greek food in a fine-dining atmosphere to Chicagoans.

Five years later he opened Santorini in what is now the heart of Greektown. Its warm atmosphere—and even warmer fireplace—have enticed diners ever since. The family still runs both places; Stefano Kontos, James's son, now manages Santorini. He describes himself as a bit of a fanatic when it comes to the food he serves and he tries to use organic produce. The approach runs in the family. "My father is very old-school. You try to stay to the old ways and do things as naturally as you can," Stefano says.

Biting into *kalamari* laden with olive oil and lemon sauce with fresh oregano, you are swept off your feet, and for good reason. The lemons were hand-squeezed; the pesticide-free olive oil was cold-pressed at the Kontos family's farm in Greece, which is also where the oregano comes from. This attention to detail carries through every dish.

Santorini is known for its seafood. The black sea bass is a rare treat, as is the fish roe spread. But it's the lamb I love. Try the lamb *paidakia*, tender, thin-sliced lamb chops by the pound. The *avgolemono* (egg and lemon soup), which can be bought by the bucketful—no joke!—is to die for.

Amid all this praise for Santorini's food comes another accolade: Its service is impeccable, among the best in the city.

NOTABLE

Athenian Room
Lincoln Park
807 West Webster Avenue
(773) 348-5155
$

Athenian Room was established in 1972 by Alex Polakis in this Lincoln Park location long before it was the bustling, high-end neighborhood that it is today. If you get a chance to visit when Alex is there, which he usually is, you may even get some picturesque descriptions of Lincoln Park's earlier, rougher personality and how he started working in Greek restaurants around town at the early age of twelve.

The place feels like a cross between a small Greek *taverna* and a Greek diner, and the Greek-American menu reflects this. The food is remarkably tasty, fresh, and inexpensive, making it a wonderful place to swing by for lunch on a busy day. The Chicken Kalamata, basted in a wonderful lemon, red wine vinegar, and oregano sauce, is tender and delicious. It is served with an order of the best Greek fries in the city (see p. 228), and at these prices, you cannot go wrong.

Barba Yianni Grecian Taverna
See "Lincoln Square: A Walk down Lincoln Avenue" in German & Austrian, p. 74.

Pegasus
Greektown
130 South Halsted Street
(312) 226-3377
$$

Pegasus is a charming restaurant with sea-blue walls that sport a mural depicting the Mykonos skyline on a summer day. Reading the appetizer list alone is like reading the front page of a newspaper. Try the *pastitsio* (pasta with nutty ground beef and lamb in a béchamel sauce); it's particularly good here.

However, the best reason to visit Pegasus is its rooftop outdoor dining area, which has its own smaller menu in the summer. This view of the city skyline makes one happy to be in Chicago and forgetful of its long winter days. In the company of friends, and surrounded by appetizers and drinks, soak up summer evenings here while they last.

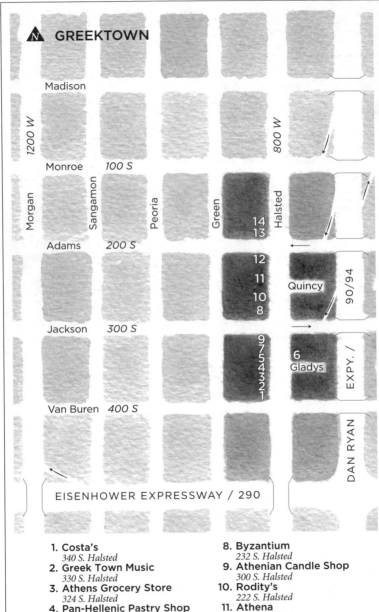

1. **Costa's**
   340 S. Halsted
2. **Greek Town Music**
   330 S. Halsted
3. **Athens Grocery Store**
   324 S. Halsted
4. **Pan-Hellenic Pastry Shop**
   322 S. Halsted
5. **Jorgio Cigars**
   320 S. Halsted
6. **9 Muses**
   315 S. Halsted
7. **Parthenon**
   314 S. Halsted
8. **Byzantium**
   232 S. Halsted
9. **Athenian Candle Shop**
   300 S. Halsted
10. **Rodity's**
    222 S. Halsted
11. **Athena**
    212 S. Halsted
12. **Greek Islands**
    200 S. Halsted
13. **Santorini**
    800 W. Adams
14. **Pegasus**
    130 S. Halsted

A WALK THROUGH GREEKTOWN

The first Greeks to come to Chicago were ship captains who arrived via Lake Michigan in the 1840s. Some of them decided to stay and became food peddlers, the progenitors of the city's modern-day restaurateurs. As the generations passed, other Greeks settled in an area of the West Side called the Delta, located around the intersection of Harrison Street, Blue Island Avenue, and Halsted Street.

In the 1960s, the Eisenhower Expressway and the University of Illinois Circle Campus were built, forcing the city's Greek community a few blocks north and creating what is now known as Greektown—the section of South Halsted between Madison and Van Buren.

Today's Greektown is a popular destination for tourists and locals alike. The neighborhood boasts a plethora of authentic family-owned restaurants that focus on fresh ingredients and Greek delicacies, as well as many retail stores that sell essential Mediterranean foods and other items.

Approaching Greektown from the south on Halsted Street, you'll first notice the stylized Grecian temples and pavilions that were erected on street corners in the mid-1990s. Depending on your perspective, they are either kitschy or incredibly tacky, but they do serve a purpose, indicating that you are indeed entering Greektown.

On the west side of the street you'll see the first of many top-class restaurants in the neighborhood. **Costa's** (1) serves traditional Greek food in a warm and inviting space. Not far from Costa's is **Greek Town Music** (2), the city's only all-Greek music store.

Right next door to Greek Town Music sits the wonderful **Athens Grocery Store** (3), family-owned for more than thirty years and now run by brothers Jim and Bill Siannas. This store carries everything Greek, from ouzo, the anise-flavored liquor, to jars of *taramosalata* (carp roe). You'll also find twenty kinds of olive oil, olives, cheeses, and lamb—even Greek Orthodox religious paraphernalia.

Just to the north, follow the incredible smells to the door of the **Pan-Hellenic Pastry Shop** (4), which sells a wide variety of Greek pastries and breads to the public, as well as supplying local restaurants. From the familiar baklava to lesser-known baked goods, this stop is a must.

If you enjoy cigars, Greektown has its own shop, **Jorgio Cigars** (5), located next door to the pastry shop. It's a great place to sip thick, strong Greek coffee and puff on a Greek cigar while visiting with fellow connoisseurs. For a less sedate experience, go across the street to the hip **9 Muses** club (6), where young Greek-speaking clubbers go in and out all weekend. And what would a neighborhood be without a coffee shop?

Back on the west side of Halsted, you'll come to the notoriously rau-
cous **Parthenon** restaurant (7), which is famous for its belly dancers,
group parties, great food, and especially the plates and plates of flaming
saganaki, wonderful Greek kefalatori or kasseri cheese that is doused with
brandy and set ablaze, typically amid cries of "Opa!" If you want to continue the party after dinner, pop in next door to the Parthenon's
Bouzouki Lounge. Or for a completely different experience, visit nearby
Byzantium (8), another trendy nightclub.

On the west corner of Jackson and Halsted, you'll find the oldest business in Greektown, a "transplant" from the old Delta neighborhood. The
family-owned **Athenian Candle Shop** (9) has been in business for more
than eighty years and in their present location for more than four
decades. Religious and home-decor candles are made here and sold in the
storefront retail shop. In addition to candles, the store also sells many religious items, such as Greek Orthodox icons, crosses, and oils that are said
to ward off evil spirits.

Rodity's (10) restaurant is another Greektown favorite, serving authentic food in a homey atmosphere. On weekends and holidays lamb is roasted
on spits in the window of the restaurant. Just next door, the patio at **Athena**
(11) is one of the largest and liveliest outdoor seating areas in Chicago during the summer months.

A family favorite is **Greek Islands** restaurant (12), at the southwest corner of Adams and Halsted. The place is huge, and can seat 450 people at
a time. Founded by three childhood friends back in 1971, it is still a wonderful place for traditional and well-priced Greek food. Their *taramosalata* is the best in Greektown.

Across Adams Street is **Santorini** (13), which specializes in seafood and
has a comfortable, fishing-village atmosphere.

Want a great view of the city? Try **Pegasus** (14). The rooftop garden
seating has a view to die for. The full menu is not served there, but a large
variety of *mezedes*—Greek appetizers similar to Spanish *tapas*—is available. Live entertainment makes this outdoor garden great for a drink and
a light summer bite.

Every year Greektown plays host to its own Taste of Greece festival, a
weekend full of Greek music, food, tradition, and heritage, and a great
time to discover the neighborhood.

INDIAN & PAKISTANI

Arya Bhavan   *(Indian, Vegetarian)*
West Rogers Park
2508 West Devon Avenue
(773) 274-5800
$–$$

Devon Avenue, on the city's Far North Side, is a showcase for Chicago's ethnic and cultural diversity; a place where Indians, Pakistanis, Orthodox Jews, and recent Eastern European immigrants, to name a few, live, work, shop, and, of course, eat. Among the many fine Indian restaurants and snack shops on Devon, Arya Bhavan, which roughly translates as "Our Home," stands out. Jayendra and Kirti Sheth warmly welcome diners to their simple yet tastefully decorated restaurant, which features pure vegetarian Indian cuisine. Jayendra and Kirti were born and bred in Indian vegetarian culture and personally oversee the kitchen and front room, blending the best of Northern and Southern Indian vegetarian cooking and spices.

Although Arya Bhavan offers a full menu, the best way to sample the broad array of well-prepared dishes is to come for the weekday lunch and dinner buffets, and especially for the grand buffets offered on the weekend. The recipes may include *uttapam*, a pancake of fermented ground *urad dal* and rice, cooked on a grill and topped with onions, tomatoes, and cilantro. As with many of the dishes, it is served with sides of *sambhar*, a thin but spicy *dal*, and flavorful, freshly made coconut, cilantro, and tamarind chutneys. If it's available, try the *uppama*, which is like Cream of Wheat mixed with mustard seeds, onion, tomato, green peas, green chiles, lentils, and cashews. It is a warm and satisfying dish. Other standouts include *paneer tikka masala*, homemade cheese simmered in a sauce of onions and tomato; *bengan bhartha*, spicy mashed smoked eggplant; and *tadka dal*, a rich blend of garlic, ginger, lentils, and spices. Arya Bhavan's *chana masala*, the simple dish of chickpeas and spices, is a cut above the usual. The breads are very good, and if you are a garlic lover, be sure to try the garlic naan.

Desserts feature a surprisingly light *gulab jamun*, made with homemade paneer and awash in sweet syrup. Fruit shakes and *lassi* (a chilled yogurt drink) are nice accompaniments to the spicy food, and a limited but well-chosen and reasonably priced selection of wines and Indian beers are available. Service is prompt and efficient, but don't be surprised if Kirti greets you at the door as if welcoming you to her home.

Indian Garden   *(Indian)*
West Rogers Park
2548 West Devon Avenue
(773) 338-2929
$-$$

Indian Garden is located in the heart of the Indian and Pakistani community along Devon Avenue; within easy walking distance of the restaurant
are some excellent ethnic markets, sari shops, jewelry stores, and music
and video vendors. Indian Garden is warm and inviting and a bit more
elegant than many of the Indian places on Devon. The tables are draped
in cloth, the room is nicely decorated with tile accents and Indian art, and
the food arrives on carts, beautifully presented in serving dishes warmed
by candles. But don't let its upscale appearance fool you: It serves some of
the best Indian food on the street.

Start with *shami kabab*, four nicely spiced patties of ground lamb,
crunchy on the outside and soft and flavorful on the inside. Another good
starter is *dahi bhala*, light lentil puffs served in a pool of citrusy yogurt
sauce and garnished with cilantro leaves. The flavorful fish Goa curry
comes with chunks of perfectly cooked fish in a rich and spicy red curry
sauce studded with mustard seeds and curry leaves. Indian Garden's
chana masala is a fiery combination of diced tomato and onion in a thick
brown gravy topped with chopped cilantro. Another well-prepared standard is the *bhindi masala*, a generous dish of small chunks of crunchy
okra, chopped tomato, and onion.

In addition to mango *lassi* and shakes, and in line with its upscale sensibilities, Indian Garden offers an attractive selection of wines and beers
as well as bar service. As one would expect, the waitstaff is professional,
attentive, and helpful—feel free to ask them for recommendations.

Kababish   *(Indian, Punjabi)*
River North
939 North Orleans Street
(312) 642-8622
$

Dhabas are roughly the equivalent of truck stops in India: roadside
restaurants providing the comfort food of Punjab to those in need of a
quick and hearty meal. In Chicago, the equivalent of the *dhaba* is the
"cabbie joint." These small restaurants smell intensely of back-home
Indian cooking, slinging out a version of fast food twenty-four hours a
day, also to those in need of a quick dose of comfort. Kababish may or
may not be the best of these cabbie places, most of which are located just

outside of downtown Chicago, but it is a very good choice—a good place to take a chance on something adventurous.

The men behind the counter warmly greet all customers and take the time to explain dishes that lack eye appeal. Regardless of how it looks, nearly everything here tastes good, in an oily, fiery, in-your-face kind of way. It's not what is usually considered Slow, but Kababish allows you to taste a type of Indian cooking that's about as real as you will find in Chicago.

Each day a steam table contains a few curries, a long-cooked, falling-apart vegetable dish, and a still-spicy yet supposedly soothing lentil dish called *dal*. In the morning the choices may include *halwa*, looking and tasting like orange Cream of Wheat. Hidden from sight, though, is the most incongruous and wonderful dish here—quite simply the best fish taco to be found in Chicago. Whole kingfish (watch out for bones) are scored, fried, doused with a secret blend of spices, and served with a homemade *chapati* that's as tasty as any tortilla you'll find in the city. For "salsa," ask for their brown sauce of indeterminate provenance. Shreds of iceberg lettuce complete the illusion. Kababish knows one price: $6. It might be the best six bucks you've ever spent.

Mount Everest   (*Nepalese, Northern Indian*)
618 Church Street
Evanston
(847) 491-1069
$

This pleasant and pretty storefront showcases the cooking of Northern India and the subtly spiced, distinctive dishes of Nepal. It bills itself as "a taste of the Himalayas," but the menu also reflects a good percentage of Indian food.

What's the difference between the cooking of India and Nepal? "Nepalese cooking is home style—with less oil and spicing—no dairy products, and more vegetables," says owner Ramakant Kharel.

This is a favorite spot of thrifty Evanstonians, including Northwestern University students who go for the daily lunch buffet, which includes nine hot dishes, salads, breads, and desserts for an all-you-can-eat price of $6.95.

When you first sit down at dinner, waiters bring out crisp *pappadam* with a pickled vegetable relish and two sauces—one peppery and hot, the other red and sweet.

Mount Everest serves an abundance of meat and vegetarian dishes unique to the Himalayas, and the menu fully explains each choice so diners aren't lost among the Indian staples. Nepalese offerings include a wide range of

meats, vegetables, and seafood in innumerable tandoori, vindaloo, tikka, and masala preparations.

A great Nepalese meal might consist of puffy naan and roti breads, spicy cauliflower, saffron rice, and *khasi ko massu* (goat meat cooked on the bone, "village style"). Finish the meal with hot *gulab jamun* (fried balls of dense dough soaked in syrup) and a nice steaming cup of Himalayan tea.

The beverage list is of interest as well, featuring mango *lassi*, Taj Mahal beers, and Flying Horse, an oversized malt lager that should easily last through the meal.

Sabri Nehari *(Pakistani)*
West Rogers Park
2511 West Devon Avenue
(773) 743-6200
$$

For years Indian restaurants in Chicago mostly dished up a version of Moghuli court cuisine, but the related Pakistani/Muslim home cooking was absent. A flux of Pakistani immigrants changed this. Most Muslim-style food is served in modest establishments (see Kababish, p. 83), but Sabri Nehari serves Pakistani food in a nice restaurant setting.

Pakistani food incorporates certain elements familiar to lovers of Indian food—primarily dishes cooked in the clay tandoor oven—but adds a range of hearty and aggressive home-style items. Even the cubes of grilled chicken (chicken *boti*) come to the table in a puddle of grease, and this is meant as a sincere compliment.

Muslim Pakistanis, unlike Hindus, have no proscription against beef, and their restaurants feature a repertoire of beef dishes. Best at Sabri is its namesake dish, *nehari*. Traditionally eaten for breakfast after a night's cooking, this goopy, not terribly attractive blend of liquid and beef shank tastes complex and special. One bowl of *nehari*, with any of Sabri's breads, leavened naan or griddled *parantha*, will leave you stuffed. From the other end of the cow comes that most neglected of parts, the brains. Sabri's brain masala—rich, fully spiced, and accented with long shards of ginger root—may convince dubious diners of the virtues of this dish.

Vegetarians have expressed frustration with Sabri, both for its lack of options and its lazy vegetable preparations. But Sabri loves meat. Entrées include intense stews and kebabs—even the innocuous-looking *seek* kebab packs lots of spice. The chicken *charga* hardly looks innocent: A whole chicken, deep-fried with subcontinental spices, soaked in Louisiana hot sauce, and wrapped in aluminum foil, it gets plunked on your table, steaming, with a knife thrust at you. End your meal with *kheer*, a pudding made of ground rice and (perhaps too much) cardamom.

Service segues nicely between modern professionalism and the staff's desire to introduce you to a cuisine that is familiar yet different. A laminated color menu with pictures of most dishes helps a lot.

Sizzle India *(Indian)*
West Rogers Park
2509¹/₂ West Devon Avenue
(773) 761-7777
$

Sizzle India threw out all the palace grandeur of the older Indian restaurants but kept the vital feature: the buffet. Do not go here for anything but the food.

More importantly, Sizzle India features the food of Hyderabad and the state of Andhra Pradesh, known as some of the spiciest in India. In the south, Andhra leans vegetarian, but a historic Mogul presence in its capital, Hyderabad, also gives the cuisine a cosmopolitan quality. And nothing says *Hyderabad* more than the dish known as chili chicken. Supposedly created by Southern Indian cooks as a version of Chinese food found in North India, it is a red muddle of chicken pieces in a sauce almost as spicy as its name. It can usually be found on the buffet.

More traditional Andhra dishes include ribbons of cabbage colored yellow from turmeric and dotted black from mustard seeds; small whole eggplants covered in a sauce thick with coconut; and *dahi bhat*, a white dish that looks like rice pudding but is instead tart and hot. On the buffet, open the rice cooker; it hides the fresh-baked, grainy but good flatbreads called chapati. In addition, someone constantly makes fresh batches of *uthappam*, small pancakes, which are marred only by the same lousy tomatoes harming every Indian (and Thai, Mexican, Middle-Eastern, etc.) place in town.

Sonargaon Restaurant   *(Bangladeshi)*
West Rogers Park
2306 West Devon Avenue
(773) 262-8008
$

Bangladeshis work in and even own many Indian restaurants, but actual Bangladeshi food is rarely seen in Chicago or elsewhere. At Sonargaon, a large, well-lit restaurant with features that belie its low prices, diners can now try the food of Bangladesh.

Bangladesh fronts the Bay of Bengal and contains a range of rivers. Bangladeshi food mostly draws from these sources, especially freshwater or "sweetwater" fish. Sonargaon presents fish and seafood more than ten ways, including fried, in gravy, and minced as *kofta*, or fish balls. The spicing is generally milder than Indian food. Much flavor comes from onions and other vegetables.

Sonargaon also has dishes typical of Muslim cooking such as *nehari* and the grain-and-meat dish *haleem*. Finally, they use their tandoor oven well. Chicken *tikka* is moist and infused from its yogurt marinade, yet fully textured. They say their *rasmalai* (a dessert made from fresh cheese and condensed milk) is the Bangladeshi version, but it tastes like most others—creamy, sweet, and fresh.

Udupi Palace   *(Southern Indian, Vegetarian)*
West Rogers Park
2543 West Devon Avenue
(773) 338-2152
$

Udupi has broken away from the dominant Indian restaurant mode. It offers no tandoor chicken—no meat at all, in fact, and none of the familiar curries. Instead, Udupi specializes in the vegetarian dishes of the southern states of India. Vegetarian cooking has been practiced in India

for millennia, and it is incredibly rich and diverse. And while it might not be particularly low calorie or fat-free, it is blessedly devoid of sprouts and soy franks.

A meal at Udupi takes up a lot of room on the table. Most diners get *dosais*, huge pancakes made from fermented rice-lentil flour that reach well past the plate on each side. In addition, the table gets strewn with cups of *sambar*, a spicy soup-sauce replacing the syrup, plus cups of chutneys, pickles, and the spiced yogurt known as *pachadi* (also known as *raita*). Try the "paper" *dosai* if you like crunch. The *pesarattu* gains a greenish tint from mung beans and provides a huge jolt from lots of thinly sliced jalapeños.

Udupi serves vegetarian dishes from other regions of India, such as *matter paneer*, (peas and cheese), but these dishes do no justice to the skills of the kitchen. For something besides *dosai*, try the *channa batura*, a large, puffy bread (expertly described by food writer Jonathan Gold as looking like a deflated basketball) served with a mess of chickpeas. For dessert, try Mysore (Karnataka) coffee. If the *batura* tastes likes an elastic beignet, then the Mysore coffee is a spicy version of café au lait. If you need something else, their *rasmalai* (fresh cheese and condensed milk) is very good. Servers helpfully explain the dishes, but can get a bit harried when the restaurant fills up.

A WALK DOWN DEVON AVENUE

Devon Avenue starts in the wildly diverse Rogers Park neighborhood and ends in some of the most suburbanized parts of Chicago. The most interesting and ethnically diverse portion of Devon stretches from Damen on the east (2000 West) to Kedzie on the west (3200 West). There's about a mile and a half of sari shops, multilingual bookstores, Bollywood movie rentals, jewelry emporiums, combined travel agency–beauty parlors, and stores selling everything from cricket paddles to yarmulkes.

For many years, this portion of Devon was nearly all Jewish. Today the western end holds a few kosher shops, but the entire stretch has given way to all the groups that have poured into Chicago in the last twenty years. The core is Indian and Pakistani, but other groups on Devon include Turks, Arabs, Assyrians, Russians, Georgians, Croatians, and probably several other nationalities.

Several small butchers have shops all along Devon selling halal (kosher for Muslims) meat. **Farm City** (1) (2255 West Devon) may be the best. Their freezer contains camel meat, but the refrigerators feature mounds of beef, goat, lamb, and veal, mostly in primal cuts. A quartet of Mexican butchers will carve and ground to your wishes. Plenty of fresh parts including hearts, kidneys, and giant cow's feet go to the less squeamish.

Atour (2) (2301 West Devon), a tiny Assyrian grocery store, does not tempt shoppers with a large inventory, but Sam the owner is so friendly and he will probably have already given *you* enough things that you will *have* to buy something. Do not worry, because his homemade *gamour*, a Middle-Eastern clotted cream, will have you waiting for your next piece of toast, and his *torshi*, mixed puckery pickles, will produce an entirely different sensation in your mouth.

Zam Zam Sweets & Grill (3) (2500 West Devon) is one of several snack or *chat* shops on Devon. With Muslim owners, Ujala differs from other *chat* shops by offering meat items, including delicious spring rolls filled with *keema* (ground beef). Nearby **Noor Meat Market** (4) (2505–07 West Devon) sells whole and half lambs and goats. I asked what happens to the other half if someone only buys half, and they told me the "first half" gets the liver and kidney; the "second half" the head. Timing is everything when buying meat here.

The **Patel Brothers** (5a) may have been the first to bring Indian staples to a large audience in Chicago. Their small shop at 2542 West Devon exists almost as a museum, the first Indian grocery store on the avenue. It is well supplied with dry goods and spices. Their more modern outlet a block away (5b) (2610 West Devon), has a small vegetable section but a much larger selection of frozen and otherwise unavailable Indian vegetables. Their freezer sections also contain several brands of Indian ice creams. In the window of **Sukhadia** (6) (2559 West Devon), they make fresh sweets from two large vats, one containing oil and the other sugar syrup. While Sukhadia no longer makes their own ice cream, the ice cream they do sell is still plenty good; also good are the ultracheap snack plates meant to be eaten with a glass of milky spiced tea.

The undisputed king of grocery stores on Devon is **Fresh Farm North Water Market** (7) (2626 West Devon). The high demand keeps the astounding variety of produce impeccably fresh and cheap. On top of that, Fresh Farm sells more exotic items than anywhere else, including two different kinds of bitter melon. Cooks working their stash of Indian recipes can find curry leaves, taro leaves, and methi leaves, as well as a variety of chile peppers in ascending order on the Scoville heat index. There are ample selections from other ethnic groups too, including a wide array of feta cheeses. Nearby is **Kamdar Plaza** (8) (2646 West Devon), a combined grocery store and *chat* shop. The grocery store stocks a huge selection of Tasty Bite pasteurized, ready-to-eat Indian foods, so when you cannot make it to Devon for a meal, you can almost re-create the experience at home. The *chat* shop is much less chaotic than others, and the people behind the counter frequently find time to explain the wide assortment of sweets and savories.

Ebner's Kosher Meat Market (9) (2649 West Devon) marks the end of the monolithically Indian-Pakistani part of Devon Avenue. Look for the house-made *kishke* (sausage) here.

Banks mostly take up the 2700 block, but soon things get interesting again. **Argo Inc. Georgian Bakery** (10) (2812 West Devon) may be the only bakery in Chicago with an oven in the middle of its floor. This Georgian bakery turns out fresh and yeasty breads in round and long shapes, as well as *hachapuri* (cheese pies) and other treats. **Best Food of the Mediterranean** (11) (2816 West Devon) stocks all manner of Turkish items, and brews a strong glass (yes, glass) of tea at its small snack counter for a mere fifty cents. **Three Sisters** (12) (2854 West Devon) sells all things Russian, including cakes, smoked fishes, sausages, and candies.

An observant Jewish community still flocks to Devon for books and other religious items at **Rosenblum's World of Judaica** (13) (2906 West Devon); baked goods, especially breads and rolls at **Tel Aviv Kosher Bakery** (14) (2944 West Devon); and fish at **Good Morgan** (15) (2948 West Devon). Sadly, there is no outstanding deli left in the neighborhood, and the kosher grocery stores, while well stocked, are not particularly nice.

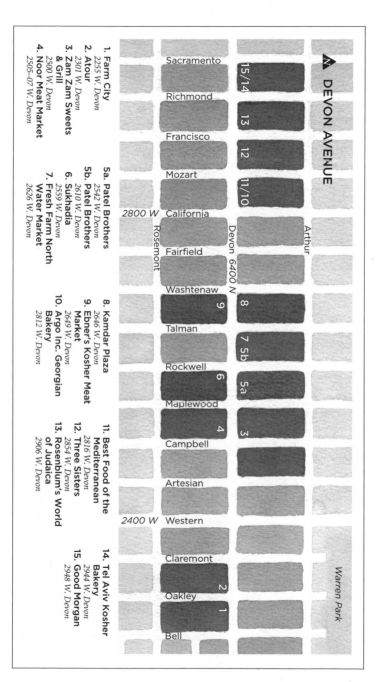

1. Farm City
2255 W. Devon

2. Atour
2301 W. Devon

3. Zam Zam Sweets & Grill
2500 W. Devon

4. Noor Meat Market
2505–07 W. Devon

5a. Patel Brothers
2542 W. Devon

5b. Patel Brothers
2610 W. Devon

6. Sukhadia
2559 W. Devon

7. Fresh Farm North Water Market
2626 W. Devon

8. Kamdar Plaza
2646 W. Devon

9. Ebner's Kosher Meat Market
2649 W. Devon

10. Argo Inc. Georgian Bakery
2812 W. Devon

11. Best Food of the Mediterranean
2816 W. Devon

12. Three Sisters
2854 W. Devon

13. Rosenblum's World of Judaica
2906 W. Devon

14. Tel Aviv Kosher Bakery
2944 W. Devon

15. Good Morgan
2948 W. Devon

DEVON AVENUE

Sacramento
Richmond
Francisco
Mozart
California · 2800 W
Fairfield
Washtenaw
Talman
Rockwell
Maplewood
Campbell
Artesian
Western · 2400 W
Claremont
Oakley
Bell

Rosemont
Devon 6400 N
Arthur

Warren Park

15/14 · 13 · 12 · 11/10 · 9 · 8 · 7 · 5b · 6 · 5a · 4 · 3 · 2 · 1

ITALIAN

FINE DINING

Carlucci
1801 Butterfield Road
Downers Grove
(630) 512-0990
$$

Don't let its two suburban locations fool you: Carlucci is anything but a chain restaurant. Executive Chef John Coletta prides himself on using only the highest-quality ingredients available in season. Coletta brings fine Italian cooking techniques to the Carlucci kitchen to create dishes that represent the best in simple, regional Italian food.

Among the antipasti, be sure to try the Oven-Roasted Sea Scallops Wrapped in "Guanciale" (prosciutto from the jowl) with Fig Vinaigrette. The "guanciale" is dried for five weeks and cured in-house. All of the pastas are similarly made from scratch.

The Braised Pork Ravioli with Fava Beans and Swiss Chard is incredibly smooth and tasty. The ravioli floats in the natural juices of the vegetables and pork, with a touch of white wine and extra virgin olive oil.

The restaurant's desserts are also made in-house, including the ice cream. The Mascarpone Cheesecake with Caramelized Bananas and Pine Nuts is luscious, and the Meyer Lemon Tart is combined with the sweetest, creamiest meringue and a raspberry sauce.

Carlucci isn't trying to re-invent the wheel or to present flashy combinations. The prices are reasonable and the setting is comfortable. Traditional recipes made with integrity are its trump card.

Other Location
6111 North River Road, Rosemont; (847) 518-0990

 ## Merlò
Lincoln Park
2638 North Lincoln Avenue
(773) 529-0747
$$$

It all starts with Silvia Marani's handwritten bible. Forty years ago as a teenager in Italy, she started writing down bits of knowledge from her mother, grandmother, neighbors, and friends. After all, she points out, "cooking is just something people do in Bologna." Gradually her red notebook filled up with the homegrown recipes of Emilia-Romagna, organized meticulously by courses, ingredients, seasons, and holidays.

Now it is the foundation of the restaurant she, her husband, and son started two years ago, bringing traditional and authentic Bolognese cuisine to Lincoln Park.

Husband Giampaolo Sassi and son Stefano run the front of the house with aplomb and an almost military-like precision. The dining room is a re-created salon from an Emilia-Romagna villa, filled with furniture brought over from their house in Italy. On the walls—painted the yellow ocher of stone baked by the Italian sun—are exquisite watercolors painted by Silvia's father. "It's the color of Bologna, the color I've lived with for sixty years," she explains.

If Silvia's red notebook is the New Testament, the Old Testament in her kitchen is a cookbook published in 1896, *La Scienza in Cucina e L'Arte di Mangiare Bene* by Pellegrino Artusi. It's a thick tome that tells the history of Italian cooking through story, culture, custom, and tradition, and sets the historical precedent for everything she does now. Nothing is bought premade, everything is made from scratch, and "you can *never* scrimp when it comes to the quality of the ingredients—never, never." Her masterful use of herbs, butter, mushrooms, cognac, and flame works its magic on muted winter fruits and vegetables. And yes, while three-day-old *mozzarella di bufala* may be a tragedy in Italy, it's the best anyone can do with express deliveries from Campania, and in Silvia's hands none of the flavors are allowed to suffer. The menu changes seasonally, nothing will disappoint, the *streghe* are addictive, and the rabbit ragout is very, very rich.

Other Location

Merlò on Maple, 16 West Maple Street, Chicago (Gold Coast);
   (312) 335-8200

Sparacino Ristorante
6966 West North Avenue
Galewood
(773) 836-2089
$$

Mark Sparacino doesn't like being awakened by a 6:30 A.M. phone call, but when it's his mother calling to tell him about the eggplant she just found at the local farmers' market, he accepts it as part of the price he pays for quality. Sparacino is nothing if not a family restaurant. Mark is usually in the kitchen, his sister Stefania works the front of the house and occasionally makes desserts, and every morning his mother, Darleen, makes the rounds of the local farmers' markets, following them from neighborhood to neighborhood, picking the fresh daily harvest.

The menu at Sparacino reads classically Italian, but don't expect classical treatments of these dishes; this is not your mother's Italian food. Rather, at its base are classical French techniques slightly modified for use with the fresh ingredients Mark assembles. The basic stocks are made from scratch every couple of days, and these yield a lot of reduced sauces, perhaps with cream or champagne. The results are rich and complex versions of standard, familiar dishes, with many surprises for the palate.

An unusual ingredient might give subtle undertones to a sauce, or an unexpected substitution in a recipe might give surprise and relief to palates weary of the same old preparations. Such are the caramelized onion mashed potatoes. Snails might be added to sautéed pancetta and garlic, but then finished with flambéed brandy and cream. A sauce for *orecchiette* is made from long-simmered sun-dried tomatoes, cremini mushrooms, cream, and black truffles. Brightness is added at the end with fresh grilled asparagus. Imagine seared sea scallops sitting in a vanilla-scented champagne reduction.

Lest the place gets too stuffy from all these continental influences, a friend of Mark's comes in every other week to sing Rat Pack music during the dinner hour. Mark patrols the room, making sure every diner is satisfied. Be warned that if you ask him how something is prepared, he'll likely give you the unabridged Julia Child version, at a speed commensurate with his frenetic drive.

 **Spiaggia**
Gold Coast
900 North Michigan Avenue
(312) 280-2750
$$$$

If life is a beach, I want to spend mine here. Spiaggia sits at the top of the Magnificent Mile overlooking the Oak Street Beach and Lake Michigan beyond. Executive Chef Tony Mantuano is something of a living landmark himself—a fixture at local farmers' markets, both as a shopper and educator. All fruits and vegetables on the menu are seasonal and bought as much as possible from local growers.

Nothing is spared with the selection and treatment of ingredients. To understand Spiaggia's commitment to quality at all levels, begin with the cheese "cave," the first temperature and humidity-controlled cheese environment in Chicago. Mike Farrell, the full-time *formaggiao*, stocks it with not only imported cheeses, but also with fine artisanal varieties from regional producers in Wisconsin and Indiana.

Tony travels to Italy every year to personally select the restaurant's private-label olive oil. Sicilian sea salt from the village of Menfi is the kitchen staple and is also on every diner's table. Seafood comes in daily from the Mediterranean, and octopus from the Canary Islands. There are white Piedmontese truffles for shaving on pastas, and black Umbrian truffles for flavoring sauces and filling ravioli. And seven days a week for the last fifteen years, a small cadre of ladies has worked the kitchen's pasta station, hand making *agnolotti, papparadelle*, ravioli, *spaghetti alla chittara*, or *bigoli* from the Veneto.

The sommelier, Henry Bishop, has been at Spiaggia for twenty years, ever since its inception. In that time his wine list has expanded from a sixty-item, all-Italian offering to more than six hundred vintages of Italian wine and Italian varietals. He came to eschew rigid political boundaries in favor of recognizing the ambiguous geographical boundaries of European viticulture. Now wines from Slovenia, Croatia, Switzerland, Austria, and

France can be found here. Just as importantly, he has a passion for discovering small, unrecognized American vineyards and ardently promotes wines from California, Arizona, the upper Midwest, Virginia, Baja Mexico, and Canada. A double magnum of Nebbiolo Reserve from Virginia, humorously priced at $1,000,000, is, however, a very serious reflection of Bishop's estimation for the wine.

Café Spiaggia
(312) 280-2755

$$

Tucked off in an intimate corner behind Spiaggia's wood-burning oven is its chic though decidedly less formal (and less expensive) offspring, Café Spiaggia. Heading up the café kitchen is newcomer Richard Camarota (just arrived from stints in Belgium and Italy), who admirably follows Tony Mantuano's lead with his attention to quality ingredients and preparation. The dishes here, while no less flavorful, are perhaps a little simpler and more rustic than at Spiaggia. If you want a pizza, you'll find a great one here. Occasionally the restaurants' menus overlap, giving diners the chance to sample the brilliance of Spiaggia's four-star kitchen at a fraction of the cost.

TRATTORIAS

A Tavola
Ukrainian Village
2148 West Chicago Avenue
(773) 276-7567
$$$

In 1987, navy electronic warfare technician Dan Bocik spent his days watching electrons zip by on his oscilloscope, and reading *Rolling Stone* magazine in his spare time. One day an article on the Culinary Institute of America (CIA) caught his eye, and after his six-year hitch in the navy was over, he ended up at the California Culinary Academy in San Francisco. Stints in Paris, Milan, and the Caribbean followed. He eventually returned to Chicago and opened A Tavola restaurant in the Ukrainian Village in 1995. Four years later he bought the quaint row house next door and then personally renovated it into the intimate and elegant space that A Tavola is today.

The menu is brief, which Bocik explains was originally born out of the need to run a frugal kitchen. Without a walk-in cooler, he survived the crucial early years of the restaurant by shopping the markets daily, some-times with just the previous night's receipts in his pocket. The limited menu allowed him always to use the freshest ingredients and to consis-tently showcase what he was best at—treating ingredients as simply as possible to bring out their full, rich, and unmasked flavors.

Most of Bocik's dishes are classics and remain on the menu year-round. His Gnocchi with Browned Sage Butter and Parmesan are considered among the city's best, and the high-temperature Roasted Chicken with Polenta and Garlic Spinach crackles with flavor. The specials are seasonal and might include a grilled sardine appetizer, or braised short ribs cooked *osso buco* style over saffron risotto, or assorted shellfish in a classic Ligurian treatment of oil, garlic, wine, spicy marinara, and parsley. In the fall his signature gnocchi are prepared with pumpkin or butternut squash; in winter there's a citrus risotto, with tangerine and grapefruit. For dessert, the perfectly caramelized apple pie and flourless chocolate cake are divine. In the summer, Bocik's herb garden in back shares space with tables for dining alfresco.

La Bocca della Verità
Lincoln Square
4618 North Lincoln Avenue
(773) 784-6222
$$

"Don't throw away the pig's head!" Cesare D'Ortenzi used to have to scream at the butcher around the corner. Who wouldn't know that the pork jowl has the very finest fat content, and is what gives the *spaghetti alla carbonara* its silky smooth texture?

La Bocca della Verità has been in the Lincoln Square neighborhood for almost fifteen years, since long before the area became fashionable and trendy. Owners Cesare and Liz D'Ortenzi deserve credit for not only sticking it out when the neighborhood was a bit sketchy, but also for con-sistently serving authentic Roman cooking during all those years. At the beginning it might have taken them six months of testing to get every-thing right—making ten pounds of practice gnocchi every day, or giving the butcher case after case of wine to make the custom sausage. In Italy there was one kind of flour and one variety of potato. In Chicago there were eight different kinds of flour and umpteen varieties of potatoes, all to be tested in a tiny kitchen alternately cooled and warmed by the extremes of weather.

The space feels like an old apartment as it rambles from room to room, each filled with an assortment of odd tables, chairs, family photos, mis-matched tablecloths, and antique dressers. Don't miss a framed 1929 first

edition of *Cucina Italiana* on the wall. Some of the recipes are still pretty good, and they've occasionally put them on the menu.

Cesare works hard at searching out the best ingredients locally, and tries to educate both purveyors and diners on what to expect. And even though the regular menu is satisfyingly familiar and traditional, the kitchen doesn't stick to standbys. There are always rotating specials on and off the menu, according to season or availability of fresh ingredients.

Befitting the charming irregularities of the decor, the kitchen and service can sometimes get a little scattered. But a leisurely two-hour lunch here comes naturally. Great food, friendship, and conversation all seem to flow spontaneously in this homey space where everyone is family.

La Piazza
410 Circle Avenue
Forest Park
(708) 366-4010
$$

Gaetano di Benedetto, from Bagheria, Sicily, opened La Piazza in May 2003. After more than twenty years of experience in other kitchens, he has created this place to express his idea of the social and cultural traditions of Italian cooking. The restaurant's interior is, in fact, painted to resemble the atmosphere of an Italian piazza. In summer and fall, di Benedetto extends this sense of community connection to the nearby Forest Park farmers' market, where one often finds him demonstrating how to make fresh mozzarella, ricotta, and goat cheese. What cheeses he doesn't make in-house he tries to buy from local artisanal cheese makers.

The restaurant's table bread is a focaccia, trays of which he bakes every day from a starter he's nurtured for the last seven years. Italian charcuterie—prosciutto, *soppressatta*, and *cotechino*—are all made in-house, as are most of the pastas and pastries. Di Benedetto is even experimenting with aging his own wine vinegars.

Although most of his recipes are based on local and family tradition, di Benedetto enjoys fusing the cuisines of other Italian regions with that of his native Sicily. So the menu is a relief to bruschetta- and marinara-weary diners, as it offers uncommon regional dishes such as Sicilian *timballo* (layered pasta cake), sea bass *al cartoccio* (cooked in a foil packet), and an inspired appetizer of encrusted blue corn oysters, called La Piazza oysters. And notwithstanding the reasonably priced menu, di Benedetto uses a few precious ingredients appropriately. White truffles, *bottarga* (pressed and dried tuna roe), and a balsamic vinegar aged more than sixty years are all brought in from Italy.

Service is warm and attentive, with the chef personally coming out to check on diners and suggest variations on the printed menu or just to inquire if there is something special he could make for them. In one case, when it was clear there would be no room for dessert, the waiter brought out several small, complimentary tastes of the entire *dolci* menu.

La Piazza is child friendly. One of the chef's tricks is to let kids make their own pizza, for which servers deliver a squishy ball of dough to the table. Little ones can form their own crust, and eventually their handiwork is whisked away and finished (or restarted) in the kitchen.

Mia Francesca
Lakeview
3311 North Clark Street
(773) 281-3310
$$

In 1992, Scott Harris opened a small trattoria in the middle of rapidly gentrifying Lakeview, just a few blocks south of Wrigley Field. With its geographical advantages, a casual yet cool interior, and outstanding, reasonably priced food, the news spread quickly. Within weeks, the wait on a weekend night easily reached an hour or two.

Eleven years later, Mia Francesca has expanded from that single storefront into a mini-empire with twelve restaurants in Chicago and the suburbs. Remarkably, in spite of this phenomenal growth, the common refrain given by locals is usually "I've had some of my best meals in Chicago there."

The menu, which changes weekly, is seasonally inspired. Good appetizer options include the mussels marinara, the calamari, and the salmon pastrami. Also superb is the carpaccio, sliced to a weblike thinness and strewn with shards of Parmigiano Reggiano cheese, arugula, and basil. Second courses include scrumptious pastas, offered in full and half orders, hearty risottos, and thin-crust pizzas. Sauces over the fish and meat entrees are wonderfully rich and complex. And Bittersweet Bakery, a Lakeview neighbor, makes all of the desserts.

Unified only by a few decorative details, each member of the Francesca family functions as an individual location, with each of its spaces charmingly reflecting the personality of the surrounding neighborhood. It's amazing to see how Harris maintains such quality and consistency over his small empire.

While the often loud, frenetic scene may disguise its Slow sensibilities, Mia Francesca has remained true to its philosophy of "honest, clean cooking, robust flavors, great service, and good prices."

Other Locations

Francesca's on Taylor, 1400 West Taylor Street, Chicago (Little Italy); (312) 829-2828

Francesca's Bryn Mawr, 1039 Bryn Mawr, Chicago (Edgewater); (773) 506-9261

For a complete listing of other Francesca restaurant locations in the Chicago suburbs, go to www.francescarestaurants.com.

NOTABLE

FINE DINING

Caliterra
Streeterville
633 North St. Clair Street
(312) 274-4446
$$$-$$$$

Chef Rick Gresh uses fresh, organic ingredients and seasonal specials to dazzle diners at Caliterra. Start with the delicious "trilogy of soups" (typical offerings include creamy spiced apple, a frothy salsify and thyme "cappuccino," and savory semolina with brown butter). Among the entrees, the Pan-Roasted Veal Sweetbreads are smooth and gentle, served with organic apples, chestnuts, and sage. Don't miss the Pecorino and

Ricotta Cheese-Stuffed Tortellini with braised organic turkey, morel mushrooms, and spring peas. The salt and natural juice of the turkey permeates the tortellini so that they melt in your mouth. Monkfish, served with mussels, potatoes, spring onions, and chorizo, could almost be considered a bouillabaisse. For dessert, the White Chocolate Bombe, with its interior pistachio custard, is served with strawberry sorbet and makes a superb finale to the meal.

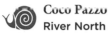

Coco Pazzo
River North

300 West Hubbard Street
(312) 836-0900
$$$

The simplicity of Tuscan cooking and its strong connection to the earth resonate deeply with Coco Pazzo's executive chef, Tony Priolo. This bond was strengthened a few years ago when Priolo spent several weeks at Da Delfina, a renowned Slow Food–rated restaurant in Artimino, Italy, just outside Florence. The trip, he says, changed his life. It reconnected Priolo to the simplicity of Tuscan food and its emphasis on seasonal, locally produced foods, and it renewed his commitment to those culinary principles.

Priolo is a big supporter of Chicago's Green City Market, where he buys lots of organic produce. He favors local producers, with the exception of his prized San Marzano tomatoes, which are flown in from southern Italy. These tomatoes, grown in the shadow of Mount Vesuvius, are raised in soil rich with volcanic ash, which makes them especially sweet for sauces. The kitchen bakes salty, chewy bread twice daily, spins its own ice cream, and makes its own sausages and delicate handmade pastas.

Va Pensiero
Inside the Margarita Inn
1566 Oak Avenue
Evanston
(847) 475-7779
$$$

Like the Verdi opera chorus for which it was named, Va Pensiero can banish your daily worries for a few hours, and immerse you in a world of comfortable and comforting Italian cooking. Since taking over Va Pensiero in 1997, owner/executive chef Jeff Muldrow's vision for the restaurant has been to recreate a romantic 1920s Italian villa, and the large space he's carved out of the adjacent hotel is warmly evocative.

The restaurant's menu changes daily, with a spectacular selection of both rustic and nouveau preparations. Chef de cuisine Jesse DuMais's mantra is to "use as little finished product as possible," by sticking to what's fresh and seasonally available. In the summer he and Muldrow frequent local farmers' markets (Evanston's may be the best), and actively support the Green City Market. All pastas are handmade every morning. Desserts by pastry chef Tanya Singer are all standouts.

TRATTORIAS

Follia
West Loop Gate
953 West Fulton Avenue
(312) 243-2888
$$–$$$

Follia has as its submotto *Cibo è Moda*, or "Food is Fashion." Several years ago chef/owner Bruno Abate brought from Milan his experience in both, and then pioneered with one of the first ultrahip dining outposts to stake a claim in the meatpacking district. The decor is starkly urban chic, with mannequins twisting on wire in the front window and posing in strategic niches throughout the restaurant. It's all very cutting edge, with Abate asking design students from Columbia College and the Art Institute to dress the mannequins in clothing of their own invention, and on occasion taking the fashion show live out on the street.

All of this is in stark contrast to Abate's menu, which could have been lifted from any trattoria in Italy. It is everyday food, in a non-everyday setting. There are half a dozen simple appetizers, a full line of pizzas, four straightforward pastas, and four meat/fish dishes.

312 Chicago
Loop
Hotel Allegro
136 North LaSalle Street
(312) 696-2420
$$$

At 312 Chicago, Chef Dean Zanella's aim is to get people to understand that Italian food is not a gut-busting heap of pasta covered in red sauce but a cuisine based on what is available in season and in the local vicinity: food that is connected to the land, the farmers, and produce around the restaurant.

Since this is Chicago and not Italy, it's not so easy to eat this way year-round. However, Chef Zanella is doing his best to change that. Zanella works closely with the Land Connection, a downstate organization that cultivates healthy farms, healthy food, and healthy communities by, among other initiatives, creating links between rural growers and urban eaters of local organic foods. While the produce, poultry, and meat Zanella serves to his guests at 312 Chicago may not have come from his own backyard, diners there are getting the next-best thing.

Trattoria #10
Loop
10 South Dearborn Street
(312) 984-1719
$$-$$$

Walking down the stairs into Trattoria #10 is like falling down a rabbit hole and landing in a Roman grotto, miles and years away from the sky-scraper canyons you left behind at street level. The tiled rooms are warm and ochre-toned, and there is a distinct lack of formality—the hallmark of a good Italian trattoria. Under the guiding hand of a new chef, Trattoria #10 has awakened from a long slumber and is making a renewed commitment to excellence and seasonality.

The menu is guided by a belief in authenticity, which is reflected in the variety of handcrafted pastas that the chef makes daily. A few standouts from a recent visit were baked *mozzarella di bufala* wrapped in zucchini, roasted peppers and pesto sauce on crostini, and light-as-a-feather ricotta gnocchi. In addition to a seasonal menu, six or seven special items are added to the menu, reflecting what's in season and available in the area. A well-rounded wine list featuring many Italian favorites—both old and new—provides the perfect balance to the food.

Trattoria Roma
Old Town
1535 North Wells Street
(312) 664-7907
$$

Trattoria Roma was one of Chicago's first trattorias when it was opened in 1985 by the late Franco Zalloni and his charming and vivacious wife, Laura, who currently runs the restaurant. Laura and the rest of the Trattoria Roma staff treat you like family in this lovely yet casual setting. Every dish here is consistently excellent, from the roast chicken and pota-toes with an earthy olive oil, lemon, and garlic sauce; to homemade pas-tas that melt in your mouth; to fresh and simply prepared fish entrées, such as rainbow trout, salmon, and sea bass.

Tufano's Vernon Park Tap
Little Italy
1073 West Vernon Park Place
(312) 733-3393
$

The third generation of DiBuonos is carrying on the family tradition of running Tufano's. Politicians, reporters, beat cops, and street-smart Chicagoans have been eating for more than seventy years at this classic Italian family restaurant in the old Italian neighborhood near the University of Illinois campus.

The way to truly appreciate Tufano's is to bring a group and eat family style. The wine list on the blackboard is limited, but adequate for a family style restaurant. As in the old country, the wine is served in small water glasses.

Via Carducci Trattoria
Lincoln Park
1419 West Fullerton Avenue
(773) 665-1981
$$

Giovanni Scalzo brought the flavors of Calabria to Lincoln Park when he opened Via Carducci in 1996. What started as a small storefront has grown over the years as the popularity of Via Carducci demanded more space for this friendly, well-staffed trattoria. Now the adjacent property is being developed into an *enoteca* (wine bar) with an outdoor grape arbor.

The menu selections are typical rustic dishes featuring plenty of natural ingredients. The synergy in pairing regional Italian wines with the dishes is evident.

LITTLE ITALY: THE NEAR WEST SIDE

Taylor Street and Grand Avenue

Starting in the latter part of the nineteenth century, Italian immigrants began settling in a large area of the Near West Side of Chicago. By the 1940s it was a vibrant and vital community, more Italian than American, encompassing several square miles. Then, beginning in the 1950s, a series of cataclysmic urban-renewal projects uprooted the tight-knit community, eventually causing a huge Italian-American diaspora throughout Chicago. The Eisenhower Expressway, the University of Illinois campus and hospital, and the Cabrini Green housing project all contributed to this upheaval, and eventually only a few pockets of Italian settlement remained. The remnants of that once large and proud community are still here, but there is very little of its original character left. What remains of the district's heart can be mostly found on a short stretch of Taylor Street, between Halsted and Ashland, and along Grand Avenue a few blocks north. Of the dozens of restaurants, shops, cafés, and bakeries in the area, several are notable.

Al's #1 Italian Beef
1079 West Taylor Street
(312) 266-4017
Al's is a perennial favorite among aficionados of Chicago-style Italian beef. It is a particularly enjoyable destination in the summer months, when the picnic tables outside are mobbed.

Conte di Savoia
1438 West Taylor Street
(312) 666-3471
An extremely well-stocked deli with many imported goods, including meats and cheeses. Many items are made in-house, such as sausage, ravioli, pasta sauces, and desserts. Great bread, fresh sandwiches, and several kinds of marinated salads make it extremely popular at lunchtime.

Ferrara's Bakery
2210 West Taylor Street
(312) 666-2200
Ferrara's has managed to thrive at a location about a mile west of the Taylor Street epicenter by relying on the strength of its pastries, cakes, and candies, and on its long, well-respected, hundred-year history in the community. They also offer a good but limited selection of foods for take-out and delivery.

Mario's Italian Lemonade
(Outdoor stand across the street from Al's #1 Italian Beef)
Open May to October
On hot summer nights, nothing beats Mario's shaved ice infused with fresh fruit juices. Their signature shaved ice is made with fresh lemon, sugar, and bits of lemon peel. But as the summer harvest progresses, their flavors will keep apace; fresh watermelon, cantaloupe, honeydew, and so forth might be added to the mix.

Patio, Italian Beef and Sausage
1503 West Taylor Street
(312) 829-0454
Excellent Italian beef sandwiches with a very good accompanying *giardiniera*. Neighborhood businessmen are usually in the back room discussing strategic plans over coffee and cards.

The Grand Avenue Corridor

As the Italian community began to disperse in the 1950s, some of the migration moved just a mile or so north, to a stretch of Grand Avenue. Along Grand Avenue today, nestled among a few bakeries and restaurants that have been there for decades, is a small resurgence of newer Italian shops and cafés.

Bari Foods
1120 West Grand Avenue
(312) 666-0730
Here for decades, this grocery store, butcher, and deli is famous for its submarine sandwiches and bottled *giardiniera.* There are long lines at the lunch hour, awaiting sandwiches made to order using bread from D'Amato's bakery next door.

D'Amato's #1
1124 West Grand Avenue
(312) 733-5456
D'Amato's bakes excellent Italian sourdough breads, sheet pizza (all day long), and rich cookies.

D'Amato's #2
1332 West Grand Avenue
(312) 733-6219
The story is told of a family feud years ago, which resulted in this second D'Amato's bakery, just a few blocks west of #1. The bread is still good here, but they also offer freshly made sandwiches and a small selection of Italian dry goods.

LITTLE ITALY: THE SOUTHWEST SIDE

Oakley Avenue, around 24th Street

The Southwest Side neighborhood around Oakley Avenue was settled more than a hundred years ago by immigrants who found jobs in the nearby Cyrus McCormick factory. Eventually a solid pocket of Italians grew up along the blocks north of Blue Island, and although very little of the community remains today, the stretch of Oakley Avenue from 23rd to 25th Street seems charmingly stuck in time as a remnant of that once grand culture. A walk up and down the block will remind you of a bygone era, or perhaps of something manufactured on a Hollywood back lot. Prominently anchoring the street is the West Town Funeral Parlor. It's perfectly framed by the simple lines of immaculately maintained row houses. Just up the block is the still active neighborhood social club, The Po-Piedmont Society (members only, please).

Years ago restaurants sprouted up on the lower floors of the buildings, primarily to serve factory workers who lived in apartments above. There are now about a half dozen of these restaurants still lining the block, a few with decor seemingly little changed from an era seventy or eighty years ago. The cooking is very basic here, but dining in any of them will be pleasant and fun, if only to experience the Old World charm of a 1930s classic "red-sauce" joint. Waitresses have been here for decades, and will answer any questions about the menu with a gravelly voiced "Everything's good here, honey."

The back room at **Bruna's**, on the corner, is worth a visit just to see the faded wall-to-wall murals of a cherubic Italian lake district, framed in fake pilasters and purple neon. Across the street, in the bar area at **Bacchanalia** a local artist has painted an impressive wall-size triptych of the restaurant's namesake, Bacchus. Best of all, every June the neighborhood hosts the Heart of Italy Food & Wine Festival with live entertainment, kids' activities, circus performances, glorious street food, and an outdoor café dominated by a re-creation of Rome's Trevi Fountain.

Bacchanalia Ristorante
2413 South Oakley Avenue
(773) 256-6555

Bruna's Ristorante
2424 South Oakley Avenue
(773) 254-5550

N HARLEM AVENUE

Cornelia

Roscoe

School

3200 N

Belmont

Barry

Wellington

Overhill
Ottawa
Oriole
Oleander
Olcott
Osceola
Oketo
Odell
Octavia
Oconto
Harlem
Neva

George

2800 N

Diversey

7600 W

7200 W

Schubert

Wrightwood

1. **Caffé Italia**
   2625 N. Harlem
2. **Il Giardino Bakery**
   2859 N. Harlem
3. **Riviera Market**
   3220 N. Harlem

4. **Caponie's Trattoria**
   3350 N. Harlem
5. **Pasta Fresh**
   3418 N. Harlem
6. **Gino's Italian Import Foods**
   3422 N. Harlem
7. **Nottoli & Son Sausage Shop**
   7652 W. Belmont

A WALK DOWN HARLEM AVENUE

As Italian-Americans returned home from World War II with the benefits of the G.I. Bill, they moved from the inner city to the western border along Harlem Avenue, where they could afford to buy new homes to raise their families. Another surge of Italian immigration into the area occurred in the 1960s, when the building of the Chicago campus of the University of Illinois disrupted the old Taylor Street neighborhood. The Montclare neighborhood is on the east side of Harlem Avenue, and the suburbs of River Forest and Elmwood Park are along the west side. Roughly between North Avenue and Addison Street, the neighborhood is sprinkled with Italian cafés, gelateria, bakeries, pasta shops, sausage shops, produce and imported food markets, restaurants, and gift shops. If you want to practice your Italian or are in search of any items from Italy, take a walk down Harlem Avenue and the surrounding streets.

In addition to the shops mentioned below, there are dozens of other shops along Harlem in which to poke around. Many spill over onto the side thoroughfares of North Diversey and Belmont as well.

Caffé Italia (1)
2625 North Harlem Avenue
(773) 889-0455
They arguably serve the best espresso in the area, along with a small selection of biscotti.

Il Giardino Bakery (2)
2859 North Harlem Avenue
(773) 889-2388
Il Giardino offers excellent confections, sweets, birthday cakes, cookies, and cannoli shells. There is a small coffee bar, and sheet pizza comes out of the kitchen around lunchtime.

Riviera Market (3)
3220 North Harlem Avenue
(773) 637-4252
This small market is a good source for Italian newspapers and Italian soccer jerseys. The butcher counter offers a good homemade sausage, in addition to a nice selection of cheese, vegetables, and house-made deli meats. For a great sandwich, pick a roll out of the bread bin and hand it over the counter to the deli man.

Caponie's Trattoria (4)
3350 North Harlem Avenue
(773) 804-9024
Caponie's is a *Goodfellas* type of place, with tongue firmly planted in cheek.

There is lots of Chicago gangster memorabilia on the walls, and in addition to simple trattoria fare they make very good wood-fired pizzas.

Pasta Fresh (5)
3418 North Harlem Avenue
(773) 745-5888
You can watch the pasta being made through the window separating the small retail area from the kitchen. In addition to the perfectly fresh home-made pasta, there are a few excellent southern Italian prepared and fried goods—*arancini*, *panzerotti*, and so on.

Gino's Italian Import Foods (6)
3422 North Harlem Avenue
(773) 745-8310 or 745-8311
Gino's is a very well-stocked deli of specialty goods, including Italian ceramics and cookware. The prepared-foods counter at the back of the store has an excellent selection of cheeses, salamis, and homemade sausages. They'll be happy to make a lunch for you, out of anything they have in stock.

On Belmont, West of Harlem

Nottoli & Son Sausage Shop (7)
7652 West Belmont Avenue
(773) 589-1010
The Nottoli family has been making sausages and salamis here for more than fifty years.

Heat
Old Town
1507 North Sedgwick Street
(312) 397-9818
$$$-$$$$

Kee Chan, the president and executive chef of Heat, is an intense guy with a Zen-like devotion to finding the very best ingredients to prepare his exquisitely presented Japanese cuisine. Seasonally available fish is flown in from Japan, the beef is Kobe, and even the freshly prepared wasabi, rarely found in other Japanese restaurants, is made with horseradish brought in from Japan or Oregon, depending on the season.

The dining room at Heat is beautiful and sedate, with dark wood table-tops and a sushi bar set off against a wood-and-tile floor and pale yellow, maroon, and beige walls. Mirrors and recessed lighting create a soft glow in the room. Table settings, from the plates and stemware to the chopstick rests, are gorgeous.

The menu features traditionally prepared dishes and well-executed modern combinations. If you can't decide where to start, one of the chef's choice menus is a good option. Live fish, kept in tanks at the base of the sushi bar—a special offering—are immediately dispatched and served, often in two courses. Chopped Flying Fish Sashimi, seared with butter, garlic, chives, and enoki mushrooms, is served wrapped in a leaf with the head and tail of the fish arranged as if swimming through a large bowl of crushed ice. Pristinely fresh pieces of superwhite *toro* arrive at the table on an elegant platter. Enjoy the fish dabbed with the freshly prepared wasabi; it is a revelation. Lightly seared portions of Kobe beef tenderloin are

served in a red grape reduction accompanied by a purple potato and an endive leaf filled with salmon roe. It is a striking combination of textures and flavors.

Heat has the most extensive sake offerings in the city and an interesting and well-chosen, if pricey, wine list. The staff is polished, professional, and extremely knowledgeable about the food, wine, and sake. The very informative monthly sake tasting, served with food pairings, is a real bargain.

Katsu
West Rogers Park
2651 West Peterson Avenue
(773) 784-3383
Closed Tuesday
$$-$$$

Inviting, conversation friendly, and relaxed compared to many of the ultrahip places around town, Katsu serves some of the very best Japanese food in the city. West of Western Avenue and a bit off the beaten path, this small but comfortable restaurant is attractive, with exposed brick, a tile floor, and gold, black, and red accents. The lighting is soft and the music is jazz. There are a few seats available at the sushi bar in the corner, but regulars taking their time while conversing with the amiable sushi chef and owner, Katsu Imamura, often occupy them.

The menu features an assortment of tempura, grilled meats, and seafood salad appetizers, as well as noodle dishes. Entrées include beef, chicken, and fish teriyaki, salt-grilled fish (*shioyaki*), and sukiyaki. Diners may start with a complimentary dish of lightly dressed bean sprouts, but don't pass up the excellent miso soup. Daily specials from the kitchen deserve attention, and might include such interesting offerings as fresh monkfish liver and an *unagi* egg custard of eel, fish cake, ginkgo nuts, and shiitake mushrooms. A salt-grilled baby yellowtail jaw comes to the table perfectly cooked; salt grilling keeps the fish moist, and the light saltiness plays off the sweetness of the fish. Specials from the sushi bar include pristinely fresh superwhite *toro* topped with crunchy black *tobikko* (flying fish roe), and salmon mounded with *ikura* (salmon roe). Sashimi carpaccio is served with tuna, flounder, and salmon, garnished with avocado, wasabi, and a spicy sauce. All of the food is beautifully prepared and nicely presented on an array of attractive plates, dishes, and bowls.

Katsu's small, well-chosen wine list features a number of food-friendly whites by the glass and bottle, but only two reds. It also offers a nice selection of hot and cold premium sakes and Japanese beers, plus several interesting Japanese liquors by the glass and bottles of Japanese vodkas. The staff is friendly and helpful with suggestions, even when the place gets hopping.

Mirai Sushi
Wicker Park
2020 West Division Street
(773) 862-8500
$$

Just west of Damen Avenue, on a stretch of Division Street exploding with trendy bars, restaurants, and boutiques, Mirai Sushi gets nods from just about everyone for the high quality of its food and well-executed presentations. The space is hip and relatively comfortable with muted colors, dark accents, soft lighting throughout, and votive candles on the tables. An artfully displayed fish tank backs the sushi bar. The music beat is equally hip. If you prefer something a bit more intimate or crave a smoke, ask to be seated in the dimly lit upstairs sake bar and lounge.

Executive Chef Jun Ichikawa knows his fish, some of which he brings in from Japan, some of which is farm-raised, but all of which is sparklingly fresh. The menu features a number of chef's specials. *Kani nigiri* is lightly baked king crab with a spicy marinade, topped with chives and wrapped in *nori*. Served warm, the marinade compliments the sweetness of the crab. Spicy *maki mono* is chopped octopus topped with spicy tuna and rolled over rice. Cut into pieces and geometrically arranged on a plate drizzled with a sweet *unagi* sauce, the dish is an interplay of spicy and sweet.

You have the option of having your fish served as either *nigiri* sushi or sashimi. Incredibly fresh *kanpachi*, Japanese amberjack, and *madai*, Japanese red snapper, arrive on an attractive serving platter, beautifully sliced with just enough of the skin intact to identify each fish. *Maki mono* options include fish, tempura, and a number of vegetarian rolls. Soft-shell crab tempura *maki*, perfectly sautéed and wrapped in rice, is served topped with the crab legs, white sesame seeds, and a creamy fish roe sauce.

Service is generally helpful and efficient, but pacing can be a bit too quick, especially if you are looking to slowly contemplate and savor each dish. Mirai offers an extensive wine list with an emphasis on wines from the American Northwest, Australia, and New Zealand, as well as many premium sake options.

Oysy
South Loop
888 South Michigan Avenue
(312) 922-1127
$$

A relative newcomer, Oysy is a welcome addition to the emerging South Loop restaurant scene. Oysy bills itself as a contemporary take on an *izagaya*, a Japanese bistro serving traditional fare at reasonable prices in a relaxed setting. Done in greens and grays and shimmering with colored light, the space is a sleek and contemporary stunner. Screens made of green panels framed in metal are suspended from the sushi bar, and the open kitchen is wall-to-wall stainless steel. Its corner location allows for an expanse of floor-to-ceiling glass windows.

Oysy's menu offers a nice selection of grilled, tempura, cooked, and cold dishes in small portions, as well as traditional *nigiri* sushi and *maki* rolls and many over-the-top special *maki* creations. Dishes appear on beautifully simple white plates. Tuna Spring Roll is served as pieces of green soy paper wrapped around red tuna and white cucumber, standing in a puddle of red chile sauce. It's a tasty combination of colors and textures. Lotus Root Tempura is seasoned chicken and diced vegetables sandwiched between rounds of lotus root, held together by a light tempura batter; it is served with two dipping sauces. Fresh homemade seafood dumplings, stuffed with shrimp and grouper, are a study in subtlety and restraint, served unadorned with a light dipping sauce. A large slice of grilled superwhite tuna comes nicely seared and lightly coated in a citrusy *yuzu* dressing. The intriguing and artfully presented special *maki* include Black Pearl (eel, avocado, and spicy sauce topped with black *tobikko*) and Tiger Eye (smoked salmon, squid, tempura crunch, chile *tobikko*, and green onion). Prices are reasonable.

Oysy's wine list, with offerings by the glass and bottle, is small but well paired to the food. Servings by the glass are generous and the stemware is contemporary and attractive. Hot and cold sakes, Japanese beers, and numerous martini and cocktail choices are available. Service is very friendly and accommodating.

NOTABLE

Naniwa
River North
607 North Wells Street
(312) 255-8555
$$

Located just a short walk from the Merchandise Mart, amid a number of upscale restaurants, Naniwa serves well-prepared Japanese food in a pleasant and tasteful setting. A clever water wall separates the main room from the entrance. The sushi bar is well staffed with chefs serious about their fish; they turn out well-executed sushi, sashimi, and rolls. The menu features appetizers such as beef wrapped around asparagus served with a light teriyaki sauce, and numerous seafood entrées such as seared tuna and grilled black cod with miso dressing. Naniwa's tempura is very good and can be ordered by the single piece—a nice touch. Japanese pumpkin tempura is served as a large horseshoe slice of pumpkin, perfectly crunchy on the outside and moist and tender on the inside. Prices are very reasonable.

Naniwa offers a very good if small selection of moderately priced wines, most of which are available by the glass, as well as sake, beer, and spirits. Service is attentive. If you are looking for hipper and trendier, try owner Bob Bee's popular sushi place in Wicker Park, **Bob San** (1805 West Division Street; 773-235-8888).

Renga Tei
3956 West Touhy Avenue
Lincolnwood
(847) 675-5177
$-$$

Renga Tei is a warm neighborhood spot popular with Asian diners. The restaurant has comfortable booths and tables and is nicely closed in with Japanese paper screens. It is brightly lit and child friendly. Renga Tei specializes in traditional Japanese dishes. The miso soup is rich and flavorful, and the house salad comes with a well-made and very refreshing sweet ginger dressing. A few special *nigiri*, sashimi, and *maki mono* supplement the traditional offerings, but the real draw here are the cooked dishes, such as lightly battered tempuras, fried oysters served with shredded cabbage, and excellent *nabeyaki udon*, brought piping hot to the table in an iron pot, filled with shrimp tempura, chicken, egg, and fish cake in a shiitake-infused broth. Many of the noodle dishes can be ordered with either udon or soba noodles. Renga Tei also offers combinations, bento

box dinners, and belt-busting "sets," as well as Japanese beers, hot and cold sakes, and one or two wines.

Tampopo
Peterson Park
5665 North Lincoln Avenue
(773) 561-2277
$

Located on the City's Far North Side, Tampopo serves hearty, well-prepared traditional Japanese dishes at very reasonable prices. The restaurant is simply but tastefully done in light lacquered woods and cream-colored walls. Wooden dividers add intimacy to an otherwise open room. Meals start with small bowls of bean sprouts in a sesame dressing, green beans topped with miso paste, and a macaroni salad. The menu features a nice assortment of appetizers, such as *wasabi shumai* and broiled squid served with ginger sauce, as well as a variety of *donburi*, *katsu*, teriyaki, and tempura. Portions are generous.

Tampopo has a sushi bar with all of the standards, but as in the movie of its namesake, noodle dishes of every kind play a starring role here. Tempura Udon is a bowl of perfectly cooked noodles in a rich and slightly sweet broth served with nicely crunchy shrimp and vegetables on the side. *Gomuko ramen* is a huge bowl of light egg noodles heaped with cabbage, bamboo shoots, and shrimp, swimming in a pork-infused broth. Tampopo offers wine, Japanese and Korean beers, hot and cold sakes, and an interesting selection of Korean liquors. The friendly service here will make you feel welcome.

KOREAN

Jang Mo Nim
Peterson Park
6320 North Lincoln Avenue
(773) 509-0211
Closed Sunday
$$

Jang Mo Nim has been one of the mainstays of the Korean dining community in the city for more than fourteen years. It is known for its excellent homemade meals—they even make their own soy sauce! The winning restaurant team is headed by Sun Pak, who cooks authentic Korean foods with "exotic yet familiar flavors" in the kitchen, and her daughter, Rachel Hyun, the hostess in the pleasant dining room, who is able to translate the menu for novices. She greets diners with a glass of toasted barley tea to begin the meal.

The black-and-white dining room is divided into individual alcoves on each side with tabletop gas grills, plus bamboo and other plants, cooling fans, and fish tanks. Service in Korean restaurants is often brusque. Not so here. The staff is friendly, eager to please, and helpful with their suggestions.

Luncheon specials include seasoned *kalbi* (meaty short ribs), marinated *bulgogi*, beef that is both tender and lean, and hot pots filled with tofu, spicy cabbage *kim chee*, and pork.

Besides the traditional *hanshik*, Korean food that shows up on most restaurant menus, Jang Mo Nim offers excellent *gul jun* (plump, tender, pan-fried oysters), plus other fresh seafood appetizers. Chicken stuffed with chestnuts, ginseng, and glutinous rice, and potato stew with pork are specialties not found on most Korean menus. Fish entrees include *sam chi gui*, a delicately flavored, lightly breaded, and pan-fried fish with a buttery-smooth texture.

Barbecue entrées are prepared for tabletop cooking for two orders or more. Besides beef entrées, there are chicken, pork, or spicy octopus pan-fried with cabbage, onions, and mushrooms, or goat meat with vegetables. Servers will help with the cooking at your table if desired.

With the helpful service and extensive menu, Jang Mo Nim is a great place for both first-timers and aficionados of Korean cuisine.

Jin Ju
Andersonville
5203 North Clark Street
(773) 334-6377
Closed Monday
$$

For those unfamiliar with Korean dining, this restaurant would be a good place to start. Co-owner Peter Mah, along with his brother-in-law, Executive Chef Yun Jin Hong, have created a comfortable, contemporary setting for their Korean-inspired menu, with a lively waitstaff who are more than happy to translate the dishes into English, explain the ingredients, and make recommendations. They have Westernized the menu somewhat, but most of the dishes are traditionally Korean. Their goal was to present authentic Korean food in a welcoming setting, emphasizing the presentation and freshness.

Located in what at one time was the Swedish neighborhood of Andersonville, the area is now an eclectic mixture of different cultures, and Jin Ju fits right in. The storefront urban space is uncluttered and modern, with polished oak floors and an exposed ceiling and brick walls.

Although they do offer an adequate list of wines and beers, the specialties of the house are *soju-tinis*, martinis made with a vodkalike Korean liquor made from sweet potatoes. The *soju* is combined with a wide assortment of fruits, vegetables, and other flavors, such as Asian pear and cucumber, to begin your meal, and chocolate to complement the ending.

Appetizers include the lovely traditional *pajuns*, scallion pancakes served plain or with *kim chee*, squid, and mussels. The traditional *mandoo*, steamed or fried dumplings filled with beef and vegetables and presented in bamboo steamers, are some of the best in the city. Fried white fish, seafood, and vegetables; batter-dipped chicken wings; and *daeji kalbi* (barbecued chicken wings) are also part of the extensive offerings.

For the main course a good choice is the ever-popular tender and mildly flavored *kalbi*, braised beef short ribs served without bones for easy eating and surrounded by the traditional greens. Other traditional entrées include the hot pot of *bi bim bap* served with soybean paste soup and the *o jinga bokum*, squid in a spicy-sweet red pepper sauce. A small list of pickled vegetables with contrasting flavors accompanies the entrées. Several salads and soups complete the menu, with green tea, red bean, and ginger ice cream offered for dessert.

Jin Ju is a welcome addition to the Chicago dining scene, and it offers a nice introduction to the fresh and flavorful cooking of Korea.

So Gong Dong Tofu House
Hollywood Park
3307 West Bryn Mawr Avenue
(773) 539-8377
Closed Wednesday
$$

If it's tofu you want, there's no better place than So Gong Dong, which offers no fewer than eight different tofu soups. The restaurant is widely regarded among Chicago's Korean community as one of the favorites. Located in the midst of the Korean area on the north side of the city, it stands out as one of the most popular dining spots, bustling with activity from midday through dinner.

Don't let the dreary street-front appearance deter you; inside it's pleasant, clean, and bustling. There are a few semiprivate alcoves with tabletop grills, comfortable wood paneling, and an airy latticed ceiling. The employees are friendly and efficient, but be advised that the language spoken here is generally Korean, and there is little explanation of the food served.

The traditional menu includes some of the most authentic *kalbi*, barbecued braised short ribs, in the city, along with well-seasoned *bulgogi*, barbecued beef and pork marinated with garlic-sesame oil. But the meal-in-a-bowl soups are the highlight of the menu. Choose from ginseng, seafood, beef, spicy cabbage *kim chee* and pork, miso, wonton, seafood, and vegetable tofu soups—all served in an authentic hot pot and accompanied by at least ten various *panchan* (side dishes of pickled vegetables, seafood, fish cakes, and even potato salad to complement the soup) and, of course, sticky rice. They are also happy to tone down the seasonings to your taste, so try to make your wishes known to the kitchen.

NOTABLE

Cho Sun Ok
North Center
4200 North Lincoln Avenue
(773) 549-5555
$

The decor is definitely not a priority at Cho Sun Ok, but the Korean community doesn't seem to mind and keeps this corner storefront bustling. The Formica tables are supplied with electric grills for tabletop cooking, or the kitchen will prepare the many authentic dishes for you. Entrées include seasoned marinated meats, fish, and seafood, plus a wide assortment of rice and noodle dishes. Specialties include pheasant stew and quail. All entrées include ten *panchan*, small dishes of pickled and marinated vegetables that add spiciness and unique textures to the meal, and sticky rice as well.

The service is quick, almost brusque, and most servers speak limited English. This is probably not a place for those who need to be guided through their first experience with Korean cuisine, but the Koreans in town rate it highly.

Hai Woon Dae
West Rogers Park
6240 North California Avenue
(773) 764-8018
$$

Located in a strip mall in the ethnically diverse north side, Hai Woon Dae offers large portions of authentic home-cooked Korean dishes at reasonable prices. For those looking for the true Korean barbecue experience, three private dining rooms are available by reservation. Diners remove their shoes at the door, are seated at low tables for up to eight on cushions, and grill beef, chicken, pork, or seafood marinated in a tasty sesame-garlic sauce over tabletop charcoal grills. A wide variety of *panchan*, side dishes, and steamed sticky rice accompany these entrées, including pickled radishes, shredded carrots, and bean sprouts with chiles and garlic, creamy potato salad, and an intensely spicy cabbage *kim chee*.

San Soo Gap San
Ravenswood
5247 North Western Avenue
(773) 334-1589
Open 24 hours
$$

For those who crave Korean barbecue or tofu hot pots in the middle of the night, this is the place for you! Drop by anytime to sample authentic traditional Korean food. The seasoned barbecued meats and seafood are served with rice and soup. The menu includes the spicy hot pots of fish, seafood, and meats, as well as sizzling rice pots with vegetables, meats, and seafood and a variety of steaming, spicy, meal-sized soups. All of these are delivered with a dozen or so little side dishes, *panchan*, of vegetables and fish in contrasting flavors to complement your meal.

If you're looking for something less filling, the *haemoul pajun*, a scallion pancake topped with squid and other seafood, or the beef and vegetable fried *goon man du* dumplings might hit the spot late at night or even early in the morning. This place is popular with the Korean community and is generally bustling late at night. The service to the semiprivate dining spaces with tabletop charcoal grills is quick and efficient, but don't expect too much help with the menu from the staff, who speak limited English.

Irazu   *(Costa Rican)*
Bucktown
1865 North Milwaukee Avenue
(773) 252-5687
Closed Sunday
$

Located on an odd stretch of Milwaukee Avenue, Izaru could easily be overlooked. With its green roof, it hides between auto-parts dealers and repair shops. Miriam and Gerardo Cerdas opened the Costa Rican eatery in 1990. You can often hear patrons asking Miriam—better known as Mom to the regulars and local artists—what to eat, and they should listen; Mom knows her cuisine. Her fried or boiled cassava (a root that tastes sort of like a potato) is one of the dishes for which people flock here. Ambience is not the focus, and don't expect to get in and out very fast. Also be prepared to settle into a "cozy" seating arrangement.

Once you get past the aesthetics, the food is brilliant and the service very personable and sincere. *Comida tipica*, or native dishes, rely heavily on rice and beans, the basis of many Costa Rican meals. *Gallo pinto*, the national dish of fried rice and black beans, is as common as the hamburger is in North America, particularly as a breakfast staple. Here it is served with care and pride. If you have room for something sweet don't miss out on the *licuados*. These icy fruit-milk concoctions come in every flavor from oatmeal to *guanabana*.

La Fonda Latino Grill   *(Colombian)*
Edgewater
5350 North Broadway Street
(773) 271-3935
Closed Monday
$$

Originally located on Clark near Lawrence, La Fonda Latino Grill reopened in the Edgewater neighborhood after a fire 16 years ago. Chef Herbert Delgado and his wife, Beatrice, own this family-run establishment that serves authentic Latin fare. Once inside, it feels like you have ventured south of the border. The pastel paintings and bronzed tin ceiling invite you into the cozy space, with its split level and exposed brick walls, Colombian folk art, and *carrieles* (handcrafted bags) hanging from the walls. There is no other place in the city that screams *Colombia* louder.

Mostly Colombian dishes, such as empanadas of spinach and mushroom, and white corn cakes topped with cheese and mushrooms, dominate the menu, but more creative dishes, such as the *lengua en salsa roja* (beef tongue

simmered in a creamy tomato sauce with peas) offer the more adventurous eater something special. Not to be missed are the *arepas*; delicious little cornmeal pancakes that are very popular in Colombia. If you're feeling more ambitious and hungry, try the lunch buffet Tuesdays through Fridays for $7.50. It provides patrons with the opportunity to sample several different dishes all at once.

Service here is shy yet competent. The staff is well versed with the menu and will happily answer any questions.

La Humita *(Ecuadoran)*
Avondale
3466 North Pulaski Road
(773) 794-9672
Closed Monday, BYOB
$$

Nestor Correa worked in the restaurant industry for many years after coming here from his native Ecuador before realizing his dream and starting a restaurant of his own. His experience paid off, for he has created a real winner. Correa's concept is to serve flavorful Ecuadoran food with an American standard of service in a European setting. The good-looking storefront location is clean, modern, and altogether pleasant, from the polished wooden tables to the Ecuadoran crafts and art decorating the walls (some of it for sale).

Begin with the tender, moist *humita* that lends the restaurant its name. It's the Andean region's answer to our bread, made from cornmeal dough surrounding mild cheese and steamed in a cornhusk. Ecuadoran *aji* sauce

on the table adds spice to this mild appetizer. The sauce is made from hot chiles and onion combined in a tropical fruit juice. It's used throughout the meal to add heat to the foods as desired.

Though the menu is not large, it includes seafood, chicken, beef, pork, and lamb. *Llapingachos*, potato pancakes stuffed with cheese, are served with the traditional accompaniments of peanut sauce, fried egg, chorizo, and avocado. The Americanized version of roasted lamb offers several well-cooked, tender baby lamb chops with roasted potatoes and seasonal vegetables. Other entrées include a typical shrimp-and-rice combination flavored with coconut milk.

Although there is no liquor license at this time, you can bring your own. Or better still, try one of the wonderful tropical fruit juices that Ecuador is known for—*mora* (like our blackberry), *tomate de arbol* (a tangy tamarillo), or *naranjilla* (a tangy, sweet fruit from the Amazon Basin). Nestor has used this lovely tropical *naranjilla* juice to flavor the restaurant's signature cheesecake dessert with its chocolate wafer crust.

All the food is fresh and lovingly presented. Diners on Saturdays are treated to weekly specials such as *seco de chivo*, a richly flavored lamb stew in a thick tomato sauce that is one of the premier dishes of Ecuador.

Mas *(Brazilian, Chilean, Argentine)*
Wicker Park
1670 West Division Street
(773) 276-8700
$$$

It's no wonder Chef John Manion has several followers. Having spent part of his childhood in Brazil, he has captured the essence of Latin cuisine. Nowhere is it more evident than at Mas (meaning "more" in Spanish). Nestled on the edge of the Wicker Park neighborhood, this hip, swanky eatery offers a menu no one can deny.

If you're looking for a nice sit-down experience, make your way to the dining area in the back, which affords a view of the open kitchen. For the bar experience, grab a seat in the front of the restaurant to indulge in some great people watching out of the huge picture window that dominates the bar area. The authentic Brazilian cocktails such as *caipirinhas* and *batidas* that are served nightly only add to the ambience of the space. The wine list is Spanish, Chilean, and Argentine in focus and surprisingly low priced, with only a few bottles more than $30.

Mas offers familiar dishes with flair. The black bean soup is served with a shot glass of *cachaca* (a sugarcane distillate). Other, more inventive dishes, such as lime-marinated tuna tacos with papaya, mustard, and rosemary; chile-cured pork tenderloin; or sautéed tilapia *a la chorrillana* are worth a try. Also on the menu is an array of small-plate choices that make it easier to sample the seasonal menu. There is always a *ceviche* of the day, and people flock here for it.

Pastry Chef Kim Stewart creates several sensational desserts, including a light pastel *tres leches* cake. Or try the banana–chocolate chip empanadas with pistachio ice cream and coconut-caramel sauce.

Rinconcito Sudamericano *(Peruvian)*
Bucktown
1954 West Armitage Avenue
(312) 489-3126
$$

This "little corner of South America," as the name translates, has been
serving authentic Peruvian food to Chicagoans since 1980. The decor has
improved over the years, and the menu continues to offer a great variety
of well-prepared Peruvian specialties, including flavorful soups, tangy
ceviches (marinated seafoods), a great array of other seafood specialties,
and, of course, potatoes.

The family-run storefront is pleasantly decorated with white tile floors,
high-backed Latin American pine chairs, a red tile roof, and mirrors, plus
louvered window shades to add airiness to the dining room. The service
is attentive and informative. Both Spanish and English are spoken here, so
you will have no problem getting answers to your questions about the
menu items.

Two fixed menus for two people are available with four different menu
selections, one with more seafood and the other with more chicken
entrées. The seafood menu begins with a typical potato in mild cheese
sauce, a large chicken corn *masa tamal*, and a nice portion of mixed
seafood *ceviche* with plenty of pickled onions. On the table you'll find hot
homemade jalapeño sauce that can be used to add spiciness. The seafood
menu is topped off with a lovely seafood paella brimming with all types
of shrimp, oysters, clams, squid, and mussels.

Also try the *anticuchos* (braised beef heart kabobs), *conejo al mani*
(rabbit in peanut sauce), *arroz con pato* (duck with rice cooked in wine),
or *picante de camerones* (shrimp in a nut cream sauce on rice). The por-
tions are more than generous and the service is prompt and professional.

NOTABLE

La Pena *(Ecuadoran)*
Portage Park
4212 North Milwaukee Avenue
(773) 545-7022
$$

Live Andean music on weekends makes this a great spot to sample typical Ecuadoran food and culture. The dining room is beautifully decorated, and the staff is friendly and eager to please.

Meals begin with a basket of *chiefles* (fried plantains) with spicy *aji* (hot chile sauce). Appetizers include five different seafood *ceviches* topped with traditional toasted corn kernels. Entrées include flavorful roasted meat and chicken, the traditional *llapingachos* (cheese-filled potato cakes), plus seafood and rice dishes. Although a full-service bar is available, lovely, frothy, tropical nonalcoholic juices are an outstanding alternative, including passion fruit and *mora* (South American blackberry).

Restaurant El Tinajon   *(Guatemalan)*
Roscoe Village
2054 West Roscoe Street
(773) 525-8455
Closed Sunday and Tuesday
$

Named after the traditional handleless clay pot used to hold drinking water, El Tinajon is a brightly decorated space that features authentic Guatemalan cuisine. Owner Olga Pezzarossi, a native of Guatemala, has operated El Tinajon for more than ten years. House specialties include *churrasquito*, a four-ounce rib eye steak served with black beans, plantains, and rice, and *pepian antiqueno*, a Mayan chicken stew with potatoes and green beans. An outdoor patio is open during the summer months and offers great alfresco dining.

Tango Sur   *(Argentine)*
Lakeview
3763 North Southport Avenue
(773) 477-5466
BYOB
$$

This storefront BYOB restaurant is a meat lover's dream, grilling large cuts of Argentine beef topped with *chimichurri* (a pestolike mixture of garlic, oil, onion, and herbs). Appetizers and entrées include deep-fried empanadas stuffed with beef, chicken, or ham and cheese; *matambre* (rolled veal cooked with vegetables); and *milanesa a caballo* (fried breaded beef topped with two eggs).

Argentine beef and *parrillada* (mixed grill) served on tabletop braziers steal the show here. Start with the *provoleta*, grilled provolone with olive oil and roasted red peppers, and finish with the killer *flan con dulce de leche*. Romantic mood lighting warms the recently expanded space (waits aren't what they used to be). There's even live tango music on Wednesdays.

MEXICAN

Carnitas Uruapan
Pilsen
1725 West 18th Street
(312) 226-2654
$

The Michoacán state in Mexico, southwest of Mexico City, is famous for its pork. It is well represented in Chicago by Carnitas Uruapan, a tiny restaurant in the center of 18th Street. For about thirty years the owners have been preparing pork as they did in their native town. The spotless kitchen is visible through a window to the back. There, three huge cauldrons sit atop gas burners, where various cuts of pork simmer for three hours. When done the meat is placed in a heated case in the front window. Now the fun begins. Before an order is taken a piece of pork is hacked off with a cleaver and proffered for a taste. It is succulent and delicious. Ordering is by the pound, and the pork is served in pieces with tortillas, salsa, and a medley of marinated peppers, as in Michoacán.

The rest of the menu is limited. There is a huge case of *chicharrones*, or fried pork skins. Occasionally there is a cactus stew. The soft drinks reflect the restaurant's Mexican roots with a selection of lime, tamarind, and other fruit sodas. The *carnitas*, though, are definitely the main event.

Frontera Grill/Topolobampo
River North
445 North Clark Street
(312) 661-1434
$$–$$$

Fans of Chef Rick Bayless's two celebrated restaurants (in the same location), Frontera Grill and Topolobampo, unreservedly praise them as serving some of the best Mexican food in America. Patricia Wells of the *International Herald Tribune* called Frontera Grill "the third best casual restaurant in the world." *The New York Times* called Topolobampo "the most elegant and serious Mexican restaurant in the country."

Bayless is known for his books like *Authentic Mexican* and *Rick Bayless's Mexican Kitchen: Recipes and Techniques of a World Class Cuisine*. His commitment to local and authentic Mexican flavors and seasonality and his support of local farmers makes the restaurants "about as Slow Food as you can get," in the words of one insider.

Housed in the same building, Frontera Grill offers more casual but no less exquisite, authentic, and creative fare than Topolobampo. From mahi mahi in a green *mole* of sesame seeds, almonds, peanuts, and poblanos to their signature chili—cubes of charcoal-seared pork and lamb simmered

with or without heirloom white runner beans, ancho chiles, roasted garlic, herbs, spices, and dark beer with a jicama salad and plantain tostadas—innovation as well as reverence for tradition are evident.

Topolobampo's offerings are equally eclectic and enticing, like the Crawford Farm Leg of Lamb with its Oaxacan black *mole* (containing twenty-nine ingredients and taking all day to cook) or the *achiote*-marinated Alaskan black cod with roasted tomatoes, parsley, poblanos, and sour orange juice in banana leaf.

Bayless goes out of his way to create good relationships with local farmers and involves his staff extensively in his philosophy of authenticity and local sustainability. Each year Bayless takes his staff to various parts of Mexico to learn hands-on how food is grown, purchased, prepared, and enjoyed. Following each trip, a new menu will highlight dishes from each respective region. After a trip to the Yucatán, chefs played with a dish of *cochinita pibil* modeled after local chef Silvio Campos's version. Whole local Berkshire pigs were butchered, coated with *achiote* spice marinade, placed on banana leaves, and covered with a rich pork stock, sour orange juice, and *poblano rajas*. The pig typically is cooked in the ground overnight, but Frontera cooks improvise with a similar slow, long cooking in the oven. The tender, flavorful meat is served on fresh tortillas with habanero salsa, definitely not for the faint of heart.

The food is simple, fresh, and traditional. Certainly people go for the margaritas, which by now are nationally famous, with accolades from nearly every publication including *Playboy* magazine. The key is the lime juice that is squeezed fresh every day. Freshly made tortillas are another key to the success of the Bayless empire. The restaurant orders its *masa* (corn flour) daily, mixes it, and prepares tortillas and tamales all day long.

This simple, fresh way of cooking is important to Rick Bayless and his staff—almost as much as his customers' happiness. Frontera is a restaurant with integrity, and their support for local farmers displays this belief clearly. Their Farmer Foundation has raised thousands of dollars for farmers. The restaurant throws events that pair chefs and farmers to teach customers exactly how their entrée begins and ends. In the end, whether you go to Frontera to have a drink and a laugh or you go to support your local farmers and ensure sustainable agriculture, you are guaranteed to have a great meal.

La Oaxaqueña
Kilbourn Park
3382 North Milwaukee Avenue
(773) 545-8585
$

La Oaxaqueña serves the traditional cuisine of the Mexican state of Oaxaca. The small storefront restaurant delivers large portions of Oaxacan favorites: grilled cactus pads, *sopes* (thick *masa* dough topped with your choice of chicken, chorizo, or beef), *ceviche*, Oaxacan tamales wrapped in banana leaves, *chilaquiles* in green salsa, *cecina* (marinated grilled beef tenderloin), *chiles rellenos* stuffed with *picadillo* (ground meat and potatoes sweetened with pineapple, raisins, almonds, and cinnamon), *conejo adobado* (skinless whole rabbit in a spicy chile marinade), and chicken served with La Oaxaqueña's own deep red mole sauce.

Huatulco, on the west coast of the Oaxacan state, is known for its fresh Pacific seafood, and La Oaxaqueña dishes up Botano Huatulco, an appetizer of shrimp, squid, and octopus flavored with garlic, red onions, and olive oil that is enough for the whole table to share. In addition, they prepare Camarones Huatulco, shrimps sauteed in onions, cheese, and brandy. Seafood cocktails, salads, and soups are also available. *Huachinango*, whole red snapper, is offered fried, with *pico de gallo*, or à la Veracruz. La Oaxaqueña boasts that its Super Tortas are unique in Chicago—they are a meal in themselves, and a bargain at $5 to $6! A good selection of Mexican beers and tequilas round out the menu, as do desserts such as flan, *tres leches* cake, and apple pie.

Other Location
6113 West Diversey Avenue, Chicago (Montclare); (773) 637-8709

MAXWELL STREET

Even though the Maxwell Street Market sees thousands of visitors every Sunday morning, it always feels like an undiscovered treasure. No longer located on Maxwell Street, and no longer the Jewish peddlers' market of seventy-five years ago, it is now located on Canal Street and has metamorphosed into a vibrant Mexican flea market with outstanding street food.

The flea market serves up lots of used tools, cheap toys, tube socks, Laserjets, and personal hygiene products (possibly also used). The produce stands feature a glorious choice of dried chiles, *nopales*, tamarind pods, and hibiscus flowers, with other foreign and local fruits and spices scattered throughout. But it is the food stands that have taken on a life of their own, becoming outdoor restaurants complete with seating, tableware, arrays of condiments, and a trail of generally satisfied city health inspectors.

To say you've done it, try the cow's eyeball taco or the brains empanada, or the grilled corn (good start) slathered with *adobo* spices, squeeze margarine, and cheap grated cheese (bad finish). To discover a mother lode of rich indigenous cooking, try Rubi's pork and red *mole* in a handmade tortilla fresh off the griddle, or the goat consommé, or some hot, greasy *churros*, or the shrimp and octopus soup, or a Oaxacan tamale, or a Salvadoran cheese-infused *pupusa*.

It can take two or three hours to ferret out these places, and even then you'll never be lucky enough to find them all on your first visit to the chaos of this street market. Maxwell Street is its own *olla podrida*, always tempting with the promise of something not yet tasted.

La Pasadita
Noble Square
1132, 1140, and 1141 North Ashland Avenue
(773) 278-0384
Open 9:30 A.M. until 1:30 A.M. weekdays, until 3:00 A.M. on weekends
$

The intersection of Ashland Avenue and Division Street boasts no fewer than three La Pasaditas. Ask anyone which restaurant they consider the best, and you will get passionate and reasoned responses in favor of each of them.

The 1140 location is situated in a funny-looking bright yellow bungalow and features tacos and burritos. And that's it. Steak, cheese steak, tongue, or soft beef are a few of the different kinds of meat and preparations you can order wrapped in soft, warm corn tortillas that are redolent of lime, along with a generous sprinkling of chopped onions and cilantro. All of these options cost $5.50 or less, including tax. The restaurant has a total of eight stools, and half of them belly up directly opposite the busy grill, which fills this joint with aroma and atmosphere. To accompany your tacos, order a glass of *horchata*—vanilla-scented rice milk served with a soup ladle from a big white bucket.

This restaurant's twin, just across the street at 1141, offers an identical menu, although the meat here has a slightly more pronounced, char-grilled dimension.

The La Pasadita at 1132 has a larger menu with table service. Some say it has sold out and gone "yuppified," offering charming tables and cute paintings on the wall, but others swear by the burritos, and the home-made smoked jalapeño salsa alone is a good reason to check it out. Avoid the vegetarian burrito here, though, which is extremely disappointing.

La Quebrada
4859 West Roosevelt Road
Cicero
(708) 780-8100
$

La Quebrada—with its barred windows and dinerlike feel—is an oasis in the midst of an otherwise dreary industrial strip strewn with shuttered factories. Often bustling, always good, it is worth taking a trip to this near-west suburb. Try anything with seafood in it, as it's bound to be fresh and tasty. *Filete al ajillo* or *filete de chipotle*—both catfish dishes—are smothered in a tangy pepper sauce so tasty you'll want to lick your plate. Red-meat lovers should try the ever-so-delicate *barbacoa de chivo* (steamed goat). All dishes are served up with fresh house-made tortillas.

Upon arrival, warm tortilla chips with a hint of lard are served up alongside a fiery salsa. If spice isn't your thing, order a glass of the very cinnamony *horchata*, a sweetened rice drink, to take out the sting. Service is friendly but can be a bit inattentive after the meal arrives.

Restaurante y Pozolería San Juan
Humboldt Park
1523 North Pulaski Avenue
(773) 276-5825
$

No celebration in the Guerrero region of Mexico is complete without *pozole*, a traditional stew made with pork and hominy, flavored with the salsa (pepper sauce) of one's choosing and served as is or dressed with diced avocado. Whether it's a simple family gathering or a more formal celebration, a steaming pot of *pozole* on the table signifies festive times ahead.

The *pozole* at Restaurante y Pozolería San Juan, among other dishes on the menu, makes this humble spot worth a visit. Here at San Juan, the *pozole* is made Guerrero style, and can be ordered in green (very, very spicy), red (very spicy), or white (some spice)—are you thinking of the Mexican flag yet? Different regions of Mexico vary the exact ingredients, but the constant is the *patitas* (pig's feet), or the head, for flavor, and the peppers that dress the soup to the eater's preference. Optional garnitures include *chicharrones* (fried pork rind) and avocado. Regardless of the degree of heat, the flavor is key, and San Juan has it down. The menu also features a large variety of other traditional Mexican dishes, all worth sampling, at an average of $6 to $7 per item. Portions are generously sized and served without smoke and mirrors—just pure flavor.

Salpicón
Old Town
1252 North Wells Street
(312) 988-7811
$$$

The Spanish word *salpicón* means "a splash," and Salpicón's menu describes itself as "a splash of Mexico in Chicago." What distinguishes Salpicón from other Mexican fine-dining establishments is its concentration on contemporary Mexican cuisine. Salpicón celebrates the cuisine of the regions of central Mexico. The menu changes weekly with the availability of seasonal ingredients.

The menu may include roasted butternut squash soup with just a hint of the smoky flavor of chipotle peppers, or a selection of *tamalitos* (little corn cakes), each with its own filling and matching sauce. Main entrées could be rack of lamb encrusted with toasted pumpkinseeds in a pasilla-tomatillo salsa, or *chiles rellenos* stuffed with the Mexican delicacy *huitlacoche*, the earthy, smoky corn mushroom. Charcoal-grilled fresh fish or chicken in a classic mole sauce are usually found on the menu. Don't overlook the desserts, many of which are updated Mexican favorites.

The desire to please the guest's palate extends to Salpicón's wine list (thirty pages long), which has received the *Wine Spectator* Award of Excellence. The tequila selection is likewise impressive, and tequila and mezcal flights are available for tastings.

All of this fine dining occurs in the Old Town neighborhood, in a bright, festive room decorated with Mexican paintings and artifacts. Service is friendly yet professional. Alfresco dining is available as the weather permits.

Taqueria Puebla-Mexico
Humboldt Park
3625 West North Avenue
(773) 772-8435
$

Traditional *cemitas* and *tacos arabes* may be rare in Chicago, but they can be found. Taqueria Puebla-Mexico, near Humboldt Park, serves Pueblan specialties under the watchful eye of the Zurita family. The food here is authentic with a capital *A*.

A *cemita* is a multilayered composition on a dense, toasted sesame-seed bun, a crunchy thing that softens under the oily heat of its filling. The *cemita* roll is sliced, crisped on the stove, and crammed full of good ingredients: avocado, *panela* cheese, and a riot of pickled onions, carrots, and jalapeño peppers. Any authentic *cemita* will also have a few leaves of *papalo*, a peppery herb with a certain resemblance to watercress. Finally, there is the meat: your choice of *carne asada*, *milanesa*, *jamon*, and *carne enchilada*.

Likened by many to the Greek gyros, the *tacos arabes* (pork and onion layered on a spit) are sliced beautifully on large flour tortillas. A variety of other traditional dishes, many also flavored by *papalo*, are offered in this corner restaurant frequented by many local families. An adjoining *lavanderia* is a conversation piece, as are the tons of sports (especially soccer) memorabilia that wallpapers this place.

NOTABLE

Adobo Grill
Old Town
1610 North Wells Street
(312) 266-7999
$$

Adobo Grill's trademark is the guacamole prepared at tableside. Watch as the fresh garlic, onions, peppers, cilantro, avocado, tomatoes, and more get mixed together in the traditional *molcajete*, a bowl made of lava rock; taste the transformation of these ingredients into the otherworldly medley of flavor that is guacamole. For this reason alone it is worth a trip.

Chef Freddy Sanchez has taken Adobo Grill to new heights. He searches for the best traditional and local ingredients, which in the early summer might include an omelet that features *huitlacoche*, the corn fungus available for such a short time. In the fall look for crispy taquitos stuffed with wild mushrooms, potatoes, and tomatillo-serrano salsa.

The atmosphere is contemporary Mexican: Exposed brick walls are accented by sun-drenched colors and vividly hued artwork. The two beautiful vintage bars boast more than forty tequilas and an extensive margarita menu.

Chilpancingo
River North
358 West Ontario Street
(312) 266-9525
$$

Chef Generoso "Geno" Bahena, steeped in the philosophy of Topolobampo and Frontera Grill, brings his own spin to authentic Mexican cuisine. Specialties include *moles* over delicate meats like quail, squid, rabbit, or lamb (sometimes pit roasted or smoked). Bahena's other restaurant, Ixcapuzalco (see below), is modern and bright, and features formal service and a more upscale backdrop for his authentic regional Mexican cuisine.

Ixcapuzalco
Logan Square
2919 North Milwaukee Avenue
(773) 486-7340
$$

Ixcapuzalco was the first restaurant Generoso "Geno" Bahena opened after working for twelve years under Rick Bayless at Frontera Grill and Topolobampo. With a somewhat smaller kitchen and more laid-back atmosphere than his subsequent creation, Chilpancingo, the daily *moles*—many said to be his mother's own recipes—are nonetheless famed in Chicago. Duck in prune *mole* is particularly scintillating. Sunday brunch here is an exciting change of pace.

MIDDLE EASTERN

A la Turka   *(Turkish)*
Lakeview
3134 North Lincoln Avenue
(773) 935-6101
$$

A la Turka is the kind of place that seems so focused on environment that
it's almost a surprise that the food is very good. When the place changed
ownership in 2001, the new proprietors gave the room an Arabian Nights
feel: lots of draped fabric, plenty of tables where customers can sit on ele-
vated platforms, reclining on pillows, and a proliferation of fake firepots.

When ordering appetizers, be sure to try the fabulous hummus and the
eggplant dip (just a little different from and chunkier than baba ghanoush).
Though not the most vegetarian-friendly place (most of the vegetarian
options, though well-labeled, are just appetizers), there are a few eggplant-
based dishes on the menu. Most entrées, however, involve some combina-
tion of beef and lamb, or chicken. They're known for their Lavash kebab:
beef and lamb skewers served with mozzarella cheese and tomato sauce. In
fact, many of the dishes involve some variation on their tomato sauce, and
rightfully so: It's a perfect balance between sweet and tangy, with the proper
herb usage to differentiate it as Turkish.

Dessert options change daily and are presented on a tray. The baklava
is spongier than what most people may be used to, but is still very good.
After dinner, if so inclined, try a bar- or table-side hookah, filled with
apple tobacco. A la Turka offers a full bar and some surprisingly good
Turkish wine. Belly dancers perform Thursday through Sunday; when
they do, be prepared for twenty minutes of very loud music. On weekends
the place can get a little rowdy, but the atmosphere is a lot of fun. The
service can be a bit leisurely at times, and you may have several different
people waiting on you. If notified in advance, A la Turka can easily
accommodate very large parties.

Isabella's Estiatorio   *(Mediterranean, American)*
330 West State Street
Geneva
(630) 845-8624
$$

British-born Chef Sean Eastwood, having spent a number of years cooking
in Europe and most recently San Francisco, is devoted to the Slow Food
philosophy. All food in this comfortable country Mediterranean restaurant
is made from scratch except the bread, which comes from Red Hen bakery.
Produce is procured from local and organic suppliers whenever possible.

Starters may include a sampler plate of Mediterranean spreads (hummus, *taramasalata, melitzanosalata*) with house-made pita; confit of Moroccan spiced duck with red grapefruit, shaved fennel, and pomegranate dressing (enough for a light entrée); or their excellent flatbread topped with caramelized onions, kalamata olives, and *idiazabal* cheese.

Popular entrées include the Wild Mushroom Risotto; Olive-Brined Pork Fillet with Sweet Potato Gratin, Brussels Sprouts, and Pear-Ginger Chutney; house-made meat lasagna with spinach, mushrooms, and Lebanese yogurt béchamel; and roasted Amish chicken from Wisconsin with olive oil mashed potatoes. They seek out suppliers of line-caught fish, and the *dorade*, which is grilled and served whole, and the John Dory are flown in from the Mediterranean.

The waitstaff has been trained to know the menu through and through, and can helpfully describe a dish or ingredient. The wine list is ample, categorizing the offerings by body and featuring Californian, French, and Italian producers that complement the food.

Kabul House *(Afghani)*
3220 Dempster Street
Skokie
(847) 763-9930
, $$

Abdul Quazi grew up just north of the Afghan capital of Kabul, in a hard-working family of grape growers. He brings the wonderful tastes of his homeland to the Chicago area with the opening of Kabul House, which last year opened a second location in Old Town.

If you have never tasted Afghan cooking, it is a cross between Indian and Middle Eastern, especially Persian, cuisine. This authentic restaurant gets rave reviews from the Afghan community in Chicago, and for good reason. The spices are subtle but flavorful. The complimentary strips of warm, slightly chewy Afghan bread are good to sop up the mildly spicy meat sauce and homemade yogurt that tops the *mantu*, delightful steamed dumplings of ground beef and onion. *Kadu*, billed as the house specialty, is a slightly smoky-tasting, honey-sweetened, sautéed mashed pumpkin seasoned with cardamom and other spices and also drizzled with yogurt. Both of these dishes make great appetizers.

Another good reason to make the trek to Kabul House is for the chicken and lamb kebabs grilled over an open fire, which makes the ginger, garlic, cilantro, and onion flavors shine through. The *qabili palau* features moist, tender shredded lamb buried under a mound of rice topped with sweet julienne carrots and raisins, served with a side of spicy mint-coriander-chutney sauce. To top off your meal, have the *dough*, a smooth, cooling beverage that blends yogurt, milk, and spices, or try a cup of the strong black cardamom-flavored tea. The tea goes well with *firni*, a cornstarch-based pudding flavored with the favorite Afghan spice, cardamom. Topped with a rosewater-scented syrup and crushed pistachios, *firni* is a deliciously sweet way to end your meal.

Other Location

1629 North Halsted, Chicago (Old Town); (312) 751-1029

Maza   *(Lebanese)*
Lincoln Park
2748 North Lincoln Avenue
(773) 929-9600
$$

Maza offers some of the finest Lebanese food you can get in Chicago. Many people are drawn to it for the tapas-style appetizers (a hot and cold variety of very sharable, small-portioned dishes), but Maza has as much to offer for entrées and desserts as it does up front.

The room is comfortable, upscale, and dimly lit—a great place to bring a date. Service is not rushed but quite attentive; the owner checks on each table, suggesting dishes or maybe comping you some baklava if you weren't planning on ordering dessert. The wine list is well rounded, but try a bottle of the house Lebanese wine. It goes very well with almost everything they serve, especially the olives and pickled vegetables that are presented to each table upon seating.

Besides the expected baba ghanoush, hummus, and falafel, the appetizer list features some traditional regional dishes not frequently spotted on menus: *ful medames* (slow-cooked fava beans with lemon and garlic); *loubieh* (string beans), and *makanak* (fresh homemade lamb sausage). Be sure to try the spinach pie; it will take a little while, but that's because it's prepared fresh with each order, served steaming and flaky-crisp right from the oven. The phyllo dough crunches while it melts on the tongue. One of the best fried appetizers is the *kibbe meklya*, served with lemon wedges, which is also great with a little *labneh* (fresh yogurt cheese).

In addition to the attention paid to spicing, preparation, and plating, a nice aspect of the entrées is that they aren't huge. The portion sizes are reasonable: not stingy, not gluttonous—the owner expects his customers to have a fair amount of appetizers in their bellies when the meal arrives. Lamb is featured heavily, even served tartare (*kibbeh nayeh*). The standard kebabs are offered, some seasoned with mint. When ordering brochettes, customers are asked how well-done they prefer meat. Seafood also features prominently on the menu, with a wonderful dish of jumbo scallops in a light cheese sauce, whole red snapper, broiled trout, and more. All entrées come with a cup of almost-creamy curried lentil soup.

Save room for dessert if you can. Traditional baklava is served with a swirl of raspberry and lemon sauces for dipping. In addition, there are several specialty items: *mamoul bi tamr* (a baked fruity couscous served flambé tableside) and *halawat al-jubn* (sweet rosewater cheese topped with pistachio nuts and served with poached figs and raspberry sauce).

NOTABLE

Anatolian Kabab   *(Turkish)*
Lincoln Square
4609 North Lincoln Avenue
(773) 561-2200
$-$$

Anatolian Kabab brings warming, authentic Turkish fare to cozy Lincoln Square. The room can feel somewhat sterile when empty and the friendly service might be somewhat slow, but the food more than makes up for it. An extremely vegetarian-friendly restaurant, Anatolian Kabab clearly labels all items that are vegan; most vegetarian dishes can be made without cheese to further expand the vegan options. Even the carnivores get a nod to good health, with Anatolian Kabab proudly serving hormone-free beef and lamb kebabs.

Cousin's Turkish Fine Dining   *(Turkish, Mediterranean)*
Irving Park
3038 Irving Park Road
(773) 478-6868
Closed Monday
$$-$$$

At Cousin's the emphasis on freshness and innovation makes for an ever-changing menu. The chefs manage to elevate traditional ingredients to a whole new level: olives, chickpeas, eggplant, spinach, bulgur, rice, feta, and yogurt are prepared and combined in exciting ways not usually seen, even in Turkish restaurants. First-timers would do well to order the appetizer sampler, which has hummus, some slightly sweet *dolmas*, *ezme* (finely chopped seasoned tomatoes with onions, peppers, and walnuts), and a baba ghanoush–like spread called Harem's Secret.

Cousin's offers a full bar as well as a decent wine list, though you can bring your own at no extra charge. However, the drink to try is the Black

Sea: a hot drink made with Turkish *cay* (tea) and Kahlùa. For those unaccustomed to hot alcoholic drinks it can be served over ice, but it is pleasantly warming, particularly in winter months. Service is attentive and helpful—very courteous to those unfamiliar with Turkish cuisine.

Middle Eastern Bakery
See Take-Out Food, p. 260.

Noon O Kabab   *(Persian)*
Albany Park
4661 North Kedzie Avenue
(773) 279-8899
$$

Located in northwest Albany Park, Noon O Kabab offers wonderfully authentic Persian food in a comfortable setting at a decent price. It's owned and operated by a father-and-son team, the Naghavis from Iran, who will greet you warmly upon your entrance. It feels like a family place: pink-tile walls, camaraderie among customers, lots of kids. A great place to find Persian home cooking, recipes prepared as passed down through the family for years.

Try visiting Noon O Kabab for lunch, when a scaled-down, even less expensive version of the menu is available in addition to the regular one. There are plenty of appetizers, including the smokier-than-usual baba ghanoush, *borani* (boiled spinach and yogurt), and *kash-ke-bademjan* (eggplant, mint, and onion). If it's lunchtime, patrons have the choice of hummus or soup with their order. In addition, all the usual kebabs are offered, a few as sandwiches on *tandouri*, a large, warm, thin, pitalike bread.

Oasis Café   *(Pan-Arabic, Israeli)*
Loop
21 North Wabash Avenue
(312) 558-1058
Closed Sunday
$

Most people wouldn't find Oasis Café by chance; it's the kind of place you just have to know about. Situated in the back of a jewelry mall, customers walk past aisles of gold watches to get to one of the best and cheapest lunches in the Loop. The clientele ranges from students at the nearby Art Institute to businessmen, all enjoying a range of vegetarian and meat-centric lunches.

If you're broke, a lentil soup that comes with a side of pita and lemon slices makes a filling lunch for $1.75. Sandwich choices range from falafel to one of the day's specials, such as the somewhat salty portobello mushroom sandwich or the roasted eggplant. Kebabs are also on the menu: slow-roasted lamb, beef, and chicken *shawerma*.

Pita Inn   *(Lebanese)*
3910 West Dempster Street
Skokie
(847) 677-0211
$

Pita Inn has been churning out high-quality, inexpensive, unpretentious yet delectable Middle Eastern/Lebanese food for two decades. Several years ago it was remodeled, with the decor changing from dingy to friendly. The service is efficient, if a bit brisk: Place an order, take a number, and wait for them to call it out. You can watch as they shave lamb from the skewer, shape and deep-fry falafel, or steam huge batches of fragrant jasmine rice. Even late at night the place is bustling, packed with customers waiting their turn at a seat, though table turnover is regular.

Pita Inn's falafel is some of the Chicagoland's best. Made to order, green inside and perfectly crispy on the outside, served in a sandwich with hummus for less than $3 or on a plate with rice for less than $4, it's the thing to order at Pita Inn. Living up to its name, Pita Inn opened a bakery to make their own pita bread, which can also be bought at the Pita Inn Market next door to the Skokie location (along with imported olives, spices, cheeses, coffee, cookware, and take-out foods from the restaurant).

Sultan's Market
See Take-Out Food, p. 257.

POLISH

More than two-thirds of the Chicago metropolitan area's Polish-Americans live in the suburbs, and there has been a rapid growth of bakeries, delis, and restaurants in southwestern and western suburbs such as Burbank, Lemont, Orland Park, Burr Ridge, and Streamwood, as well as in northwestern suburbs such as Niles, Mount Prospect, Arlington Heights, Schaumburg, and Mundelein. While it is impossible to compare and sample them all, this section focuses on the proven establishments that consistently provide a homemade, tasty product. The majority of these places are located in established Polish neighborhoods on the northwest and southwest sides of Chicago.

Halina's Polish Delights
Jefferson Park
5914 West Lawrence Avenue
(773) 205-0256
Open daily 12:00–8:00 P.M.
$ (Cash only)

The northwest Chicago neighborhoods of Jefferson Park and Dunning are home to vibrant Polish communities, and the main streets are lined with delis, bakeries, shops, and restaurants catering to this clientele. Tucked into a strip mall on Lawrence Avenue, the sunny and welcoming Halina's Polish Delights offers the comforts of home to those who are far from their homeland.

Halina's owner has been a professional cook for thirty years (the last ten years in the United States), and the quality of the food shows it. She shops daily for fresh ingredients, butchers her own meat, and bakes all desserts on the premises. Only the rye bread accompanying all soups comes from the Delightful Pastries bakery across the street (see note below). There is a lunch menu offering everything from ham-and-cheese sandwiches to julienne salad to accommodate the many neighborhood residents who meet to eat here on a regular basis, but the true Polish treasures are found in the soups and dinners, which can be ordered all day.

The clear red *barszcz* (borscht) served with a *krokiet* (breaded, meat-filled blintz) literally sings with flavor, and is one of six soups offered daily. The *zurek* (white borscht) with smoked red kielbasa comes with a whole sliced boiled egg and has the required tangy taste from its sour starter. *Rosol* (chicken), *flaczki* (tripe), and *pieczarkowa* (mushroom) soups round out the menu, supplemented by a daily special.

Dinners can be ordered either à la carte or "complete," which includes tea, soup, and dessert. Menu items, just like Poland's history, are from all over the European map. *Kotlet schabowy* (pork cutlet), traditional or Viennese or Swedish style; *szaszlyk* (Turkish shish kebab); *placek po*

wegiersku (potato pancake with Hungarian-style goulash) and *cyganeria* (Gypsy stew) are just some examples of the various ethnic threads woven throughout Polish cuisine. All entrées come with assorted *surowki* (salads) and a choice of homemade mashed potatoes, *kopytka* (dumplings), or kasha. Desserts vary daily—the apple *szarlotka*, a perfect blend of tangy, sweet apples and pastry, is heavenly. The owner spends seven days a week in the kitchen, and the tasty, home-cooked food is a reflection of her love of cooking.

Note: When you're in the area, check out **Delightful Pastries**, 5927 West Lawrence, and **J & J European Deli**, 5960 West Lawrence—known for its ample homemade sausage selection.

Hortex Restaurant
Belmont Heights
7419 West Irving Park Road
(773) 625-1200
$

Despite a name reminiscent (to English speakers, at least) of a chemical plant, Hortex is an ambitious, bistrolike restaurant serving high-quality "nouvelle" Polish food. Fear not—in this case, that simply means fork-tender pork ribs cooked in honey-wine sauce and spinach-stuffed pierogi, to name a few of the innovative items available here. The pierogi, also offered with more traditional fillings such as meat, mushroom, sauerkraut, and potato-cheese, are particular standouts, well seasoned and encased in an exceptionally light dough.

Diners weary of the chilled, shredded side salads that accompany every Polish meal will be delighted to learn that Hortex serves fresh, sautéed vegetables with many of the entrées. It is also a good place to try slightly more adventurous items, such as the tripe soup, which at Hortex consists of inch-long, thinly sliced beef tripe in a fragrant, peppery broth, or the quail roasted in cranberry glaze and wrapped in bacon.

Hortex is somewhat unusual in that it offers vegetarian selections as well as several game dishes; aside from the quail, there is roasted rabbit and duck cooked in honey wine. The kitchen has a real flair for presentation—entrées are served on enormous, colorful square plates and are fancifully garnished.

Hortex is housed in a small storefront, with a brick interior and original art on the walls. Order a Polish beer and enjoy the scenery and people watching.

Smak Tak Polish Restaurant
Jefferson Park
5961 North Elston Avenue
(773) 763-1123
Open Tuesday–Sunday 12:00–7:00 P.M., closed Monday
$

Located on a quiet residential stretch of Elston Avenue on Chicago's far northwest side, Smak Tak is a destination for those seeking authentic Polish home cooking. The primarily Polish clientele ranges from the sharply dressed businessman raving to his companion about the *rosol* (chicken soup) and *szarlotka* (apple charlotte cake) to the three working men who dig into the daily special of soup, salads, pork cutlet, and dessert with gusto.

Soups are a mainstay of Polish cooking, and this cozy storefront offers three choices each day from its repertoire of twenty favorites. The owner maps out her soups on a monthly spreadsheet, rotating them to offer a large variety to her regulars. She routinely calls customers to let them know when their favorite red *barszcz* (borscht) will be served. On a recent visit, excellent *zupa ogorkowa* (dill pickle soup), served with a basket of fresh rye bread, included chunks of potato in a sour cream–thickened stock with finely chopped dill sprinkled on top. In the summer, *chlodniki* (cold fruit soups) feature whatever is in season.

Most main courses, ranging from the flavorful ground veal cutlet with sautéed mushrooms to the stuffed cabbage (*golabki*), come with mashed potatoes and three composed salads, or *surowki*. Banish all thoughts of iceberg or romaine lettuce—Polish salads delight in combining diced fresh or cooked vegetables in either a sour cream, vinegar and lemon juice, or mayonnaise base, and have entire sections of cookbooks devoted to them. Selections one day included a crunchy carrot and raisin salad and a sweet beet medley. Five *surowki* are available daily, and customers can request their favorites.

The menu, which is printed in both Polish and English, offers a good selection of the basics: *nalesniki z serem* (cheese blintzes), *placki ziemniaczane* (potato pancakes), pierogi with a choice of eight different fillings, *bigos* (hunter's stew), and grilled sausage and *kopytka* (potato dumplings). Everything is made on the premises from scratch daily. Smak Tak is family friendly, and even offers chicken fingers and hamburgers for picky eaters. Catering and take-out are available, including special à la carte holiday menus for those who want a traditional Polish thirteen-course meatless *Wigilia* (Christmas Eve dinner).

Szalas Restaurant
Garfield Ridge
5214 South Archer Avenue
(773) 582-0300
$

Chicago's southwest side is home to the *gorale*, or Polish highlanders, who hail from the mountainous regions of southern Poland. These hardy shepherds are known for their expert woodworking and homemade sheep's-milk cheese (*oscypek*), which is a Slow Food Presidium product. Perhaps the most extraordinary thing about Szalas is the sheer folkloric stylishness of it all. The spacious yet cozy interior is decked out in fine *Goral* style—a soaring wooden cathedral ceiling, exposed log walls, elaborately carved wood doors, and to top it off, a partition dividing the bar and restaurant area, designed to look like a highlander mountain home, complete with ruffled curtains and flowers in the window.

The waitstaff (all Polish, dressed in authentic highlander folk costume) start off by serving moist rye bread and *moskol*, a kind of dense highlander griddle cake made from potatoes, flour, egg, and sour cream. The real treats, however, are the accompaniments: silky homemade lard studded with flecks of bacon (*smalec*), and *bryndza*, a salty, creamy sheep's-milk

cheese produced in Poland's Tatry Mountain region. Do not overlook the soups: Polish cuisine pays lots of attention to soup, and Szalas is no exception. Try the white borscht, a hearty, slightly sour white soup made with fermented rye meal and served with a hard-boiled egg and sausage, or the *kwasnica*, a *Goral* specialty containing smoked rib meat (a fact the English-language version of the menu neglects to mention).

The entrées veer somewhat from the traditional stuffed cabbage–pierogi axis, although these items are offered as well. Dinners are, unsurprisingly, on the meaty side: pork cutlet stuffed with *bryndza*, beef medallions with cherry sauce, lamb roast, and in an apparent concession to local tastes, chicken tenders with coconut. Plop yourself down in a velvet-upholstered sleigh (which doubles as a booth), listen to live *goral* folk music (weekends only), and you would swear you were in Zakopane, Poland's "winter capital."

NOTABLE

Andrzej Grill
Ukrainian Village
1022 North Western Avenue
(773) 489-3566
Open until 8:00 P.M., Sunday until 6:00 P.M.
$ (Cash only)

Do not be fooled by the Cherry Master video game or the spartan atmosphere—Andrzej Grill offers some of the most delicious home-style Polish food in the city. Andrzej started out as a Polish workingman's joint, where temporarily wifeless immigrants could purchase a meal plan, read the Polish paper, and avoid American fast food.

Presided over by the melancholy Andrzej himself, the restaurant dishes up all the classics, in large quantities. The football-size potato pancake folded over pork goulash filling is delectable, as are the pierogi, which are never leaden or water-logged, a failing often encountered in Chicago's buffet-heavy Polish food scene. *Kopytka* (finger-shaped potato dumplings) in mushroom-dill sauce is also a standout. All the soups are clearly home-made, including a delicate *rosol*, golden chicken broth dotted with tiny flecks of chicken and carrots. Bigger appetites may want to take on *flaki* (tripe soup) or *kapusniak*, a thick, fragrant cabbage soup.

Bobak's
Garfield Ridge
5275 South Archer Avenue
(773) 735-5334
$

The Bobak family has been in the sausage and deli business on the south-west side since 1967, and has created a new segment of the Polish buffet restaurant market. By adding a sit-down restaurant with liquor service to its superdeli, it created an added destination for customers.

If you're hell-bent on preparing tripe soup, hunter's stew, or any other Polish delicacy yourself, however, your first stop on Chicago's southwest side should be Bobak's Supermarket and Deli. Bobak's is spacious, well organized, and chock-full of all the Polish specialty products you'll ever need. In addition to prepared products such as *kluski slaskie* (Silesian dumplings), *pyzy* (potato dumplings stuffed with meat), *nalesniki* (blintzes), and traditional Polish vegetable salads, Bobak's has an unusu-ally rich selection of homemade Polish sausage, including country (*wiejska*) sausage, cherry-smoked pork sausage, and a truly delectable *kabanos*, a smoky, dried pork sausage. As is the norm in most Polish gro-cery stores, Bobak's makes its own brine- and vinegar-cured cucumbers and sauerkraut—scoop your own out of large pails located in the rear of the store.

The Burr Ridge combination deli/grocery store/take-out buffet/sit-down restaurant has been so incredibly successful that it is now being replicated in the Naperville location. For those who don't want to eat in, all food is sold by the pound for take-out—$3.49 per pound Monday through Saturday, and $3.99 per pound on Sundays.

Other Locations
100 Burr Ridge Parkway, Burr Ridge; (630) 655-2100
955 West 75th Street, Naperville; (630) 961-9200

Old Warsaw Buffet
4750 North Harlem Avenue
Norridge
(708) 867-4500
$

A fixture on Harlem Avenue—where Chicago meets Norridge—for thirty-four years, Old Warsaw Buffet has thrived because customers recognize the quality of its food and keep coming back for more. The buffet is filled to the brim with soups, *surowki* (salads), homemade pierogi and *nalesniki* (blintzes), and many types of meats ranging from the *kotlet mielony* (ground veal pattie), ribs, and pork cutlets to an exceptionally tasty version of *golabki* (stuffed cabbage). On weekends, the buffet is expanded to include roast duck and smoked salmon, several kinds of homemade *pasztet* (pâté) and *zimne nozki* (literally, "cold feet," i.e., pigs feet in aspic). All food and desserts are made in-house by cooks from Poland.

Old Warsaw is known for its *paczki* (bismarcks), prepared according to a traditional Polish recipe. Denser and smaller than the *paczki* found in bakeries, their version is a treat. The manager, who has supervised the dining room for twenty-five years, and her crew of experienced waitresses navigate the restaurant smoothly, making sure that customers of all ages and nationalities have everything they need. Catering, take-out, and banquet space are also available.

Red Apple Restaurant
See "Family-Friendly Dining," p. 225.

SCANDINAVIAN

Svea
Andersonville
5236 North Clark Street
(773) 275-7738
Open Monday–Friday 7:00 A.M.–3:00 P.M., Saturday–Sunday
   7:00 A.M.–4:00 P.M.
$

This family-owned storefront restaurant, serving breakfast and lunch only, is decked out with blue-and-yellow-checked tablecloths, blue wood-paneled walls, and a diner-style lunch counter that is generally flanked with neighborhood regulars, some even speaking Swedish. The food is the epitome of hearty and traditional Swedish fare, with such items as the Viking Breakfast: two eggs any style, Swedish-style potatoes, grilled *falukorv* (a mild pork sausage), crêpelike Swedish pancakes with lingonberry sauce, and *limpa*, a light rye bread flavored with fennel and made down the street at The Swedish Bakery (see p. 334).

To sample a bit of everything at lunch, try the Three Crown Special: salt pork, brown beans, Swedish meatballs, mashed potatoes, a vegetable, and a choice of appetizer. This is simple, honest Swedish home cooking with a family-style, neighborhood atmosphere to match.

Tre Kronor
Albany Park
3258 West Foster Avenue
(773) 267-9888
BYOB
$$

This outstanding Scandinavian restaurant is considered by many to be the city's best. Tre Kronor is owned by Patty Rasmussen, who is of Norwegian descent, and her husband, Larry Anderson, who is of Swedish descent. The cuisine is clearly Scandinavian, but Anderson and Rasmussen have done a terrific job updating traditional favorites and creating new ones.

The menu for dinner changes all the time, but diners can count on *smorgasbord* sandwiches, pickled herring, *potatiskorv* (potato sausage), *falukorv* (pork sausage), and gravlax (cured salmon). Specials may include such entrées as roast duck breast with lingonberries or pan-fried rainbow trout. The breakfast menu includes Danish pastry, omelets, French toast, and Swedish pancakes with lingonberries. All baking is done in-house daily and is delicious.

Tre Kronor's now famous *Jul Bord* boasts a truly impressive *smorgasbord* of Swedish holiday specialties—including sixteen styles of herring. This very special event runs throughout December.

SEAFOOD

Avenues
Gold Coast

The Peninsula Hotel
108 East Superior Street at Michigan Avenue
(312) 573-6754
Open Tuesday–Saturday for dinner, Sunday for brunch, closed
   Monday
$$$$

Dining at Avenues is like taking an exotic excursion. Every bite offers a song of flavors from around the world: the freshest fish from New Zealand, luscious Caribbean fruits, French-accented sauces, and live scallops shucked right at the restaurant itself. As you walk through the door, the smell of pan-seared foie gras is enough to send the senses wandering.

Located in the Peninsula Hotel, Avenues opened in 2001 and, along with the hotel, seemed immediately destined for success. It is currently under the vision of Head Chef Terry Crandall, who was sous chef when the restaurant opened. The decor is done in light squash colors, and the atmosphere is a bit bland, with plenty of space between tables to keep every dining experience private and focused on the magnificent food.

Before you even have a chance to pick one of the many culinary prizes from the menu, the *amuse bouche* arrives: Fresh Snapper Tartare with Citrus Fruit in a coconut milk sauce with curry and mint. Refreshing, delightful, and surprisingly harmonious, with no taste drowning out another, it's a small sign of all the glorious combinations to come.

The appetizer menu is broad and appealing: seared *loup de mer*, Porcini Potage, and Peekytoe Crab Salad with Papaya and Buttermilk-Vanilla Drizzle. A degustation menu of six courses ($105) is heavy on the choices from the appetizer list, and this may be the best way to approach dinner here, where every option sounds better than the previous one.

The entrées don't make the choice any easier: John Dory in a Basil and Goat cheese Coulis with Ratatouille; Couscous-Crusted Skate Wing with spinach, tomato, and onion amid Yukon Gold potatoes and eighty-year-old balsamic vinegar; Marinated Loin of Venison in Caramelized Quince and Cognac Cream. Two large fillets of Baked Turbot, served over porcini-ricotta gnocchi and crispy potato bits in a truffle and chive sauce, is light, flavorful, and delicate. The savory sturgeon is the *pièce de résistance*. Floating in a foie gras purée with cannellini beans, veal cheek, and mushrooms, every mouthful is a symphony of flavors.

Be sure to save room for dessert. Suggestions such as the Coconut Steam Cake with date compote and lemon verbena ice cream, and the Thyme Parfait and Meringue with almond ice cream and caramel sauce will confirm your decision to visit Avenues again to try everything you didn't get to taste on your first stop. Little parting gifts of chocolate and caramel bonbons and white toffee leave you feeling spoiled and happy.

Avenues is for the sophisticated diner who enjoys exploring new tastes and discovering culinary delights, and is willing to pay for them. At a time when globalized cuisine has standardized food options and menus from many different restaurants that look like carbon copies of one another, Avenues is a creative awakening for the senses and offers both original dishes and the use of the freshest, purest ingredients from around the world.

Oceanique
505 Main Street
Evanston
(847) 864-3435
$$$

Traditional French food is presented with care and soulfulness in Mark Grosz's restaurant, Oceanique. After working with Jean Banchet at Le Français in Wheeling and expanding his skills in France and Hong Kong, Grosz opened Oceanique in 1989 with three partners. Five years later as sole proprietor, he and his wife Renee, the general manager, turned this 1920s Spanish-style building into a warm, comfortable spot. The ceiling is draped with fabric, and the dark walls create a beautiful ambience for the food. The waitstaff is young and professional, and the service is crisp.

Traditional starters include chilled Maine lobster and a salad of grilled shrimp and calamari with daikon. Make sure you check out the daily specials. The salad of roasted yellow beets and scallops is generous and beautiful in presentation. Three perfectly seared dry scallops tossed with beets, blanched beans, mixed organic greens, radish, tomato, and tarragon-saffron dressing are topped with a fried quail egg and presented on beautiful china dancing with tiny fish. Lobster is presented again as an entrée, along with seared yellowfin tuna. The classic bouillabaisse is quite nice, with shrimp, salmon, snapper, turbot, and mussels. Desserts are presented on a platter and are heavy on the tarts and cakes, but do not miss the classic crème brûlée. Oceanique has been a mainstay of traditional French dining in Chicago for more than a decade, and it does not disappoint.

Spring
Wicker Park
2039 West North Avenue
(773) 395-7100
$$$

Open since June 2001, Spring is a relatively new addition to the food scene in Chicago. With an educated, helpful, and entertaining staff and seasonally inspired food, it has become a dining destination.

Upon entering what was once the old North Avenue Bathhouse, you are greeted in a small, tranquil rock garden. You then descend into the bar, once the swimming pool, which is framed in the original pearly white tile. The below-street-level dining area is done in soothing shades of light green, tan, and eggplant, with nicely angled banquettes, making the room feel warm and inclusive; a beautiful setting for Chef Shawn McClain, formerly of Trio, to present his subtle but flavorful Asian-influenced work.

McClain, a supporter of sustainable seafood and seasonal foods, demonstrates his philosophy in the menu, which changes daily. A morsel of raw ahi tuna with fresh mint and soy sets the stage. Shellfish is done with skill and grace; the freshest, most succulent Kumamoto oysters prepared with shaved wasabi and diced cucumber; plump and meaty Prince Edward Island mussels with Thai basil, kaffir lime, and sake; and rich, earthy scallop-and-potato ravioli are just a few options. Scallops appear again, paired with slow-cooked oxtail, and the Sturgeon with Puy Lentils and Caramelized Salsify is very satisfying. Wonderful meat entrées are also presented, such as Poached Beef Tenderloin with Short Rib, Roasted Shiitake, and a Red Wine–Mushroom Reduction. The wine list created by partner Sue Drohomyrecky, also formerly of Trio, spans the globe with interesting and food-friendly pairings. Dessert should not be missed. The Valrhona chocolate cake was almost like a soufflé, and paired beautifully with sesame ice cream and sesame candy. The final touch was a tiny cup of the most intense hot chocolate with a hint of orange. Walking into the Zen-inspired Spring brings a sense of calm to the soul, but the food will leave you breathless.

Tin Fish
18201 South Harlem Avenue
Tinley Park
(708) 532-0200
$$

A lively and innovative sustainable seafood haven in chain-heavy Tinley Park, Tin Fish specializes in fish that is flown in daily. Co-owner and chef Colin Turner, formerly of 120 Ocean and Shaw's Crab House, and his partner Curtis Wierbicki (Shaw's Crab House and North Pond) have a long history and great knowledge of seafood. They strive to bring in product only when it's in season, including fresh Georges Bank scallops and wild king salmon.

The main dining room is jumping with energy, like the eponymous tin fish swimming overhead, yet it affords a comfortable dining atmosphere. Start by ordering something from the oyster bar. Tin Fish serves super-fresh cold-water oysters from both coasts, by the dozen or half-dozen. The briny Imperial Eagles from the West Coast and the bigger, meatier Wellfleets from the East Coast are both amazing. You can also get wonderful clams, and the varieties change daily.

Our server told us that some of the dishes, especially the starters, come out of a contest that they hold periodically in the kitchen. Whichever dish wins the taste test makes it onto the special menu—then, if it's popular there, onto the regular menu. One contest winner we particularly enjoyed was the Salmon Blini, wonderfully light pancakes layered with smoked salmon, capers, crème fraîche, and small sticks of Granny Smith apples, all drizzled with a chive pesto. Another past winner is the Cuban Black Bean and Shrimp Salad—spicy red chiles and honey-tossed black beans with fresh, sweet shrimp, topped with a cumin-coriander crisp.

The menu at Tin Fish changes frequently, and there are quite a few specials every day, depending on what kinds of fish are currently in season and available. The Florida swordfish we tried was fabulous; perfectly grilled and moist, served with a slightly sweet brown balsamic vinaigrette and topped with frisée. The grilled Georges Bank scallops, served with sinfully rich puréed parsnips and a wild mushroom vinaigrette, were wonderfully balanced and delicious.

The wine list is well chosen and well priced, with more than twenty selections available in half-bottles. Be sure to save room for dessert, especially the Bourbon Pecan Pie, which is a standout.

NOTABLE

Calumet Fisheries
South Chicago
3259 East 95th Street (at the bridge)
(773) 933-9855
Take-out only
$-$$ (Cash only)

Remember the drawbridge that the car jumped at the beginning of *The Blues Brothers* movie? That bridge is right next to Calumet Fisheries, and they still have the clippings on the wall to prove it. Chicago used to have lots of riverside fish shacks, but only a handful remain (Goose Island Shrimp House and Lawrence's Fisheries are two others). Calumet may be the best of the bunch.

They serve the usual breaded and deep-fried shrimp, fish, and scallops, plus a few less-common offerings like frogs' legs and oysters. Fish is fried to order and is generally reliable or better. Unfortunately, the sauces are lousy and the accompaniments are few and include low-end choices like sleeves of saltines. A big reason to visit Calumet—aside from the spectacular industrial scenery—is the smoked fish, done each week in a little brick smokehouse on the banks of the Calumet River. Salmon and trout steaks, each threaded with a loop of twine for hanging, are usually available, but the standout is their absolutely incredible shell-on jumbo smoked shrimp. The food is take-out only. Many people just pull over by the bridge and chow down.

Cape Cod Room
Gold Coast
The Drake Hotel
140 East Walton Street
(312) 932-4615
$$$

A Chicago landmark dating back to 1933, the Cape Cod Room harks back to a different time and place. Not much has changed in this Old World setting of dark wood, with its gingham-checked tablecloths and stuffed fish on the walls. It is a wonderful backdrop for Oysters Rockefeller, Bookbinder Red Snapper Soup, Lobster Thermidor, and fresh Dover sole flown in from Holland. The cuisine is traditional, and the service is polished and friendly.

McCormick & Schmick's
Gold Coast
41 East Chestnut Street
(312) 397-9500
$$

Although it is a national restaurant chain, McCormick & Schmick's takes a proactive stance on the company's buying practices for its seafood. Strict guidelines in environmental policies and strong support of sustainability are not just buzzwords, but required of all their purveyors. In fact, the chain supports only fisheries that can show they don't—or won't in the future—compromise any species' survival or the integrity of the surrounding ecosystem. As a rule they also avoid any and all species that are overfished or endangered, or whose habitat is being damaged.

Perhaps the best way to enjoy McCormick & Schmick's is to sit in its hopping bar and sample the wide variety of fresh oysters flown in daily from around the world. Chef Mark Mavrantonis not only runs the

kitchen, but also takes pride in personally handling all the requisitioning of shellfish and seafood, keeping an eye on weather conditions, supplies, and the practices of providers all over the world. The menu is so up-to-the-minute that it changes *twice* daily. Fresh, real fruit juices used for drink mixers are another excuse to linger for a while and slurp up another platter of oysters.

Shaw's Crab House
River North
21 East Hubbard Street
(312) 527-2722
$$$

Without a doubt some of the best and freshest oysters in town are found at this old-time seafood restaurant. They celebrate the oyster every October with a boisterous street fair, but every day you can enjoy oysters flown in directly from both coasts. They work with many fishermen to bring in the freshest halibut, wild king salmon, and crab legs, among other delicacies.

The Nantucket Bay scallops are an amazing special when you can find them. For a casual lunch or a light bite with drinks after work, the Blue Crab Lounge next door offers an oyster bar and hearty, steaming bowls of chowder and gumbo.

Arun's   *(Thai)*
Albany Park
4156 North Kedzie Avenue
(773) 539-1909
$$$$ (prix fixe)

Growing up as a firstborn son in Thailand, Arun Sampanthavivat was given a place at his grandfather's table at a very young age. Luckily for Chicago diners, it was at that table where Sampanthavivat's passion for food flourished. The University of Chicago also lent a helping hand; its Ph.D. program in political science first brought the young Sampanthavivat to the United States. Surprisingly, it was not until he actually opened his namesake restaurant in 1984 that he actually started cooking.

Arun's current Albany Park location is an upgrade from its original tiny space. Filled with rich fabrics, carved woods, Thai antiques, and many of Sampanthavivat's brother's paintings, it seems part restaurant, part museum. Two levels and several romantic nooks make for an intimate mood. The exterior, although still modest, has been revamped to bring it more in line with the lavish dining space. And the Sampanthavivat family's artistic tendencies continue in the kitchen with intricate, thought-provoking presentations. Even the quiet, respectful service is a creative blend of European and Asian traditions that Sampanthavivat calls a "sequential banquet."

Don't worry about having to decide which dishes to choose. There's only one choice here: the multicourse prix fixe menu (although Arun's will make substitutions for dietary restrictions). Expect a leisurely progression of a half-dozen small appetizers and several entrées served fam-

ily style along with rice, followed by a dessert selection. Sure, there are expertly prepared standards like *tom yum*, *shu mai*, *pad thai*, or *massaman* curry. But higher-end options set Arun's apart: Dungeness Crab Spring Rolls with Tamarind Sauce, Roast Duck Medallions with Scallion Pancake Rolls and Fresh Fruit Chutney, or Lobster Tail in buttery Ginger-Curry Sauce. The wine list also offers some interesting selections that match well with the food and cool off the authentically powerful heat of Sampanthavivat's creations.

Deftly prepared and artistically served, Arun's food is not about fusion or daring experimentation. And although Arun's may need to justify their prices in the face of more modern competitors like Erawan, it still remains an award-winning landmark of Thai dining in Chicago.

Erawan Royal Thai Cuisine   *(Thai)*
River North
729 North Clark Street
(312) 642-6888
$$$

With its location in the bustling, stylish River North neighborhood, you might expect Erawan to be more about Western fashion than Eastern authenticity. But one taste of Executive Chef Art Lee's creative Thai preparations and you just might swear off people watching.

There's an intensity about the service here that resonates with partners Anoroth "Noth" Chitdamrong (an Arun's veteran) and Ken Lim's passion for their culture and attention to detail. Even the use of the sacred name Erawan wasn't taking the easy road—it required a Buddhist religious ceremony. Erawan is the mythical name of the three-headed elephant used by the god Phra Phrom, a Hindu and Buddhist symbol for good fortune. And although the decor here is quite lavish—including deep purple and golden walls, intricately carved teak furniture and screens, paintings, and tapestries, not to mention brass flatware and custom porcelain—the attention to detail extends right to the menu.

Selections, which change slightly with each season, range from the recognizable to the pleasantly esoteric. An adventurous take on *shu mai* includes a rich, silky filling of foie gras and shiitake mushrooms plated over decorative ribbons of shallot-balsamic reduction. Other starters from the generous list include a green papaya salad with grilled honey pork—the crisp, julienned papaya tossed with chile-lime dressing, the marinated pork pounded thin, skewered, and artistically balanced against the salad and a small mound of coconut-infused sticky rice. There's even Larb Alligator—spicy minced alligator loin seasoned with fresh herbs, chile, and lemongrass.

House specialty entrées include expert preparations of Three-Flavored Red Snapper, a crispy whole red snapper dressed with a sweet chile-shallot sauce; and Turmeric Lobster, sautéed lobster tail in a luxurious turmeric cream sauce garnished with *tobikko* caviar; plus a good sampling of curries, including green chicken, *panang* shrimp, and lamb *mussaman*. Surprises include the Peppercorn Wild Boar, sliced and sautéed with bamboo shoots and eggplant in a spicy chile–green peppercorn sauce. Even the *pad thai* has character, with the addition of prawns, garlic chives, and sweet turnips to the typical rice noodle, bean sprout, tofu, and peanut mix.

The royal degustation menu, which changes monthly, is a great, broad-brush sampling of Chef Lee's artistry—even better when paired with the optional suggested wines from the award-winning list. And a raised area of the dining room proves a romantic enclave with its traditional canopy and floor-cushion seating. If you're looking for the refinement of Chicago landmark Arun's coupled with nontraditional ingredients and unique, modern flavor combinations, this is the place.

Penang Restaurant   *(Malaysian)*
Chinatown
2201 South Wentworth Avenue
(312) 326-6888
$-$$

Located in the crossroads of Southeast Asia, Malaysia is geographically gifted in terms of food culture. The foundation of Malaysian cuisine is built on the indigenous Malay culture, with its abundant diet based on regional foods like rice, fish, coconut, and tropical fruits. Spicy influences come from nearby Thailand, Indonesia, and India. In certain parts of Malaysia, where Chinese workers settled years ago and married local women, a complicated hybrid type of cuisine emerged called *Nyonya*, or "grandmother." Also present are colonial influences from England, Portugal, Holland, and the Islamic world. All the flavors from these cultures come together in such interesting ways that one could go on for a long time trying to taste everything unique.

Penang Restaurant, located in the heart of Chicago's Chinatown, makes it possible to sample the full extent of Malaysian cuisine. The huge dining room is sparsely decorated in a tropical theme. The menu is diverse, with more than 150 choices organized as appetizers, noodle dishes, soups, curries, seafood, stir-fries, traditional Malaysian foods, desserts, and a sushi bar. Sushi in Malaysia? It must be one of the newer trends. There is also a full bar offering tropical drinks, beer, wine, and sake.

Menu highlights include the delicious, ubiquitous Malaysian street food *roti canai*: a large, thin pancake with a light crust that comes mounded on a plate with a small bowl of chicken curry for dipping. *Laksa* is a spicy and sour coconut fish soup from the south of Malaysia. *Char kway teow* is a rice wheat–noodle stir-fry with vegetables, eggs, and shrimp. On the menu curry dishes characterized by their dry texture are explained; also indicated are spiciness or whether the meat has bones. *Nasi lemak* is a taste of common Malaysian cuisine. It comes as a plate of coconut rice surrounded by a dollop of curry, cucumber, dried salty-sweet anchovies, hard-boiled egg, and spicy sauce.

For dessert, the refreshing *ice kacang* is part of a lineage of shaved ice sweets so refreshing they must have been created to shrug off the tropical heat. It comes as a mound of shaved ice mixed with sweet palm seeds, corn, red beans, red rose syrup, and jelly cubes, drizzled with sweetened condensed milk. But regardless of the weather outside, you'll welcome the sweet ending to a spicy meal.

Siam's House   (Thai)
7742 North Milwaukee Avenue
Niles
(847) 967-2390
$

Siam's House is a pleasant, modestly appointed Thai restaurant in the near northwest suburbs, catering to both American and Thai customers with equal ease. For the unadventurous Siam's House does good versions of the now ubiquitous standards of *pad thai*, *lard nar*, *tom yum* soup, and several mild curries, but they also have less assimilated offerings.

The regular English menu has a number of Thai gems mixed in with the standard offerings, including *yum pla dook fu*, an excellent fried (exploded) catfish salad with a light topping of ground peanut and dried fish. Grilled Issan sausage is accompanied by diced hot pepper and fresh ginger. *Larp* chicken or pork is served slightly warm, tart with lime, fragrant with herbs, and topped with ground toasted rice, which gives the dish an interesting textural counterpoint.

Siam's House also has a number of dishes that, while having the same menu description, are served in different ways. For example, Basil Chicken or Crab on rice can be quite mild, but if one orders them Thai style, the corresponding spicy boost along with the fried-egg topping and lime on the side changes the nature of the dish completely.

Spoon Thai Restaurant   (Thai)
Lincoln Square
4608 North Western Avenue
(773) 769-1173
$

When a restaurant imparts the sensation of eating in someone's home, it can either feel slightly unnerving or refreshingly real and comfortable. Thankfully, Chai and Vanna Gumtrontip's tiny, forty-seat dining room produces the latter sensation; complete with paper napkins, a countertop television, and the busy backdoor comings and goings of relatives and friends helping with the vibrant take-out business. The blond wood paneling and bright lighting lend a clean, slightly stark feel to the room, making it more uplifting and pleasant than other storefront take-out-focused eateries. A few pieces of Thai art and sculpture add warmth and character.

It was Chai and Vanna's sister who originally motivated the Gumtrontips to open Spoon Thai: She herself owns a restaurant in Bangkok, where many of Spoon Thai's recipes originated. Staying true to these northeastern Thai recipes, Chai and Vanna source many of their ingredients from the Argyle Street groceries, placing special orders for items not normally stocked.

A large, organized menu offers an easy-to-read selection of traditional dishes—from salads and soups to noodles, curries (*panang*, red, green, and yellow), and fried rice. The *nam sod* salad of chicken, onion, sliced ginger, green onion, cilantro, roasted peanuts, and lime juice is particularly refreshing and well balanced, with just the right amount of spice. Entrées include an intensely flavored Thai fried chicken marinated in lime juice, fish sauce, fresh herbs, and chiles.

The one-page special Thai menu offers more adventurous dishes, the likes of which are rarely seen in Chicago. For instance, there is *hoa mok*, a curried catfish custard steamed in banana leaf cups, or *nam tok moo*, grilled pork neck flavored with lime, ginger, onion, and rice and chile powders served over lettuce. Regulars come back for the *meang cam*, a strikingly simple dish that packs a punch of fresh, vibrant flavor: crispy shredded coconut, red onion, ginger, and roasted peanuts served in small lettuce cups with Thai dressing.

From urban twenty-somethings to families with children, Spoon Thai draws a loyal following thanks to reasonable prices, gentle service, and authentic food. There's even a small case of Thai souvenirs for those that want to go home with a keepsake. In sum, heed the instructions printed on the menu cover, to "enjoy and dine with your friends and family."

Yum Thai   *(Thai)*
7748 Madison Street
Forest Park
(708) 366-8888
$

The same way one can find decent Chinese food all around New York City, one can find decent Thai food all around Chicago. Yet once you've had truly great Thai food, you won't want to settle for anything less. Fortunately, there are a few places sprinkled around the city that really excel. Catering to a Thai clientele, these outposts produce food that not only tastes different, but better. Finding these "real" Thai gems is not always easy. Yum Thai, in Forest Park, looks like all the decent Thai places prospering mostly on delivery of Thai standards to lazy customers. What these lazy customers don't know is that behind this facade exists a very authentic Thai restaurant that is well worth a visit.

Yum Thai disguises its true fare with a menu written solely in Thai. Luckily, through the work of several dedicated chowhounds, the "secret" menu has been cracked and now everyone can sample the special foods of Yum Thai. Ask (you may have to more than once) to get a mimeographed version of the translated menu.

Except for a beef-garlic salad, order nothing from the regular menu. On the Thai menu you will find several impressive curries, the finest of which is the unique *mon* curry. Muddy in color from too much shrimp paste but offset by sweet squash and crunchy vegetables, this soup-curry will be unlike anything doled out at those ordinary Thai places. Most dishes do not deliver blistering heat, and this mars some salads like the *laab*, but the squid with lime dressing (*bplaamyyk manaow*) needs nothing extra. Curls of squid drenched in a tart and fishy sauce, plus hundreds of thin slices of garlic, make this salad complete. Excellent desserts, especially the Thai custard (*khanom maw gaeng*), are worth saving room for.

Service here is earnest but harried, due to the skeleton staff. Be forgiving; by ordering from the "secret" menu, one can sample some very special Thai food in the western suburbs.

NOTABLE

Amarind's   (*Thai*)
6822 West North Avenue
Galewood
(773) 889-9999
$

How can you go wrong when chef/owner Rangsan Sutcharit's training ground was Arun's, the veritable Thai mecca of Chicago? The answer is, you can't. Sutcharit's cooking is close to flawless, with its skilled preparation, thoughtful presentation, strikingly fresh ingredients, and authentic Thai spice level, so often ignored at other Thai restaurants.

Amarind's interior is entirely spotless (even in the nooks and crannies) and very plain, simply decorated with vases of "lucky" bamboo—all the more reason to focus on the incredible food. And the crowds (expect a wait for one of some sixty seats on busy nights) actually add a refreshing buzz not typically found in other small eateries. Be forewarned: The attention to detail results in longer wait times between courses, so sit back and relax. Amarind's is worth the wait and the drive.

Ba Le   (*Vietnamese*)
Uptown
5018 North Broadway Street
(773) 561-4424
$

Ba Le (family owned since 1989) lies in the heart of Chicago's Argyle Street Vietnamese neighborhood. Ba Le is not a sit-down restaurant but more of a take-out place that specializes in Vietnamese sandwiches and prepared meals. Sandwiches are their pride. They bake their own French baguettes and croissants on the premises with an oven that can make 450 loaves of bread a day. One of their more popular sandwiches is the Ba Le Special, which has ham, pork loin, pâté (really more like a French-style *fromage de tête*), and radishes. Ba Le is very serious about the meats and pâtés that go into their sandwiches.

Dharma Garden Thai (Thai)
Albany Park
3109 West Irving Park Road
(773) 588-9140
$

If you close your eyes and listen to the music at Dharma Garden Thai, you just might think you're dining in a day spa instead of an Albany Park storefront eatery. The meditative tunes are a relaxing touch in keeping with Thailand-born owner Surintorn Suanthont's restaurant concept of "natural healing for mind and body." In keeping with what partner Prasat Duangou Pa calls "biospiritual cuisine," Dharma Garden Thai offers vegetarian and seafood preparations using filtered water, olive oil, sea salt, soy protein, and fresh herbs, plus no MSG, fish sauce, refined sugar, or other processed ingredients.

Luc Thang Noodle (Thai, Vietnamese)
Wicker Park
1524 North Ashland Avenue
(773) 395-3907
$

Luc Thang Noodle is situated on the eastern edge of Chicago's Wicker Park neighborhood in the midst of a largely Hispanic section of Ashland Avenue. The first impression is of a clean, pared-down atmosphere. The menu offers Thai, Vietnamese, and Chinese items with at least one Philippine dish.

One of the best things at Luc Thang is their *ban xeo*, a crispy tacolike shell filled with shrimp, strips of seasoned pork, and bean sprouts. They are also a sure bet for home delivery or take-out. Somehow, the texture and flavor of the food seems to withstand the journey better than that of most other take-out places.

New Saigon (Vietnamese)
Uptown
5000 North Broadway
(773) 334-3322
$

New Saigon is located at the corner of Argyle and Broadway in the center of Chicago's Vietnamese neighborhood. The co-owner of New Saigon, who goes by the French name Antoine (he learned French while in Vietnam), was once in the South Vietnamese Air Force based near his Saigon home. His wife, Hoa, is in charge of the kitchen.

The menu at New Saigon is lengthy and it can take a while to make your selection. Among the best items on the menu are the simple egg rolls. If you ask, you can have them served with a lettuce and mint leaf wrapping (as is traditional in Vietnam). The coolness of the lettuce and the zing of the fresh mint leaves contrast well with the crispness of the fried egg rolls. All the dishes are very authentic, as is shown by the largely Vietnamese clientele.

Another sure bet at New Saigon are the *pho* (Vietnamese soups), with twenty-three combinations to choose from. The soups are all served in big bowls with fresh herbs, bean sprouts, and limes on the side.

Nhu Hoa   *(Laotian, Vietnamese)*
Uptown
1020 West Argyle Street
(773) 878-0618
$

On Argyle Street among the mostly Vietnamese restaurants, Nhu Hoa stands out because it offers Laotian cuisine in addition to an extensive Vietnamese menu. Typical Laotian dishes are relegated to the back of the large menu, which offers good descriptions and pictures of many of the dishes. There are so many good choices and portions are so generous that you might want to bring friends in order to sample as much as possible. Try any dish that says it is prepared Laotian style: the Beefy Jerky Salad, Green Papaya Salad, and Marinated Beef Salads are typical of this.

Tropical drinks are definitely a house specialty. If you are in the mood for something exotic, choose between the following juices: avocado, *guanabana*, jackfruit, durian, pineapple, and strawberry. Wine, beer, and cocktails are also served, as well as fruity ices, bubble teas, and Laotian-style coffee.

Opart Thai House   *(Thai)*
Lincoln Square
4658 North Western Avenue
(773) 989-8517
$

The ratio of staff (dressed in neatly embroidered jackets) to diners at Opart can sometimes reach 2 to 1, but all those employees are probably needed, given the restaurant's busy take-out and delivery business.

More than a hundred items on the menu give diners lots of choice, and it's hard to go wrong. Classics like *naem sod*, a salad of ground chicken, ginger, peanuts, Thai chiles, and lime, screams with refreshing flavor. And entrées like *pad kra praow lard khao* highlight flavorful sliced beef sautéed

with basil and chiles over steamed rice. A trio of interesting appetizers includes Tiger Cry, Opart Beef, and *neau sa ded*: variations of marinated and charbroiled beef with several homemade hot sauces.

Pho 777   *(Vietnamese)*
Uptown
1065 West Argyle Street
(773) 561-9909
$

Somewhat hidden on Argyle Street just west of the Red Line El stop is Pho 777. Full of Vietnamese and other Asian clientele, the specialty here is *pho* (Vietnamese noodle soups). The portions are very generous, and the menu offers plenty of choice for soups as well as for rice and noodle dishes. This allows the uninitiated the comfort of sticking with familiar dishes, while the more adventurous can sample more exotic fare. Their most popular soups are the beef noodle and the chicken noodle, which is popular with American patrons. One particularly good dish is the *bahn cuon tay ho*, which includes wide rice noodles, ham, grilled pork, and a fried shrimp cake.

Sweet Tamarind   *(Thai)*
Lincoln Park
1408 West Diversey Parkway
(773) 281-5300
$

You'll pay a dollar or two less for similar dishes at Thai spots in less gentrified neighborhoods, but the pleasant yuppie decor and generously portioned, flavorful Thai food at Sweet Tamarind makes the small price differential well worth it.

With just fourteen tables, bright orange-and-yellow walls, and plenty of little white lights and candles, the dining room is cozy and romantic. A small patio is open seasonally. A selection of eight curries includes a great *mussaman* redolent with tamarind and mixed with your choice of meat, onions, potatoes, cashews, tomatoes, and pineapple. There is also a pleasantly spicy *kaeng pa*, or fiery jungle curry.

TAC Quick   (*Thai*)
Wrigleyville
3930 North Sheridan Road
(773) 327-5253
$

One visit to TAC Quick and you'll know it isn't the typical ethnic-neighborhood Thai spot. For one, the location is almost directly under the Sheridan El stop, a popular exit for many young, professional commuters. And despite the seedy street element, its interior is all clean, modern minimalism.

TAC stands for *Thai Authentic Cuisine*, and it is exactly that. Try the *moo ping*, a starter of grilled marinated pork with an addictive sweet-spicy sauce. The Thai-language menu gives more unusual choices such as *sai krog*, a spicy fermented sausage served alongside fresh ginger, peanuts, and cucumbers. More approachable choices for the Thai novice include *pad kee mao*, wide rice noodles stir-fried with basil, tomatoes, carrots, bean sprouts, pea pods, and onions. The vegetables in all preparations are incredibly fresh.

Thai Pastry   (*Thai*)
Uptown
4925 North Broadway
(773) 784-5399
$

Don't let the name fool you; there's much more to this Uptown/Lincoln Square storefront restaurant than the entryway pastry case. The simple dining room is spacious and very bright, the service gentle and friendly, the food fresh and authentic.

Portions are fairly small and simply presented. The nearly ninety-item menu offers a good selection—everything from twenty soups and salads to noodle dishes, rice dishes, entrées, and curries. Several good seafood dishes and house specialties elevate the menu above other take-out and delivery-focused competitors, such as the Whole Red Snapper with Hot Pepper or Sweet-Sour Sauce and the Roast Duck Salad. Owner/Chef Aumphai Kusub's made-to-order lunch special (no tired buffet!) is a great bargain. In the warmer months there is sidewalk seating.

Thai Room *(Thai)*
North Center
4022 North Western Avenue
(773) 539-6150
$

Chef Chanpen Ratana cooks authentic family recipes like *ba mee janron*, stir-fried yellow noodles, pea pods, mushrooms, green onions, broccoli, sesame seeds, and your choice of meat served on a hot plate. Skip the "Thai-style" potstickers—the deep-fried mounds of spinach (frozen, not fresh) coated in thick batter are mushy and greasy. But noodle dishes have a healthy dose of fresh vegetables (ask for extra additions if you like) including a saucy *pad khee mao* (drunken noodles) with bean sprouts, peppers, tomato, onion, and fresh basil. And feel free to request extra heat for any dish.

BJ's Market and Bakery   *(Soul Food)*
Calumet Heights
8734 South Stony Island Avenue
(773) 374-4700
$-$$

Soul Food 101. Chef John Meyers, formerly at The Retreat in Pullman, opened this unintimidating soul-food restaurant about seven years ago. During the week it operates much like a Boston Market, to which BJ's bears an uncanny resemblance (except that the food is all made in-house and tastes good).

Many of the soul-food classics are here, though most are prepared with a lighter touch. For example, the very good greens are seasoned with smoked turkey instead of the traditional fatback or hog jowl. Deep-fried foods, such as green tomatoes and catfish, are generally handled very well, with a minimum of residual grease. The excellent Mustard-Breaded Catfish is BJ's signature dish, but be advised that it doesn't travel well. All baking is done in-house, and many of the desserts are first-rate.

The biggest reason to go to BJ's is the Sunday all-you-can-eat buffet offering almost everything on the menu. Each category—salads, main dishes, vegetables, desserts—is represented by more than a half-dozen examples. It's a true challenge to sample everything, but worth the effort. A few dishes, including some of the Cajun fare, may be slightly disappointing, but there are more than enough standouts to make a great meal. A newer BJ's Market is located at 9645 South Western Avenue, but it doesn't offer the Sunday buffet.

For a more advanced course in soul food consider **Queen of the Sea**, a twenty-four-hour buffet almost across the street from the original BJ's, at 8701 South Stony Island.

Other Location
9645 South Western Avenue, Chicago (Beverly);
(773) 445-3400

Davis Street Fish Market   *(Cajun/Creole)*
501 Davis Street
Evanston
(847) 869-3474
$$

Davis Street Fish Market, located in downtown Evanston, just north of Chicago, has been bringing Midwesterners to the shores of the East and West coasts with a cooking style that blends Northeastern and Cajun, firing up taste buds with the full-throttle flavors and party ambience of New Orleans.

Since the eatery's inception in 1985 chef and fishmonger Charlie Raygoza has continued to marvel customers as they are treated to some of the most memorable seafood experiences of their lives. On weekends there is usually a long wait, but you could start your evening at the Stone Raw Bar and sample some of the best oysters in town. On any given day, Davis Street Fish Market has at least sixteen varieties of oysters, including the Delaware Bay oyster, which is proudly listed on the Slow Food USA Ark of Taste (see p. ix). The bar is one of the best places to enjoy a meal, as there are at least a dozen tables with stools lining the room. Every inch of wall space is covered in some sort of fish memorabilia that has a story behind it. Daily specials are listed on the chalkboard and are usually your best bet, but the menu has an extensive list of favorites too, from Blackened Tilapia with Red Beans and Rice to Crawfish Étoufée over rice. Not to be missed is the the Old San Francisco Cioppino, which is chock-full of fresh fish and shrimp in a tomato bouillabaisse, served with a big basket of warm bread and whipped butter. They also do a great Cajun lunch featuring gumbos, chowders (seasonal, no less), po' boys, beans, rice, and andouille sausage; it's the real deal—as is the key lime pie, which is made with authentic key lime juice and is tart and sweet and delicious.

The other great thing about Davis Street Fish Market is you can purchase raw and cooked seafood (salmon, bluefish, trout, crab claws, mussels, various clams, etc.) from their counter. Stock varies based on what is fresh and available, but we have always had great luck with our raw purchases at Davis Street.

Edna's Restaurant   *(Soul Food)*
Garfield Park
3175 West Madison Street
(773) 638-7079
Open Tuesday–Sunday 6:00 A.M.–7:00 P.M., closed Monday
$

It's hard not to like Edna's, a large cheery room with floral-painted walls, large plants, ceiling fans, and a good buzz of conversation at nearly any hour of the day. Take-out is available, but it would be a shame not to choose a counter seat, table, or booth and relax with some good home cooking. Service is usually sweet and caring but can be a bit slow. Much of the food is made in-house and many items are cooked to order, so patience is in order. Edna herself is usually around, stopping by to see how things are going.

Breakfast includes the usual pancake-and-egg combinations as well as the somewhat more exotic brains and eggs. Edna's modestly advertises "the best biscuits on earth," which isn't too far from the truth. These come freshly baked—there's often a wait—and slathered with butter. Lunch and dinner entrées come with two sides. Notably, all the side dishes are vegetarian: good greens, macaroni and cheese, and various well-seasoned vegetables. Fried chicken, short ribs, and catfish are among the main dishes. It's tough to pass up the excellent peach cobbler, but all the pies and cakes, proudly displayed on a revolving cake rack, are made in-house.

Besides serving excellent food, Edna's has been an integral part of the neighborhood for its thirty-seven years of existence. It's a regular stop for politicians and community organizers, and it served as a meeting place for many of those involved in the civil rights marches of the 1960s. Edna's is located near the beautifully renovated Garfield Park Conservatory. A stroll through the gardens and glass houses is a perfect way to work off a biscuit or two.

H&A Restaurant   *(Soul Food)*
Woodlawn
432 East 63rd Street
(773) 684-8214
Open daily 7:00 A.M.–9:00 P.M.
$

Appearances can be deceiving. On a particularly forbidding block under the 63rd Street El tracks is the plain stucco facade of H&A, serving some of Chicago's best soul food since 1945. As you enter, the day's offerings are displayed on a steam table with very little effort at presentation. Indeed, in cold weather the glass may be so steamed over that it's nearly impossible to see anything. Orders to go can be placed at the front counter, or choose a seat at the well-worn counter or a battered booth.

Full dinners (less than $10) include soup, salad, or beets, "meat and two," plus rolls or corn muffins. Dishes are rotated daily. House-made soup is generally the best bet for a starter. Muffins are good, but the light, buttery dinner rolls are extraordinary. For the main course, Smothered Pork Chops or baked chicken or Cornish hen with wonderful sweet gravy are safe bets. If nothing looks appealing (remember, looks can be deceiving) fried chicken can be made to order, but expect a worthwhile wait of twenty minutes.

Sides include several long-cooked but well-seasoned vegetables. The greens are good here, but don't pass up at least one bean or pea dish, maybe butterbeans or black-eyed peas. Dessert, not included, is worth ordering. The ubiquitous peach cobbler is tasty, but don't pass up the stellar bread pudding if it's available.

Heaven on Seven   *(Cajun/Creole)*
Loop
Garland Building
111 North Wabash Avenue, 7th Floor
(312) 263-6444
Open Monday–Friday 10:30 A.M.–5:00 P.M., Saturday to 3:00 P.M.,
   closed Sunday
$–$$

In their unlikely location on the seventh floor of an office building overlooking the elevated train tracks, brothers Jimmy and George Bannos have transformed the family's coffee shop into New Orleans North. Jimmy Bannos introduced Chicago to Cajun and Creole cooking in the 1980s, and the rest is history. There are now four Heaven on Sevens, but the original restaurant in the Garland Building remains the most popular.

The U-shaped coffee shop counter is available to single diners and the overflow crowd waiting for tables. The decor can only be described as hot sauce; walls are covered with shelves full of every hot sauce ever bottled, as are the tables. But it is the food for which customers line up in the hallway on weekdays, and Saturday for breakfast and lunch (dinner is served on the third Friday of the month). Po' boy sandwiches served with Cajun coleslaw, red beans and rice with andouille sausage, crab cakes, and gumbo or jambalaya served with jalapeño-corn muffins are regular items on the menu. There are daily specials, such as corn *maque choux*, seafood enchiladas, chicken and crawfish étouffée, or voodoo shrimp with linguine. Hurricanes, those Southern rum drinks that pack a punch, are

served, as well as beer and wine. Sweet potato pie, Chocolate-Bourbon Pecan Pie, bread pudding, rice pudding, Chocolate–Peanut Butter Pie, key lime pie, and chicory coffee complete the Louisiana-laced menu.

Jimmy Bannos, enthusiastically sharing his love of Cajun cuisine, offers evening cooking classes on the first Friday of the month. Heaven on Seven is a unique and fun dining experience in the heart of downtown Chicago.

Other Locations
3478 North Clark Street, Chicago (Wrigleyville); (773) 477-7818
600 North Michigan Avenue, Chicago (Gold Coast);
   (312) 280-7774
224 South Main Street, Naperville; (630) 717-0777

The Maple Tree Inn   *(Cajun/Creole)*
13301 South Western Avenue
Blue Island
(708) 388-3461
$$$

Hidden in suburban Blue Island is a gem of New Orleans cooking. This Louisiana brasserie is a historic and memorable place that offers locals some of the best Creole and Cajun cuisine around. When you walk in, a sign invites you to "Sit long, talk much." The atmosphere is cozy and casual, with a gorgeous vintage bar offering extensive and carefully selected wine and beer lists in addition to many specialty drinks.

The menu demonstrates owner Charlie Orr's commitment to authentic cooking, artisanal preparations, and sustainability. The smoked chicken in the jambalaya is purchased from an organic farm fifty miles south of the city and is smoked on-site. In fact, many of the sausages and meats are made and smoked at the Maple Tree. This attention to detail and passion comes out in every dish. Diners can order appetizers, entrées, and desserts à la carte or with the Fixed Price Meal. The blue crab fingers au gratin, seafood gumbo, onion and andouille tart, catfish pecandine, and Mississippi Mud Pie are superb.

NOTABLE

Harold's Chicken Shack   (*Southern*)
Hyde Park
1208 East 53rd Street
(773) 752-9270
$

Love it or hate it, Harold's is a Chicago institution. With dozens of mostly family-run Chicken Shacks, mostly on the South Side, the "fried chicken king" is a local success story. The menu and food quality at different Harold's can vary significantly, but the 53rd Street outpost in Hyde Park near the University of Chicago is generally reliable and offers the option of eating at the restaurant.

A better alternative might be carrying your chicken two blocks to the venerable **Jimmy's Woodlawn Tap**, 1172 East 55th Street, where they don't mind if you bring in food, as long as you order drinks and don't make a mess. At Harold's, chicken is clearly the thing to order and it seems a shame not to get it doused with "hot and mild," a pair of sauces that soak into the thick, tasty breading and so-so fries to effect a near-magical transformation. The uninitiated may see it simply as greasy chicken, but what do they know? Deep-fried livers and gizzards are also available.

L.T.'s Grill
See Hamburgers, p. 233.

Soul Vegetarian East   (*Vegetarian*)
Park Manor
205 East 75th Street
(773) 224-0104
$

Those with a hankering for vegetarian barbecue don't have a lot of choices in Chicago. While it probably won't make devoted carnivores bypass the ribs and hot links at nearby—and great—Lem's, Soul Vegetarian East's Barbecue Twist, made with freshly prepared seitan and peanuts, is a surprisingly satisfying meal. Plenty of non-barbecue sandwiches and main dishes are available as well. Some nice salads are offered (try the Prince dressing) as well as an array of interesting mixes of fresh-squeezed juices. There is a pleasant dining room and take-out is available; expect a wait either way.

The restaurant is run by members of the African-Hebrew Israelite community. All in all, this might be one of the most interesting vegetarian restaurants in the city.

Wishbone Restaurant
See Brunch, p. 208.

STEAK HOUSES

Gibson's Steak House
Gold Coast
1028 North Rush Street
(312) 266-8999
$$$

Gibson's fits the City of Big Shoulders like a good power suit. Its style mirrors that of the city itself: boisterous, brash, and masculine, while at the same time exuding Midwestern warmth and charm. Locals rule the scene, in addition to the many politicos, power brokers, and *Playboy* Bunnies that call Gibson's home.

Your authentic Chicago experience at Gibson's starts at the bar, where the supersize martinis are professionally made and the people watching is akin to good theater. From the outside, Gibson's may not seem like a good fit with the Slow Food agenda, but their credo and the keys to their success are deliberate and honest. Customer service is high on their list of priorities, and they justifiably pride themselves on treating everyone graciously no matter what their status. Everyone from the hosts, coat checkers, and management are over-the-top friendly and courteous. The career waitstaff are all characters, iconoclasts who deliver their table-side steak spiel with individual style. But Gibson's guiding principle is their belief in great-quality food in incredibly large portions. They encourage people to share, and share you must when you find yourself staring down the W. R., also known as the Chicago Cut: 32 ounces of prime aged rib eye named after legendary local food writer William Rice.

Other signature steaks of note are the porterhouse and the filet mignon. All steaks are USDA Prime aged beef cooked at very high temperatures, charred on the outside and simply grilled to order. You can also choose from myriad special preparations. Steaks can be topped with horseradish, garlic butter, or blue cheese at no extra charge.

Sharing is advised with all the sides and desserts as well. The double-baked potato is the size of a small football, indelicately stuffed with butter, sour cream, and cheese. The creamed spinach is savory with a sweet hint of nutmeg, and is rich enough to hold a spoon upright. When ordering dessert (all desserts are made in-house), keep in mind that ordering a piece of Macadamia Turtle Pie or carrot cake will deliver a quarter pie almost a foot in height. The wine list is mostly American in origin and has many reasonably priced selections.

Overall, Gibson's believes that their large portions result in a lower check average, which keeps their customers happy, and that sharing is the key to a truly convivial experience.

Keefer's
River North
20 West Kinzie Street
(312) 467-9525
$$$$

To say that Chicago steak houses have rested on their culinary laurels for too long is an understatement. Enter Keefer's, the first chef-driven steak house in Chicago. Beloved Chicago chef John Hogan and his gracious partner, Glenn Keefer, run a seamless operation where there's more to love than just slabs of beef. Chef Hogan honors traditional steak house fare by blending his classically trained ingenuity with au courant style.

The atmosphere at Keefer's is warm, modern, and smarter than your average steak joint. Cherrywood and granite flank the bar, and their signature turquoise glassware floats like blue sparks around the room. Unlike most steak houses, which boast off-the-charts testosterone levels, this is a female-friendly establishment. The bar is open and lively, and booths surrounding the outer edge of the bar are best for catching all the action. More reflective dining takes place in the main dining room and adjacent fireplace room. The staff exudes a warm confidence; there's no need for table-side theatrics here—the food speaks for itself.

Hogan's steak portfolio is meticulous: corn-fed, locally raised, wet-aged, USDA Prime, certifiably fabulous beef. All steaks are simply seasoned with lemon-shallot butter, salt, and pepper and grilled to perfection. A cut to savor is their Kansas City strip, while the bone-in New York strip is incredibly lusty and flavorful. There is also the option of handpicking your steak depending on how marbled or lean you like your meat.

The variations on standard steak house sides come as a welcome surprise. Chef Hogan finally gives us a reason to bring peas back from our childhood boycott. No gray-green, mushy melancholy here; just freshly shelled peas baked in leek cream with lardons and pearl onions. Creamed spinach is also recommended for its texture and depth. The breadth of potato options are mostly French inspired, but not at all precious. Hearty highlights include the Potato Croquettes with Cheese Fondue, Potatoes Gratin with Gruyère, Pommes Frites, and the Crispy Potato Cakes.

Exceptional steak house fare aside, Hogan does maverick preparations with seafood. It is here he shows what a gifted wild card he can be. While Dover sole and lobster are traditionally presented, the chef prides himself on seasonal preparations. Daily specials always seem to have a certain playfulness, and you never know on any given day what he might be up to. Here is a man who clearly loves his job.

The wine list is varied, with many selections by the glass and most bottles comfortably priced below $50. Desserts are also in Hogan's repetoire.

Homemade ice cream, orange-chocolate crème brûlée, and almond cheese-cake round out the meal.

Keefer's has raised the bar high for a restaurant of any category, but rest assured they have earned their rightful place in the pantheon of Chicago steak houses.

NOTABLE

Club Gene & Georgetti
River North
500 North Franklin Street
(312) 527-3718
$$$$

Club Gene and Georgetti, often referred to as just Gene & Georgetti's, is billed as the mother of all Chicago steak houses. Established in 1941, the restaurant is now run by the daughter and son-in-law of the original owners. In many ways the downstairs section still has a clubby feel from decades gone by: Lots of tables huddle around the incredibly smoky bar, autographed pictures of faded stars hang on the walls, and a bordello-red motif runs throughout the decor. Unfortunately, much of the color and character fade when it comes to the food.

Steaks are suitably charred on the outside and tender and moist on the inside, yet they're somehow lacking in flavor. While the quality might

have slipped a bit, Gene & Georgetti's remains one of the most popular steak houses in the city, sustained by its atmosphere of bygone days and the excellent service that its waitstaff provides.

Myron & Phil's
3900 West Devon Avenue
Lincolnwood
(847) 677-6663
$$$

If there were such a thing as a Jewish Rat Pack, Myron & Phil's would most certainly be its headquarters. Inside its doors one finds a perfectly preserved 1970s-style supper club. The restaurant is second-generation family owned and hasn't changed much since it opened its doors in 1971. The Freedman family has taken the old adage "If it ain't broke don't fix it" and used it to their advantage.

The restaurant is known for the consistent excellence of its steaks and chops. The New York strip and the Romanian-style skirt steak are their signatures. Other standouts include sweet-sauced baby-back ribs and lamb chops. Preparations are simple and proportions are generous. Be sure to try their house-made Green Goddess dressing with a hint of anchovy. Also sample Chef Ronnie Lobo's potatoes, sautéed to a crisp with green onions and mushrooms. Much of the staff has clocked in twenty-five to thirty years of service and everyone is warm, attentive, and sometimes downright mothering.

Pete Miller's
See Hamburgers, p. 234.

VEGETARIAN

Blind Faith Café
525 Dempster Street
Evanston
(847) 328-6875
$

This Evanston restaurant and bakery has long been a destination for diehard vegans and vegetarians. Those new to vegetarianism can sample the joys of high-protein meals made with seitan, tempeh, and tofu, but can also go with vegetarian dishes of ethnic origins, in particular Mexican and Asian. Dairy cheeses and eggs are available and always on the menu, but can be substituted with soy cheeses and tofu for vegan dining. Huevos rancheros are a classic on the brunch menu, served with warm flour tortillas and refried black beans and brown rice.

Fresh-squeezed juices and a wide variety of baked goods and desserts round out meals. The cozy dining room underscores the restaurant's earthy appeal, with plants and quilts hanging on the walls, while the cafeteria provides a quicker, more communal dining experience.

During Sunday brunch there is a constant line in the bakery for to-go orders, made-to-order smoothies, and a variety of baked goods both sweet and savory. The waitstaff is particularly helpful in explaining the menu and, though it gets crowded, service is very attentive.

There is heavy emphasis on Mexican items on the menu, which for the nonvegetarian contributes greatly to the delivery of higher-power flavor through salsas, guacamole, and spices.

Karyn's Fresh Café
Lincoln Park
1901 North Halsted Street
(312) 255-1590
$$

One feels healthier just walking into Karyn's Fresh Café, the longest-standing raw-food restaurant in the Midwest. The food is energizing, both literally and figuratively.

Karyn's is a restaurant dedicated to the raw-food concept, which means that while food may be heated here it is never really cooked (116 degrees F is the maximum temperature to which food is heated), which would destroy its enzymes. According to raw-food advocates, all cooked food is devoid of enzymes, and cooking food changes its molecular structure and renders it toxic. Living and raw foods also have enormously higher nutrient values than foods that have been cooked.

Owner Karyn Calabrese is one of the most innovative leaders in the holistic health industry and practices what she preaches, having become a vegan more than twenty-five years ago. Like its owner, the restaurant space itself multitasks: the raw café in the front has seating for about twenty and features comfortable low lighting, elegant bronze sconces, and soft jazz in the background, punctuated by the whirr and buzz of the juicer in the adjacent juice bar and shop.

The café menu, which features all organic gourmet dishes and uniquely flavorful raw vegan ones, has a few classics that appear year-round like Karyn's House Dressing, Sweet Mango Tango Soup, and Basil-Scented Ravioli with Macadamia Whipped Crème dressed with Sun-Dried Tomato Purée. Other items change seasonally or become specials added to the permanent menu as demanded by a regular neighborhood clientele. A nonvegan or nonvegetarian would still be satisfied with the variety of choices available and the creativity of individual items.

The juice bar serves up numerous smoothies, shakes, juice cocktails, and herbal elixirs, with or without your choice of supplements; portions of soups, salads, and pastas from the restaurant menu; and a variety of enzyme powders, supplements, and books on vegan and raw diets and some on spiritual pursuits as well.

At the back of the space, Karyn's has a class space where she conducts lectures on healthful eating. There is also a studio for a variety of dance and yoga classes, which are held several times weekly. Finally, a spa features treatments like massage, ear coning, oxygen bath, lymphatic drainage, and private nutritional consultation. Karyn's also offers food prep classes.

 **Lovitt**
Wicker Park
1466 North Ashland Avenue
(773) 252-1466
Closed Monday–Tuesday, BYOB
$$

Lovitt is a BYOB restaurant that recently opened in Wicker Park, featuring seasonal American cuisine. The new owners have completely revamped the restaurant, including opening the formerly barred front windows to let in some light. Executive Chef Norman Six (formerly of Blackhawk Lodge) has designed a menu that showcases organic produce whenever possible and features plenty of variety, including vegan and vegetarian options. The menu changes almost weekly to emphasize the seasonal fruits and vegetables at the heart of the offerings.

Starters include mini profiteroles stuffed with shrimp, garlic, and fresh herbs. Entrées include Parmesan Gnocchi with Diablo Cream Sauce and

Homemade Ravioli Stuffed with Shiitake Mushrooms in a pool of tomato-basil sauce. Six also prepares all the pastries, including fresh fruit tarts, pies, and seasonal treats like strawberry shortcake. An à la carte brunch features a quiche of the day, special omelets, fresh biscuits and jam, and other traditional breakfast favorites.

As evidenced by the Wednesday through Sunday hours, the owners' dedication to doing things right means they are doing it all themselves. Though not a pure vegetarian restaurant, the quality of the food is exceptional and there is a focus on use of organic and seasonal items. And while they are now in a relatively small space (thirty-two seats), there are plans to expand in time.

NOTABLE

Arya Bhavan
See Indian & Pakistani, p. 82.

Chicago Diner
Lakeview
3441 North Halsted Street
(773) 935-6696
$$

Since 1983 the crew at this Lakeview classic has been slinging seitan and tofu for their vegetarian and vegan neighbors. Think diner faves like shepherd's pie (with lentils subbing for lamb) or a wheat-meat Philly steak sandwich washed down with organic wine or beer. The newly formed "Healthy Dining Club," a singles group for vegetarians, hosts several monthly meet-ups and dinners here, so the diner has the local vegetarians' seal of approval.

Earwax Café
Wicker Park
1561 North Milwaukee Avenue
(773) 772-4019
$$

Any good listing of burgers should by all rights include a good veggie burger place, and in Chicago, Earwax Café makes a great one. The vegetarian-friendly restaurant has a carnival feel to it, with the decor incorporating bright colors and circuslike decorations. Downstairs houses an alternative video rental shop, with lots of art and foreign films. A vegetarian- and

vegan-slanted menu draws plenty of hipsters for the Tuscan seitan sandwich, tofu scramble, and excellent smoothies. Meat options include turkey and ham, but no beef.

The veggie burger itself is made in-house, with black beans, quinoa, and mushrooms, and is served on a toasted bun. Sandwiches come with a side choice of vinegar-based (nonmayo) coleslaw or potato salad. Service at Earwax is relaxed and friendly, though certainly not fast paced. It's a great space for people watching in the Bucktown/Wicker Park community while you're enjoying some healthy dining options.

Lula Café
See American, p. 11.

Udupi Palace
See Indian & Pakistani, p. 87.

Victory's Banner
See Brunch, p. 212.

PART TWO

SPECIAL FOODS
&
NIGHTLIFE

BARBECUE

Chicago rib joints run the gamut from upscale steak restaurants posing as rib joints to no-ambience, fifteen-square-foot take-out joints with great ribs. Actually, the joints do have ambience: post-apocalyptic ambience, but ambience nonetheless. This latter type of rib joint is usually found on the far South and West Sides of the city. They are sparse in decor, running almost to coffee-shop interiors or no interiors at all, and if you're lucky there might be one or two stools. The features most common to all are probably the bulletproof glass and service carousel, through which everyone transacts their business.

In Chicago one is likely to run into two distinct types of ribs: fall-off-the-bone or "meat Jell-O" ribs, and ribs that, through proper cooking, still have texture and flavor. The "meat Jell-O" ribs are typically parboiled, slopped with sauce, and then grilled; those still maintaining integrity of texture and flavor are slowly smoked all the way through, as true barbecue should be. Be aware that while the term *meat Jell-O* is meant to be derogatory, 90 percent of Chicagoans feel that this is the *perfect* rib.

Barbecue arrived in Chicago along with the blues on the wave of black migration from the Deep South during the first half of the twentieth century. Mississippi Delta blacks followed the path of the river (and the Illinois Central Railroad) north, up past Memphis to jobs in Chicago. As they developed a new community on the south side of the city, they developed the style of barbecue cooking found here today. It generally means pork spareribs that are smoked slowly over fragrant hardwoods, usually

via direct heat, but occasionally via indirect heat. A tempered glass-and-metal pit is almost always the smoker of choice. The result should be meat that is cooked to a toothy firmness, with a noticeable pink outer edge or smoke ring, and most importantly, a smoky flavor that permeates and complements the meat throughout.

A word about barbecue sauces: The sauces that accompany almost all Chicago barbecue tend to share a common base, which is probably closest to Memphis style. They're usually sweet, bright red, and tomatoey, with hints of vinegar and Worcestershire sauce, and they are almost always offered in both mild and spicy versions. You can request either or both, slathered on the meat or on the side. (To properly measure and appreciate meat quality and cooking technique, a good rule is to always ask for it on the side.) Some might use a little honey or syrup to alter the balance of sweet and sour, others might use Tabasco sauce or ground cayenne pepper to boost the heat, but with few exceptions they generally exhibit the same basic ketchuplike character. You might occasionally find a Texas-style sauce—darker and more vinegary, with hints of garlic, citrus, and chile powder.

There are literally hundreds of rib shacks on the South and West Sides of the city, and keeping track of them is impossible. They seem to pop up and then close like short-blooming desert cacti in barren locations, and on any given day you can never be sure that the joint you liked, or meant to try last month, is still there. A few, however, seem to have gotten the formula, the business model, and the recipe down well enough to sustain themselves—and a loyal clientele.

Note that most rib shacks have not finished cooking their meat until around 1:00 or 2:00 P.M. Rib tips, perhaps more popular in Chicago than the ribs themselves, require shorter cooking times and are usually ready earlier. Closing hours vary widely depending on the day and the supply of cooked meat.

Barbara Ann's BBQ
Park Manor
7617 South Cottage Grove
(773) 723-4780
Take-out only
$

Barbara Ann's is a barbecue shack with an aroma that will drive you crazy from the parking lot. The smoke seems to shoot right up through the nostrils into the brain, and then downward to trigger the salivary glands. Mack, the personable pitman at Barbara Ann's, manages a slow, gentle fire that infuses his meat (and everything else in the area, including your car's upholstery) with a deep complex smokiness. This is some of the best barbecue in the city.

Mack, however, has one great specialty that seems to be on people's lips, figuratively and literally. While he offers an extended menu of ribs, tips, chicken, catfish, and spaghetti, the consensus seems to be that his hot links (thick, rich, spicy pork sausage) are the best in the city. What sets them apart is their coarse grind, their spiciness, and a wonderful crustiness, without the usual chunks of gristle. These links are smoked delicately on the top rack of the "aquarium" smoker, where the heat is gentler and there's less risk of drying out. When they are about 80 percent cooked, they're taken off, held until ordered, and then finished in the deep fryer. It's curious that even though Mack's sauce does little for the ribs, the combination of his sausage with sauce elevates the dish to a perfect pairing of exquisitely commingled flavors.

All orders come with fries and bread, of course, but Barbara Ann's will offer wheat bread if you like—perhaps to relieve palates weary of the standard Wonder Bread–type white. And if you'd prefer to dine indoors instead of on your car hood, the namesake Barbara Ann's Motel next door offers rooms at hourly rates.

This is high-quality, experienced, and professional barbecue, but if you want to try your hand at cooking it at home, Mack will even sell you a twenty-pound case of links.

Honey 1 BBQ
Austin
5135 West Division Street
(773) 626-5436
Take-out only
$

Robert Adams Sr. says you learn an awful lot about wood by chopping it down every week to put in your grandmother's cooking stove and to heat the family farmhouse. The family farm in this case was in Marianna, Arkansas, just downriver from Memphis, where Adams and fifteen other children helped his grandfather raise cotton, corn, and soybeans.

In 1967 Adams moved to Chicago, where he ended up working as a truck driver. But he was always cooking barbecue in his backyard, just as he learned back home from his mother and grandparents. It was usually for family, friends, and neighbors, but the barbecue was good enough for him to start a catering business on the side. Then in June of 2003, at the urging of his son Robert Jr., they opened their own place where they now work fourteen-hour days, making some of the best barbecue on the West Side.

Robert picks over his wood and meat deliveries carefully, making sure

that both are up to his standards. He prefers fresher wood with a higher moisture content, to create just the right balance of heat and smoke, and he always pays more for a better-quality meat. Nothing is precooked, and he cuts no corners with cooking times. The ribs might take three to four hours in the smoker, the tips two to three, all of it done over a perfectly managed fire. Robert's wife, Patricia, makes their sauce from scratch every day, using the not-so-secret ingredient of honey. Feel free to bring him a chicken or turkey if you want it custom smoked—he's happy to oblige and knows what he's doing.

Lem's Bar B Q House
Park Manor
311 East 75th Street
(773) 994-2428
Take-out only
$

Before you see the line of cars and customers, you can smell the wood smoke blocks away. Arguably serving the best barbecue in the city, Lem's is firmly managed by Lynn Walker and Carmen Lemons, who advise the tightly squeezed line of respectful, waiting customers, "Do you want to speak to the man in charge, or to the woman who knows what's going on?" The ribs are crispy on the outside and succulent in the center, and the rib tips exude flavor all the way through. Sauce is slathered on with a huge paintbrush, but as more than one barbecue maven has been heard to comment, "It ain't about the sauce; it's about the meat." Nevertheless, Lem's offers one of the more unique sauces around, with a flavor and consistency somewhat like a buffalo wing sauce, though a bit smokier. Standard accompaniments are spongy white bread and fries.

Leon's BBQ
Chatham
8249 South Cottage Grove
(773) 488-4556
Take-out only
$

By sheer longevity Leon Finney Sr. probably reigns as the godfather of Chicago barbecue. The story actually begins with Bertha Brody, Leon's aunt, who was cooking barbecue on the South Side in the late 1930s. Problems from a bookie joint being operated out of the restaurant's back room eventually shut them down, so in 1940 Leon bought the place for seven hundred dollars, and his aunt stayed on.

Leon's location moved around a lot in the ensuing years, and now he and his son Leon Jr. run three barbecue shacks on the South Side, each making 'cue according to the formula Leon's been working to perfect since the 1940s. That formula was devised to meet high demand without sacrificing quality control; their combined operations can go through almost five hundred thousand pounds of ribs and rib tips a year. Not to mention all the sausage made in-house a couple of times a week.

Leon's rich, deep brown signature sauce is unique and different from the standard ketchuplike sauces prevalent on the South Side. It's tangy, spicy, and above all not too sweet. This sauce actually harkens back to his aunt, who concocted the original version, but it has evolved over the last sixty-three years through trial, error, and a lot of family opinion polls.

Through his leadership of The Woodlawn Organization and its sister organization The Woodlawn Community Development Corporation, Leon Jr. has been a longtime fixture in community activism on Chicago's South Side. For the last thirty-seven years he's worked to improve job opportunities, housing, public schools, medical care, and child-care support services. But when things get busy in the rib business, he and eighty-eight-year-old Leon Sr. still get their hands dirty in the bins of spices and raw meat, making sure the product they're so proud of goes out the door right.

Other Locations
1640 East 79th Street, Chicago (South Shore); (773) 731-1454
1200 West 59th Street, Chicago (Englewood); (773) 778-7828
2418 North Ashland Avenue, Chicago (Lincoln Park);
   (773) 975-7427

NOTABLE

Carson's
River North
612 North Wells Street
(312) 280-9200
$$

The official name, Carson's—the Place for Ribs, bespeaks the respected tenure of this longstanding Chicago institution. They smoke large volumes of meat in big rotisserie-type ovens, producing a rib that is nicely balanced between the long-smoked South and West Side styles and the North Side fall-off-the-bone style. Although much of the product is precooked, it does pick up a mild smoke flavor in the process, and the meat maintains a good toothsome quality. Before serving it is covered with sauce and finished on the grill. Carson's also receives high marks for their pork chops and au gratin potatoes. There are two locations in town and two in the suburbs. All are very comfortable family-style restaurants.

Other Locations
5970 North Ridge, Chicago (East Rogers Park); (773) 271-4000
5050 North Harlem Avenue, Harwood Heights; (708) 867-4200
200 North Waukegan Road, Deerfield; (847) 374-8500

Exsenator's
3349 West 159th Street
Markham
(708) 333-1211
Take-out only
$-$$

Ask any random Chicago South Sider where the best barbecue is, and they just might answer Exsenator's, which is so far south it isn't even in Chicago anymore. But it gets mentioned frequently enough by the locals, even as far as eighty-five blocks away, that it must be doing something right. Actually, Exsenator (the owner's first name) is doing many things right. His barbecue is deep and full flavored, with just the right amount of exterior crispness, and accented by a rich rub. Pitman Dwight has been there for seven years, and is justifiably proud of what he does.

Hecky's
1902 Green Bay Road
Evanston
(847) 492-1182
Take-out only
$$

In spite of its Far North Side location, Hecky's BBQ is good enough to go toe-to-toe with some of the better South Side joints. It shares many of their reverse-charm elements: a grungy waiting area, no seating, long waits for an order. The tips especially have great flavor here, while there is a gentle smokiness that complements the rib meat. They also do chopped beef and pork sandwiches, unusual in Chicago, and a little reminiscent of Texas shacks. In all, it is rich and nicely balanced barbecue. And although some barbecue purists will always eschew the sauce, in this case Hecky's has a remarkably rich and complex sauce, more vinegar- than tomato-based and also somewhat Texan in character. It's one of the few sauces around that isn't superfluous to the meat it accompanies.

I-57 Rib House
Pullman
1524 West 115th Street
(773) 429-1111
Take-out only
$-$$

Owner Shirley Williams (along with husband Lewis) may be the friend-liest barbecuer in the historic Pullman neighborhood on the South Side. She loves to talk about her craft and can do so for hours, somehow without ever managing to divulge her trade secrets. Her most important secret may be what she does to those rib tips, which are some of the most fla-vorful of all the South Side shacks.

The Rib Joint
Chatham
432 East 87th Street
(773) 651-4108
Take-out only
$

The Rib Joint has many loyal customers, mainly for its consistency. The rib tips have that crisp, fat-in-the-fire flavor, the smoke ring lightly paints the edge of the rib meat, and a balanced smokiness runs throughout. Like Lem's, there always seems to be a crowd of people standing around waiting for their orders, whatever the hour. Most barbecue shacks offer a mild and a spicy sauce, and the spicy sauce at The Rib Joint is nicely peppery. It's best ordered on the side. The standard accompaniments come with all dishes, even with their rib-tip lunch special for a bargain $3.39.

Robinson's #1 BBQ Ribs
940 Madison Street
Oak Park
(708) 383-8452
$–$$

Robinson's is a bright and clean full-service restaurant, with an emphasis on ribs and rib tips. Sandwiches are made with sliced rather than pulled pork and served with their own signature tomato-based sauce that has a bit of kick to it. Southern roots are evident in the rest of the menu, which includes catfish, turnip greens, and black-eyed peas. Out of a building next door to their Oak Park address they run their Robinson Barbecue Sauce Company.

Definitely a local company, with its own bottled sauce business, Robinson's has expanded quite a bit, with franchises in Union Station and the Thompson State of Illinois Center. They also have two other full-service restaurants owned by the family.

Other Locations
655 West Armitage Avenue, Chicago (Lincoln Park);
(312) 337-1399
5121 St. Charles Road, Bellwood; (708) 544-6402

The Smoke Daddy
Wicker Park
1804 West Division Street
(773) 772-6656
$$

This Wicker Park haunt feels like a dimly lit blues joint from the 1950s. The crowd tends to be young, hip, and professional. In addition to good food, there is live jazz and blues every night. They call their barbecue style Texarkana, although the barbecue on the menu seems more Kansas City in style, as does the sauce. Shoestring sweet potato fries, done to perfect crispness, are a good accompaniment to any of their selections.

A POPULAR ALTERNATIVE

In the interest of fairness, we should mention a couple of Chicago institutions that serve the tender fall-off-the-bone style of rib. They've all been around for decades, and are extremely popular with North Side crowds, young and old. Instead of spareribs, all use baby-backs, which are meatier and more tender and which can also produce a flavor more like pork chops. The ribs are either baked, steamed, or boiled beforehand, then slathered with a sweet sauce and thrown onto the grill to caramelize the surface sugars. Often they are proudly advertised as "ribs so tender you can eat them with a spoon."

Gale Street Inn
Jefferson Park
4914 North Milwaukee Avenue
(773) 725-1300
$$

The Gale Street Inn (no longer on Gale Street) is a spacious family-style restaurant with good service and a convivial bar. In addition to their award-winning ribs, the menu features everything from seafood to chicken, pasta, and steaks. If this place is viewed less as a rib house and more as a typical Greek diner, but one on steroids, its appeal is readily apparent. There are enough selections to please everyone from kids to grandparents, the staff is personable and friendly, the drinks are generous, and the food tasty. They've been doing it this way for nearly forty years.

Twin Anchors
Old Town
1655 North Sedgwick Street
(312) 266-1616
$$

Twin Anchors started out as a speakeasy sometime in the 1930s, and has forever since borne the label of quaint neighborhood tavern. When Frank Sinatra used to favor the place it was a working-class corner bar with great food. Today families from the neighborhood come and endure waits of up to an hour and a half for one of the precious tables in the back room. To help pass the time, one of the local sports teams will probably be broadcast over the TVs in the bar, and there's plenty of Chicago memorabilia to peruse on the wall, most of it about Twin Anchors itself.

BARS, PUBS & TAVERNS

The Berghoff Bar
Loop
17 West Adams Street
(312) 427-3170
Closed Sunday and holidays, no food service Saturday
$

Located just 2.5 blocks west of the Art Institute, the Berghoff Bar first opened next door to its present location on the corner of State and Adams in 1898, where it sold beers for a nickel and the sandwiches were free. Even during Prohibition, the Berghoff prospered selling near beer and Bergo soda pop.

The Berghoff grew steadily from its humble beginnings and now includes a large full-service restaurant, banquet facilities, three enormous kitchens, and even its own woodworking shop to care for the extensive hardwood decor.

It is still the bar, though, that people look to for a sense of history and old, big-shouldered Chicago style. Today guests enjoy the Berghoff's full line of beers; great sandwiches; and private stock, single-barrel, fourteen-year-old Kentucky bourbon.

Goose Island Brew Pub
Goose Island
1800 North Clybourn Avenue
(312) 915-0071
$$

Fifteen years ago the Goose Island neighborhood was much like the Chicago beer scene: desolate and near ruin. Today both the neighborhood and Chicago beer are thriving, thanks in great part to the Goose Island Brewery. Father and son John and Greg Hall have created a craft-beer empire with two pubs and a large production brewery that demonstrate the artisanship of craft brewing. The flagship pub (established in 1986) on Clybourn is a classic American brewpub and now home to the Siebel Institute, the longest-running school for brewers in the United States.

The food here has a definite flair, and everyone who goes will find something he or she will like. For example, take a burger, crust it in black pepper, and cover it with garlic cloves and Stilton cheese—this is the legendary Stilton burger.

The award-winning beer is excellent and manages to span a wide range of styles while still maintaining quality. The number of beers offered at Goose Island has approached a hundred in some years, and the Halls strive to always have one cask-conditioned real ale on draft.

Particularly impressive is the Halls' support of their local neighborhood and local brewers. They are willing hosts to many beer events, including brewmasters' dinners and local beer club meetings. Patrons are also encouraged to earn their MBA—Master of Beer Appreciation—by sampling a variety of the beers. Goose Island has been a sponsor and supporter of the nationally renowned Real Ale Festival since its inception.

Need a place to watch the game? The many television sets and friendly atmosphere offer a great location at both pubs. For Cubs fans, the Wrigleyville location's proximity to the field makes it an ideal spot to meet before or after the game. Goose Island is a new Chicago classic.

Other Location
3535 North Clark Street, Chicago (Wrigleyville); (773) 832-9040

Hopleaf Bar
Andersonville
5148 North Clark Street
(773) 334-9851
$$

On the north side of Chicago, beer and food lovers will find a treasure in the historic Andersonville neighborhood. When you walk into the Hopleaf, there is a chalkboard list of the beers offered, both draft and bottled. Many of the beers are served in glassware specifically designed to showcase the color, flavor, and aroma of the beer. Long known as a bastion of Belgian beer, the Hopleaf expanded in the summer of 2003 when it opened a restaurant in its back room under the direction of Chef Monica Riley (formerly of Zinfandel). The organic, free-range menu features appetizers and entrées from Belgian-style *frites* and smoked duck sandwiches to mussels. The food beautifully complements the full range of drinks while providing discerning diners with an alternative to regular pub fare. The cozy restaurant with exposed brickwork overlooks a garden whose yield may be featured in the very meal you are eating.

Owner Michael Roeper has handpicked all of the beers offered. And while emphasizing Belgian beers, the beer menu has something to please everyone. Although service here can be slow, the meal is worth the wait while you sip on an extraordinary brew.

The Map Room
Bucktown
1949 North Hoyne Avenue
(773) 252-7636
$

To beer lovers, this bar is the mecca of the Midwest. On an easy-to-miss corner in the heart of the popular, artsy Bucktown neighborhood, this cozy "traveler's tavern" welcomes both locals and visitors alike. Its walls and furniture are covered with maps, flags, brewery signs, and even foreign currency. While many beer bars have a hundred or more taps as their claim to fame, the twenty-five or so drafts available most nights at The Map Room provide arguably the most eclectic and unique selection of beers in the city. If only one keg of a particularly rare beer comes to the Midwest, chances are it will find its way to The Map Room cellar. The staff is very knowledgeable about their wares, and the full-service bar provides a wide range of drinks. Want to learn more about what's available? The bar offers a monthly beer-and-wine school taught by industry locals.

While The Map Room does not serve food, patrons are welcome to carry in from the various local dining hot spots. In addition, a weekly International Night (free on Tuesdays with a two-drink minimum) provides an ever-changing catered plate of food from a different ethnic Chicago restaurant. At The Map Room you can "travel" to Belgium for a beer, have an excellent meal from Argentina, and end the night with a local brew, all without ever having left the city.

Come to The Map Room a few times and you'll realize that you recognize many of the faces—that's the kind of place this is. From the coffee, bagels, and muffins served in the morning to the world-class drinks served late into the night, The Map Room is a must on the Chicago bar scene.

Matchbox
West Town
770 North Milwaukee Avenue
(312) 666-9292
$-$$

One of the quirkiest, coolest watering holes in the city calls the intersection of Milwaukee, Chicago, and Ogden avenues its home. While its name may suggest a singles bar or smoking den, the Matchbox actually takes its name from the tiny, cramped interior—as in "not much bigger than a matchbox." Matchbox is one of those places that is full of stories—you just need to ask. Some of the oddities are more functional than others, like the jars of home-steeped ginger-and-pineapple vodka, which are used to make some of the best margaritas and gimlets you'll find anywhere.

Great care is taken with the drinks. The rims of the glasses may have any one of three coatings: powdered sugar for fruit drinks, salt for traditional margaritas, and cocoa for the decadent chocolate martini. While this is no place for the claustrophobe, the adventurous will find the close quarters welcoming and friendly. The crowd is a mix of all kinds of people, and the place fills at the predictable times. The full-service bar has two tap lines, thirty-four well-selected bottled beers, and a huge selection of specialty liquors they've made efforts to acquire. The owners run the restaurant next door which, in keeping with the matchbox theme, is housed in an old railcar. You'll love this tiny corner of Chicago.

NOTABLE

Brick's Pizza Chicago
Lincoln Park
1909 North Lincoln Avenue
(312) 255-0851
$$

If gentrified Lincoln Park has a basement, it's Brick's. Literally. This cool bar is entered down a stairway eye level with the sidewalk. It's not a basement in a bad sense; it's the kind of basement where people bring friends to enjoy good food and drink while having a great time. The relaxed, fun atmosphere is no accident; owner Bill Brandt is a veteran of the Chicago bar scene. The full-service bar has an attentive and friendly staff who are glad to serve label beers brewed for Brick's by Rogue Brewing in Oregon, as well as some bottled beers you're unlikely to find anywhere else.

The simple menu consists of pizzas, pastas, and salads that are hearty, homey, and pleasing. The local crowd can be pleasantly rowdy and although it can get a bit loud on the weekends, everyone is welcome. Just watch your step on the way out—that hidden stair on the way up will get you every time.

Buddy Guy's Legends
South Loop
754 South Wabash Avenue
(312) 427-0333
$$

Not too many bars greet you with the owner's Grammy award to one side and a signed Eric Clapton guitar above the bar to the other. Buddy Guy, one of the last great living legends of the blues, runs this funky bar in Chicago's South Loop neighborhood. Legends is more than a typical boozy, smoky bar; it's also a functioning museum of the blues. Guitars, awards, photos, and other various memorabilia fill Legends and sing the history of the blues.

The kitchen offers Louisiana fare, to mixed reviews. Guy himself appears every year at various times and for most of the month of January,

reminding appreciative crowds why many consider him the inspiration for Jimi Hendrix and "the world's greatest living guitarist." Notice the blue-and-white checkered floor—it recalls the historic Checkerboard Lounge, one of Guy's previous ventures and the now-gone cradle of Chicago blues. Legends is today's real Chicago blues.

Clark Street Ale House
River North
742 North Clark Street
(312) 642-9253
$

Clark Street Ale House is centrally located but just far enough from the congested streets of the Loop and the Magnificent Mile. Don't let the name fool you—this place has more to offer than ale. Owner Adam Ellis has built a bar that defies categorization. All types congregate here into the wee hours of the morning, whether they seek a special dram of Scotch (there are forty varieties here) or a last drink after a night at the adjacent Blue Chicago. Locals suspect that the seemingly out-of-place large neon sign that's never properly illuminated is a bit of urban camouflage devised to scare away all but the seasoned drinker. This is the place to drink and experience late night in Chicago.

Delilah's
Lincoln Park
2771 North Lincoln Avenue
(773) 472-2771
$$

A Lincoln Park alternative, Delilah's is a bar with attitude. Most nights a hip twenty-something crowd enjoys not only the full-service bar but DJs, punk bands, and even movie showings. This neo-Gothic, dark, quirky, and absolutely unique bar could easily be dismissed as a haven for punks and goths, but that dismissal would be your loss. Delilah's has one of the best selections of boutique liquors and beer in the city; it may be where a younger crowd learns about the finer things a great bar has to offer. Owner Mike Miller is a man of discerning tastes, and his bar is your best bet to find a rare single-malt Scotch, small-batch bourbon, or artisan tequila. Ever had vintage beer? Delilah's has a collection of bottled beers that actually improve with age. This place may not be everyone's dram of Scotch, but you won't forget you were here.

The Green Mill
Uptown
4802 Broadway
(773) 878-5552
$$

Hailed as an old Al Capone hot spot, this bar–jazz club still has the feel of the lavish 1920s, even if the once plush upholstered booths and maritime frescoes have mellowed a bit. Complete with a backdoor getaway for Capone's great escapes during Prohibition raids, the Green Mill is thick on atmosphere.

The stage easily takes up 35 percent of the navigable space, making for a very intimate libation-and-music experience. Entertainers play the piano in the middle of the bar on Friday evenings from 5:00 to 8:00 P.M. and Sunday nights usually from 11:00 P.M. on, but calling to confirm is never a bad idea. Jazz performers play here every night of the week and sometimes even on Sunday afternoons. Scoring a booth at The Green Mill is the ideal way to dazzle a first date with your ineffable coolness. Be advised, though: Lines form down the block on Broadway to get into this hideout, even on the coldest winter nights.

The Hideout
Goose Island
1354 West Wabansia Avenue
(773) 227-4433
$

The Hideout is one of those places that time and urbanization seem to have forgotten. Hidden away on Wabansia Avenue in the midst of decaying industrial sprawl, The Hideout draws a regular neighborhood crowd without the neighborhood. A small black-and-white handmade sign directs you in from Elston Avenue. The building allegedly dates back to nineteenth-century Irish immigrants who settled in this part of the city. Music and atmosphere are the real reasons to visit: The owners are enthusiastic music lovers and historians who are eager to preach the gospel of good music and the history of their unique establishment. The bar offers a standard range of drinks with some decent draft beers. If you want to explore local Chicago, The Hideout is a great place to start. You'll just have to find it first.

Le Coq d' Or
Gold Coast
The Drake Hotel
140 East Walton Street
(312) 787-2200
$$

Heading south on Lake Shore Drive toward the city, one of the most prominent sights on Chicago's nighttime landscape is the illuminated beacon of The Drake Hotel. Sitting regally on the north end of the Magnificent Mile, The Drake is a classic hotel that boasts a classic hotel bar—Le Coq d' Or. Serving Chicago since slightly before the end of Prohibition, this historic pub's wood-and-leather interior is welcoming and cozy. With impeccable service it's an inviting oasis from Chicago's wind and the crowds on Michigan Avenue. The bar covers all the bases with a great selection of high-end liquors, famous mixed drinks (the Executive Line), and decent draft beers. The Goose Island Honkers Ale poured here is one of the freshest and tastiest local brews. Great soups highlight a basic menu, but people looking for a full meal might do better in one of The Drake's restaurants. For a touch of old Chicago, check out this classic pub.

Mickey Finn's Brewery
412 North Milwaukee Avenue
Libertyville
(847) 362-6688
$

Rich history, great food, and award-winning beer combine to make Mickey Finn's a must-visit bar on Chicago's North Shore. Aside from a brief period during Prohibition when it served as a barbershop, Finn's has been a locally loved pub since the 1920s. In 1994 the classic building in old downtown Libertyville was renovated and expanded to include a brewery. You really get a small-town feel as you sit at the old wooden bar and look out across the scenic square opposite—urban sprawl has yet to completely reach this far north.

The brewery produces excellent beer and has both local and national awards to prove it. The bar is full-service; the menu offers a broad range of pub food, with fuller meals also available. An outdoor garden in front of the building can be a wonderful oasis on a hot summer day.

Mike's American Ale House
Portage Park
5737 West Irving Park Road
(773) 282-3150
$

Having replaced a longtime Portage Park watering hole, Mike's has expanded on the basic neighborhood-bar theme by adding some convivial and flavorful touches. The beer menu has something for everyone; the food menu is simple but good. Comfort food? If it were any more comfortable it would be served in fuzzy pink slippers.

If you doubt Mike's is an authentic neighborhood spot, just ask the people sitting next to you. Chances are they are local aldermen or police officers, so watch your step.

Piece
Bucktown/Wicker Park
1927 West North Avenue
(773) 772-4422
$$

Made (in)famous shortly after opening when some of MTV's *Real World: Chicago* cast worked here, Piece's real claims to fame are its pizza and beer, both done with a quirky flair. In the bustling heart of the

Bucktown/Wicker Park area, Piece (as in *piece of pizza*) fits in ably among the artsy, sophisticated, cosmopolitan city dwellers.

For starters, their pizza is based on the New Haven, Connecticut, thick-crust style. They feature two tomato-based pizzas and one "white" pizza. All pies are square and generously serve a group. The beers are made by veterans of the local craft-beer scene, and Piece can hardly meet demand. To supplement their own offerings, they provide several other beers on tap, from Pabst Blue Ribbon to rare Japanese brews, as well as a full-service bar to satisfy all tastes.

The skylit center of the oddly shaped room is a focal point for the long curving bar, sunken front room, and raised tables on either side. In pleasant weather, the swinging windows open right out onto North Avenue. Piece is popular with a younger crowd, but everyone is welcome.

Rock Bottom Brewery and Restaurant
River North
One West Grand Avenue
(312) 755-9339
$

While Rock Bottom Breweries are part of a national chain, their downtown Chicago location has distinguished itself. On almost any night of the week, this spacious bar and restaurant, in a vibrant part of the city, is bustling. Don't be misled by the brewery designation; this is a full-service bar including single-malt Scotch, small-batch bourbon, and a great depth of high-end liquors. Its menu of pub food goes beyond regular fare and incorporates the house brews in the recipes.

One of the keys to the Rock Bottom empire's success has been that it allows each local brewer a free hand, particularly in creating the seasonal beers. Brewmaster Pete Crowley has garnered many awards on both the local and national levels. If that wasn't enough, the rooftop beer garden is one of Chicago's best-kept secrets on a summer day.

Sheffield's
Lakeview
3258 North Sheffield Avenue
(773) 281-4989
$

This gem of a local bar is nestled on a quiet corner in between Wrigley Field and the theatres on Belmont Avenue. It boasts one of the finest secluded beer gardens in the city. While the crowd is often twenty-somethings in school colors, there is always a geriatric on-site in the form of the giant tree that serves as the garden's centerpiece. This place has all kinds of local charm. The former bar cat, Fang Sheffield, had free run of the joint for fourteen years and was the poster boy for the pub, as he sat on the back bar drinking water from a martini glass. The bar is full-service with a huge, notable range of bottled and draft beer, some quite rare. Questions about the beer? Refer to one of the great "almanacs" provided for your educational enjoyment.

While there is no kitchen, they are food-friendly, so feel free to bring in a meal from any of the nearby restaurants. Sheffield's is truly a local spot that caters to both a hip crowd and the locals who remember when they were the hip crowd.

Signature Lounge
Gold Coast
875 North Michigan Avenue, 96th Floor
(312) 787-7230
$$-$$$

The Signature Lounge, located on the 96th floor of the Hancock Building, commands a prominent place in Chicago's skyline. It's virtually impossible to have a drink and enjoy a view of the city that's better than this. With floor-to-ceiling windows overlooking Lake Michigan and the city, there are few places in the world with a view and ambience like the Signature Lounge.

The bar offers a full range of libations with a focus on Chicago-themed mixed drinks. Beers are limited to bottles. The prices are as stratospheric as the view, but the experience is worth the extra pennies. Up this high, even one of the world's hardest-working cities seems to slow down. In fact, the only things that seem to move fast are the clouds. So sit back, relax, and take in the great view—this is Chicago, and you're on cloud ninety-six.

Underground Wonder Bar
Gold Coast
10 East Walton Street
(312) 266-7761
$$

An unlikely fixture in its ritzy neighborhood, the subterranean Underground Wonder Bar is a simple, cool place to have a drink and soak up some authentic Chicago music. The UWB is a small, cozy, boozy, candlelit basement watering hole with a stage set in the back of the main room. Live music is performed 365 days a year, generally starting after

8:00 P.M. The music is heavy on Chicago staples—blues and jazz. There's not a bad seat in the often smoky bar. UWB welcomes the after-work crowd, but is also known as a late-night place that goes strong until the early hours of the morning. The bar has something for everyone in its full range of drinks, though there aren't any big surprises. So close to the bustle of the Gold Coast and the Magnificent Mile, the UWB still seems a world away.

BRUNCH

The Bongo Room
Wicker Park
1470 North Milwaukee Avenue
(773) 489-0690
$$

Just down the street from the heart of Wicker Park, along Milwaukee Avenue, sits an urban eatery that attracts hungry mobs anxiously awaiting such brunch treats as Banana, Ginger, and Walnut Pancakes with Warm Maple-Mascarpone Cream, or bittersweet Cocoa-Espresso Pancakes with Butterfinger-Cashew Butter. Not all brunch establishments are created alike, and The Bongo Room is a perfect example of that. Derrick Robles and John Latino joined forces after meeting while Latino was interning at The Pump Room, and together they have created a temple to brunch.

Once inside, you are instantly warmed by the pale purple, green, and yellow walls mixed with exposed brick and large murals. The antique fixtures that hang from the ceiling and adorn the walls give patrons the feeling that they have stepped into a hip grandmother's kitchen. Suprisingly, there are a variety of seating options in such a small space. The counter offers diners a quick in-and-out meal, while the tables for two provide a somewhat more romantic feel. If you're with a crowd, waiting for one of their huge booths in the center of the space (which are large enough for a dinner party) is well worth it.

The menu is mostly vegetarian with a few chicken dishes to satisfy those who need meat in their diets. The weekday menu offers what seems to be the standard brunch fare: omelets, bacon and eggs, and so forth—though the pancakes might be cranberry-buttermilk with tangerine-macaroon butter or pumpkin spice. The weekend menu, by contrast, is more adventurous.

Flo
Noble Square
1434 West Chicago Avenue
(312) 243-0477
Open daily for breakfast and lunch, Tuesday–Saturday for dinner
$

The fans are loyal and the prices are more reasonable than one could imagine. If you're looking for a Southwestern flair to kick-start your day, head over to Flo. Set off the beaten path on West Chicago Avenue in a somewhat rough-and-tumble area, this brunch spot adds bold flavors to morning staples. Whether it's bellying up to the counter or waiting for a table (and there is usually a wait on weekends—luckily, coffee is served), hunger pangs will be satisfied here.

Once inside it feels as though you have stepped into a place you have been frequenting for years. The inviting, warm colors and local art that adorn the walls soothe you in a homey way. The huge chalkboard in the center of the wall explains the specials of the day while the counter serves up coffee, juices, smoothies, muffins, and other pastries.

The menu offers everything from basic bacon and eggs to more inventive takes on traditional items. Eggs Flo, one of their specialties, is poached eggs with smoked turkey, fresh spinach, and hollandaise sauce, served on English muffins with grated Asiago cheese on top. Another dish that begs to be tried is the *chilaquiles*. This dish is frequently eaten for breakfast food south of the border, and Flo gets it right. Tortilla strips with freshly scrambled eggs, roasted chiles, and fresh *pico de gallo* all add to the Southwestern focus.

Service is extremely nice and food comes out very quickly. The tables get a little crowded by the time everything is served, but this is not a huge restaurant so every inch of space is put to good use.

Lou Mitchell's
West Loop Gate
565 West Jackson Boulevard
(312) 939-3111
$ (Cash only)

In business since 1923 and just down the street from Union Station, Lou Mitchell's is one of Chicago's most popular breakfast spots and is famous for its Sunday breakfast and homemade baked goods. While you wait for a table (on any given Sunday, the line is out the door and down the street) enjoy complimentary Milk Duds (for children and ladies only; sorry, fellas) and doughnut holes offered by the cheerful hostess.

The inside is that of an old diner, complete with brown booths and a black-and-white-speckled floor. Be prepared to make new friends, as more often than not you will be seated along a large communal table with other patrons; this only adds to the family feeling. The waitstaff is quick on the draw and wastes no time taking orders and refilling glasses. Meals are served with lightning speed and excellent precision. It's like clockwork in this place—everything from the double-yolk eggs to the toast is brought to the table piping hot and ready to be devoured.

This is definitely not the place to eat if you are counting calories. Everything served is made from scratch and in high-fat and larger-than-life portions. This doesn't seem to stop patrons from coming in droves. Lou's serves more than 1,200 customers daily. It's standard breakfast fare here: pancakes, omelets, eggs, and bacon.

In the summertime Lou's offers outdoor seating for those who don't want the experience of the bustling interior. Make sure you come with cash—they accept nothing else, but to help you out there is an ATM right inside the door.

The Phoenix
Chinatown
2131 South Archer Avenue
(312) 328-0848
$–$$

The Chinese call the little delicacies dim sum, which translates as "touching your heart." And it's no wonder: These little morsels are a great way to enjoy a weekend meal. It may take you several visits to The Phoenix to decide which ones you like best, since there are so many to choose from.

The Phoenix is just around the corner from the center of Chinatown but still in the heart of it all. The inside is nothing to write home about, but the aesthetics are not the focus for most patrons. The restaurant is divided into two levels, upstairs being more of the formal, authentic Chinese establishment, while the downstairs, known as The Phoenix Dumpling House, caters to a younger crowd wanting a good meal and a place to hang out late at night.

Shrimp *har gow, siu mai*, other dumpling-type dishes, and the sticky rice wrapped in leaves are dishes that make you feel as if you've sailed around the world and are eating in a small diner in China.

Service is speedy and friendly; communication can be tricky if you're not familiar with the menu, but the host and hostess are very helpful in explaining the different foods.

The dim sum brunch begins daily at 8:00 A.M. and ends at 3:00 P.M., but get there early if possible; the wait is long for those who decide to sleep in.

Wishbone Restaurant
West Loop Gate
1001 West Washington Boulevard
(312) 850-2663
Open daily for breakfast and lunch, Tuesday–Saturday for dinner
$

Attracting everyone from those who just rolled out of bed, to those all glammed-out and ready for the day, to Oprah Winfrey's staff, this West Loop destination offers a menu as varied as its clientele. The decor is funky and inspired. Artist Lia Nickson (mom to Chef Joel Nickson) has decorated the space with her big vegetables and one-of-a-kind chicken-and-egg art. Focus your eyes upward and notice the massive chandeliers with attached flowers made out of spoons in the center. Specials are written on a chalkboard over the kitchen with colored chalk and a little piz-zazz, while the laminated paper menu features everyday entrées.

Inside the menu there is an array of comfort foods to choose from. Everything from the traditional Denver omelet and thick biscuits and gravy to more inventive dishes such as Red Eggs and crawfish cakes. Add to any dish the hot sauce that occupies every table and you're destined to taste something straight out of the South. Fresh-squeezed orange juice and peach Bellinis make a nice addition to put out the fire. This is also a vege-tarian-friendly place, offering such favorites as bean cakes and cornflakes encrusted French toast.

Pinpointing the waitstaff is easy—just search for people wearing T-shirts emblazoned with snarling poodles. The poodle is somewhat of a mascot to this establishment, but beware: They are very proud to be sporting such a mean pooch, so insults and cracks are not welcome.

NOTABLE

Hilary's Urban Eatery (HUE)
Noble Square
1500 West Division Street
(773) 235-4327
$$

A brunch favorite in the West Town neighborhood, HUE is tucked into a little corner along West Division Street. Venture inside and something that reminds you of Grandma's house is bound to catch your eye. From the crazy chandeliers to the jars of jelly beans on the table, the space welcomes you like a mother's open arms. People flock here for weekend brunch, serving up traditional country breakfast items along with takes on *chilaquiles*, specialty egg dishes, and an assortment of fresh pastries. Service is swift, but with a personal touch; most of the time the owner is swimming through the crowd. Hilary's is extremely child friendly, but reservations are not accepted here, so be prepared to wait a bit on weekends.

Ina's
West Loop Gate
1235 West Randolph Street
(312) 266-8227
$$

One of the first people you meet when you step into this establishment is Ina herself, the "Breakfast Queen." Her breakfast menu has wonderful specialties: pancakes (either Ina's signature buttermilk or whole-wheat and oatmeal) filled with blueberries or bananas, homemade granola, and a vegetable hash steamed in cream, to name just a few.

Service is attentive and pleasant. Don't venture in here if you are expecting a cell phone call: Ina doesn't allow them, and that makes for an even more pleasant, relaxing atmosphere.

Milk and Honey Café
Wicker Park
1920 West Division Street
(773) 395-9434
$

Owners Heidi Carlson and Carol Watson, who met when they were both working at Mia Francesca, have opened up what is becoming a hot spot for breakfast fare. Using organic ingredients whenever possible, they serve everything from scones and muffins to Almond-Orange French Toast,

Ham-and-Cheese Bread Pudding, and Oatmeal with Dried Cherries, Brown Sugar, and Pecans. Open only for breakfast and lunch, Milk and Honey Café is also vegetarian friendly, with entrées such as spicy Thai Tofu Salad as well as a sandwich with roasted red peppers, herbed goat cheese, and grilled eggplant.

With wooden tables and chairs, brick walls, and a fireplace, the restaurant might seem a little too cozy for an early breakfast, but this only adds to the warmth of the space. In the warmer months the front windows open up onto a sidewalk café, allowing diners to enjoy their breakfast while watching the parade of Wicker Parkers.

Orange
Lakeview
3231 North Clark Street
(773) 549-4400
Closed Monday
$$

Orange's space has a lofty feel with its exposed brick and high ceilings, and it resembles a trendy little lounge, complete with orange seat cushions and an orange tree in the corner. The custom-order, fresh-squeezed juice bar is adorned with oranges that line the shelves on the back counter, and it provides patrons with a fun way to be creative with their daily dose of vitamins and minerals.

The menu, dependent on seasonal ingredients, is ever changing. The four-section pancake flight might consist of lavender honey, fresh strawberries, toasted candied pecans, and classic maple syrup, but may morph into something savory by the next week. For those with a sweet tooth, there are the French Toast Kebabs composed of moist chunks of challah bread speared with strawberries and pineapple.

Sweet Maple Café
Little Italy
1339 West Taylor Street
(312) 243-8908
$$

Located just west of the University of Illinois, Chicago, in the Little Italy neighborhood, this small café offers breakfast fare that would make any grandmother jealous. The menu is focused on home cooking and includes an array of omelets, fluffy biscuits, and appealing sides. As with most places serving brunch, there is a wait and it does get rather crowded. However, the staff is accommodating and eager to please once you are seated.

Toast
Bucktown
2046 North Damen Avenue
(773) 772-5600
$$

Boasting a child-friendly atmosphere and traditional breakfast fare, this Bucktown breakfast spot scores high marks with its patrons. This slightly swank eatery attracts all types with its accommodating menu that includes everything from breakfast burritos and stuffed French toast to panini, eggs Benedict, and banana-pecan pancakes. Things get a little crazy on the weekends, and it is usually packed with hungry toddlers and their mothers, but the service is efficient and pleasant despite all the racket. If you're looking for a more low-key atmosphere, in the summer months enjoy dining outside on the patio and relax with some fresh-squeezed orange juice while watching people stroll by.

Victory's Banner   *(Vegetarian)*
Roscoe Village
2100 West Roscoe Street
(773) 665-0227
Closed Tuesday
$

The vegetarian/vegan-friendly eatery in Roscoe Village remains a little-known place despite its wonderful breakfast fare. The Satisfaction Promise is a free-range scrambled-egg dish with spinach, sun-dried tomatoes, and feta. Other items include French toast served with marmalade, peach butter, and real maple syrup. There's also a hot Indian cereal known as *uppama*, which tastes like spicy Cream of Wheat and is sure to warm you up on a cold morning.

The restaurant is owned and run by students of Sri Chinmoy. Chinmoy, who was born in the small village of Shakpura in East Bengal, serves as the spiritual guide to students in some sixty countries around the world, encouraging a balanced lifestyle that incorporates the inner disciplines of prayer and meditation with contemporary life. There are several portraits of him hanging on the walls. On the tables, sugar packets with the teachings of Chinmoy add to the dining experience. Plus all the waitresses wear saris, which again enhances the ambience of the space.

COFFEE & TEA HOUSES

Aion   *(Tearoom)*
Ukrainian Village
2135 West Division Street
(773) 489-1534
$

Located in a rehabbed three-flat apartment building and somewhat hidden among the restaurants, bars, sushi joints, and boutiques on Division, you'll find Aion, which bills itself as an antiquities shop and teahouse. The seating area is spacious and comfortable, with exposed brick, a high ceiling, and large, well-spaced tables. There is also a small but charming seating area on the lower level. The atmosphere is relaxed and refined. The small collection of antiquities, nicely displayed, includes Roman glass, tiles, and maps.

The real draw here, however, is the tea. With more than one hundred high-quality loose teas, sourced from Todd & Holland and suppliers on both coasts, including many hard-to-find and unusual single-estate options, this is the best place in the city to explore the world of tea. The staff is knowledgeable and helpful and will give you a timer and steeping suggestions for your pot of tea. Aion has a small menu of soups, sandwiches, salads, pastries, and desserts, and serves a traditional high tea anytime, at the bargain price of $9 per person (two-person minimum). A great place for both novice and experienced tea enthusiasts.

Bourgeois Pig   *(Coffeehouse/Tearoom/Café)*
Lincoln Park
738 West Fullerton Avenue
(773) 883-5282
$

Occupying an old Lincoln Park brownstone near De Paul University's main campus, the Pig is a classic, and one of the few establishments that can truly claim to be a coffee *house*. The place is often packed with a mix of students, hospital workers, and neighborhood professionals. With its small rooms and tables, dark wood, and soft lighting, seating is tight but cozy. Be sure to check out the antique furnishings, including old Chicago photos and the collection of vintage coffee cans. You may also notice a sea of laptops taking advantage of the Pig's concession to modernity: wireless Internet access.

The coffee served is locally roasted Intelligentsia, and you will find a huge selection of coffee and tea concoctions and café chow, including soups, salads, and sandwiches. Choose from the extensive collection of loose teas by carefully grabbing one of the large jars from the shelf and handing it to the staff. Tea served in Chinese iron pots is a nice touch. The Pig is a great place to contemplate what you have, and have not, done with your life. A couple of tables are available outside.

Café Jumping Bean   *(Coffeehouse)*
Pilsen
1439 West 18th Street
(312) 455-0019
$

Jumping Bean, in the heart of the lively and predominantly Hispanic Pilsen neighborhood, is a decidedly urban neighborhood café, serving local businesspeople, students, and the numerous artists who inhabit area lofts and storefronts. The café feels right at home in this working-class community amid the many colorful shops and restaurants along 18th Street. The customers seem to know each other here. With its corner location, this is a bright and comfortable place. The café is decorated in deep blue, yellow, green, and gold, and features hand-painted tables. Be sure to check out the expanse of leaded stained glass, with its Arts and Crafts motifs, topping the windows.

The café serves coffee from Coffee and Tea Exchange, as well as sandwiches, focaccia, soups, salads, and baked goods. Find yourself a cozy spot to enjoy a warm cup of Chocolate Mexicano and to view the display of art on the walls and shelves. Works by local, national, and international artists often reflect the Mexican heritage of the community and Pilsen's vibrant and well-established art scene.

Caffé Italia   *(Coffeehouse)*
Monteclare
2625 North Harlem Avenue
(773) 889-0455
$

Nearly every coffeehouse and trendy restaurant in the city these days will serve you a cup of espresso, which can range from very good to downright nasty. Diehard fans of the elusive perfect cup, though, often make the pilgrimage to the strip of Italian restaurants, bars, and markets on the western edge of the city. Here, Italian is spoken in cafés over cups of espresso. Located practically across the street from the venerable Caputo's Market, Caffé Italia offers a few tables, a stand-up bar, a pool table in the back, and what those who are passionate about the stuff claim is among the best, if not *the* best espresso in the city.

Caffé Italia roasts its own beans in espresso, decaf espresso, and

Americano styles. Unlike the overroasted, thin, and astringent brews served at many places, you will find Italia's espresso to be well rounded, earthy, incredibly nuanced, and capped with a rich and surprisingly dark brown *crema*. The friendly staff will be happy to grind fresh beans for your home machine. Bar service features Italian beers and a large selection of Italian *aperitivos*. Try the homemade gelati if it's available.

Ennui   *(Coffeehouse)*
East Rogers Park
6981 North Sheridan Road
(773) 973-2233
$

A straightforward corner café near the lake and Loyola University's main campus, Ennui attracts a multiethnic crowd of young and old from its East Rogers Park neighborhood. This step-down city kind of place is nothing fancy, with its wraparound windows, black-and-white tile floor, white walls, and well-worn tables and chairs, but the conversation is lively and the sense of community is strong. Proceeds from the sale of art exhibited in the café have been used to benefit several local not-for-profit organizations.

The café serves Casteel coffee and an assortment of hot and cold drinks, imported sodas, soups, sandwiches, pastries, and desserts. Ennui offers very pleasant outdoor seating in warmer weather, and sponsors an annual neighborhood jazz festival.

Gourmand   *(Coffeehouse/Café)*
South Loop
728 South Dearborn Street
(312) 427-2610
$

Locals recommended this Printers Row spot for its laid-back atmosphere and the quality of its food and coffee. Industrial beams, exposed pipes painted black, and a cracked and patched floor preserve the commercial past of this historically significant area. It's a good thing, given the frenzied pace of demolition and redevelopment of nearby areas.

The coffee is very good and is freshly roasted for the café and its popular sister spots in Bucktown, Filter and Gallery Café. There is also a small loose-tea selection. For such a small place Gourmand offers a surprisingly large selection of well-prepared egg, sandwich, salad, and south-of-the-border options, as well as pastries and muffins. You may wait a bit for your food when things get hopping, and seating at the tables and couches

can be a bit tight, so bring a book or newspaper and relax. As one would expect, weekend brunch is very popular, and if you are looking for a little extra with your dinner, catch the live jazz on Fridays. Beer and wines by the glass and bottle are also available.

 **Intelligentsia**   *(Coffeehouse/Coffee Retail Store)*
Lakeview
3123 North Broadway
(773) 348-8058
$

This friendly Lakeview establishment serves what many consider to be the best coffee in the city. The owners are dedicated world coffee ambassadors and only sell coffee roasted in their own facility within days of roasting. TransFair officially certifies Intelligentsia as a fair-trade roaster. Patrons, including a number of the city's top restaurants, buy pounds of the single-estate, blended, organic, and fair-trade selections.

You will find an artistic presentation in your cup of latte, worthy of Seattle's best cafés, and a very good selection of high-quality loose teas by the cup and pot. Intelligentsia is a nice place to hang out if you're in the neighborhood; the café is popular with commuters, and the well-lit space, with its large tables, is a haven for students. Limited, dog-friendly seating on the street in warm weather is great for observing the neighborhood scene. Nibbles are pretty much limited to a small selection of baked goods. However, the recently opened downtown location, in the historic and architecturally significant Monadnock Building, offers a few light lunch choices, including very good panini. Intelligentsia is a must for every serious coffee lover.

Other Location
Monadnock Building, 53 West Jackson Street, Chicago (Loop);
  (312) 253-0544

Kopi Café   *(Coffeehouse/Tearoom/Café)*
Andersonville
5317 North Clark Street
(773) 989-5674
$

Part coffeehouse, part travel bookstore, part world boutique, this inviting Andersonville classic is the perfect place to plan your next adventure while sipping an herbal tea or munching vegetarian fare. Popular with locals and those looking for a genuine coffeehouse experience, the café is warm and dark, though tables are relatively well lit. The red floor, colorful accents, artful tabletops, and around-the-world clocks add to the funky, globetrotting charm of the place.

Kopi serves a nice assortment of hot and cold coffee and tea drinks featuring Coffee and Tea Exchange items, and sells organic fair-trade coffees in packages. The vegetarian offerings are extensive and the comforting food is uniformly very good. The breads are excellent. Kopi offers a relaxing break from perusing the shops and markets up and down Clark Street. Lounge on a pillow in the window up front, if you can grab a spot, close your eyes, and dream of far-off places.

Ten Ren   *(Tea Retail Store)*
Chinatown
2247 South Wentworth Avenue
(312) 842-1171
$-$$$

Located in Chicago's Chinatown on the Near South Side, this San Francisco–based purveyor has the city's best selection of teas from China and Taiwan, as well as an incredible array of ginseng, ranging from ginseng-flavored gum to ginseng powder for tea and fantastically expensive preserved whole ginseng root. Ten Ren, with stores located in a few major metropolitan areas in the United States, claims to be the largest manufacturer of tea in the Pacific Rim. The Chinatown shop, with items displayed on Chinese tables and in display cases, is attractive and inviting. Large canisters of loose tea are neatly arranged on one side of the shop, and a large display of ginseng products occupies the opposite side.

The tea choices are extensive and include green, white, oolong, jasmine, and black teas. Most teas are offered in several different grades ranging in price from around $10 to well over $100 per pound. Don't let the prices dissuade you from trying the better grades of tea; a little goes a long way, and the helpful staff will be happy to sell you as little or as much as you would like. In addition, they'll take the time to show you the teas, explain the differences, and describe the healthful benefits of each. Freshly brewed tea samples are often available. There are several organic green and oolong tea selections, and many of the teas are offered in tea bags, which are individually sealed for freshness. In addition to herbal and flavored teas and tea snacks, Ten Ren has an extensive collection of beautifully crafted Chinese teapots for sale. Whether you are a novice tea drinker or devoted enthusiast, Ten Ren has high-grade teas and ginseng to suit your taste and budget.

Uncommon Ground   *(Coffeehouse/Café)*
Lakeview
1214 West Grace Street
(773) 929-3680
$

An inviting café with attractive outdoor seating on a tree-lined residential street just west of Clark Street, Uncommon Ground offers a respite from the Cubs mania just around the block. Divided into two rooms with exposed brick walls, a gas fireplace, and comfortable chairs with matching tables, the place has evolved over the years, along with its increasingly upscale neighborhood.

The café features a sophisticated menu leaning toward the vegetarian, plus wine, beer, and bar service. Weekend brunches are particularly popular, and true to its coffeehouse roots, you are welcome to relax with a cup of Intelligentsia coffee, a pot of tea, or a bowl of very good hot chocolate. But what makes Uncommon Ground truly uncommon, and one of the city's best coffeehouses, is its ambitious commitment to showcasing local artists and musicians. Stop by any evening and you will likely find an acoustic performance going on. Dinner reservations are recommended. Gallery displays change monthly, and the café hosts an opening reception for each artist. Check the information-packed Web site for details: www.uncommonground.com.

Unicorn Café   *(Coffeehouse/Café)*
1723 Sherman Avenue
Evanston
(847) 332-2312
$

Here's a place, located within blocks of Northwestern University's main campus, where you could find yourself discussing politics, science, or law with one or more experts on the subject. This is the regular hangout for students and professors, many of whom have one eye on their books and newspapers and the other on each other. The space, with its floor-to-ceiling windows, orderly benches and chairs, marble-topped tables, and worn floor, is a good spot for reading, writing, and conversing.

Unicorn brews a respectable cup of locally roasted Casteel coffee, and sells a small selection of bagged and loose black, green, and flavored teas. The café serves particularly fine and very refreshing lemonade. The food, consisting of a limited menu of soups, sandwiches, and baked goods, is pretty good. Unicorn is a pleasant retreat for those looking for some relief from the malls of downtown Evanston. A street-side table offers a good view of the patrons scurrying in and out of the Starbucks and Dunkin' Donuts franchises across the street.

NOTABLE

Café Colao   *(Coffeehouse)*
Humboldt Park
2638 West Division Street
(773) 276-1780
$

Coffee culture has moved west with the addition of Café Colao to the slowly-but-surely gentrifying Humboldt Park neighborhood. This is the place to order a rich and earthy *cafe con leche*. Traditional Latin American baked goods and pastries are showcased on trays and in built-in glass cases lining one wall of this small and cozy café. Try the *quesita*, a pastry similar to an éclair, baked with lightly sweetened cream cheese filling.

Café Marianao
See Caribbean, p. 35.

Casteel Coffee   *(Coffee and Tea Retail Store)*
2924 Central Street
Evanston
(847) 424-9999
$

Established in 1993, Casteel roasts a wide variety of single-estate and blended coffees in small batches six days a week, and claims it usually sells its coffees within three days of roasting. It produces its decaf coffees by a chemical-free CO_2 process. Casteel also sells loose teas and gift baskets. It supplies a number of area coffeehouses and restaurants, and offers discounts and specials through its e-mail club. All coffees are certified kosher.

Coffee and Tea Exchange   *(Coffee and Tea Retail Store)*
Lakeview
3311 North Broadway
(773) 528-2241
$-$$

The Coffee and Tea Exchange, an institution in Chicago, has been roasting coffee since 1975 and sells it in bulk from barrels and sacks at its neighborhood retail store. TransFair USA officially certifies it as a fair-trade roaster, and several fair-trade offerings are usually available. A number of the coffees and teas are organic, and the shop also stocks flavored coffees and herbal teas, as well as a variety of spices.

Todd & Holland Tea Merchants   *(Tea Retail Store)*
7577 Lake Street
River Forest
(800) 747-8827
$$

Located in a lovingly converted home just west of downtown Oak Park, Todd & Holland is a purveyor of high-end teas and tea blends, including a few organic teas, all nicely packaged and displayed. They also carry a large assortment of tea-making accessories, including a selection of beautifully crafted teapots, cups, and mugs. The teapots alone make the trip worthwhile, but if you can't visit, they'll be happy to ship to you. Attractive gift packages are available.

DELIS

Alpine Food Shop
7538 West North Avenue
Elmwood Park
(708) 453-3505
$

At Alpine Food Shop the sandwich is king, and each one is king-size: Their sandwiches come in small, medium, and large, with the large topping out at a whopping eighteen inches. Eighteen wonderful inches, especially when it's the Alpine Sandwich, the quintessential Italian sub with capicola, prosciutto, mortadella, Genoa salami, shredded lettuce, and paper-thin tomatoes drenched in oil and vinegar.

Aside from the sandwiches everything else here is small. Alpine carries a small selection of olives and pasta salads, and has a small freezer with pasta sauce and dishes like lasagna and baked clams. To go with your sandwich there are the requisite "pop and chips," as we say in the Midwest. In the little room they have left at Alpine, shelves line the wall with imported Italian canned goods like tomatoes and artichoke hearts.

Chaim's Kosher Bakery
4956 Dempster Street
Skokie
(847) 675-1005
$

Chaim's Kosher Bakery is a requisite for anyone who keeps kosher in Chicago. Serving the large Jewish population on the North Shore, Chaim's has everything from kosher meats to frozen kosher meals. The deli counter boasts meat and cheese by the pound, freshly made sandwiches and salads, and hot entrées like barbecue short ribs, beef brisket, roasted chicken, knishes, and even a chop suey casserole. The freezer section has homemade chicken stock and matzo balls along with frozen hors d'oeuvres, entrées, and meats. Chaim's also has a bakery with frosted sugar cookies in every color, challah bread, bagels, and a display of specialty cakes for weddings, birthdays, and bar mitzvahs.

The fact that the store is unadorned and sometimes poorly organized is overshadowed by the largest selection of kosher foods this side of the Great Lakes.

Kaufman's Bagel and Delicatessen
4905 West Dempster Street
Skokie
(847) 677-9880
$

Kaufman's Bagel and Delicatessen is one of two delis found on Dempster Avenue in Skokie. The small, neat store is divided between deli area and bakery. As you enter, it's hard to decide where to go first. The deli counter has meats and cheeses by the pound, sizable sandwiches, and a variety of impeccable-looking smoked fish. Their prepared foods are an appetizing array of noodle kugel, beef brisket, knishes, and meatloaf, among others. Their freezer case carries an expansive selection of soups and entrées like chicken *paprikash* and boiled cabbage. The bakery at Kaufman's carries countless varieties of rye bread, in addition to inventive loaves such as onion-pumpernickel. Beyond the kaiser rolls and bagels are the delectable coffee cakes, strudels, danish, and *rugalach*.

Manny's Coffee Shop and Deli
South Loop
1141 South Jefferson Street
(312) 939-2855
$

There's no deli counter at Manny's Coffee Shop and Deli, but they do serve some of the best sandwiches in town. On any given afternoon you might bump into your alderman, your rabbi, your lawyer, your local weatherman, or even your favorite uncle. This no-frills Chicago institution may not look like much with its linoleum floors and stark fluorescent lighting, but it has been catering to the West Side for ages.

The busy cafeteria line serves up homemade hot dishes like spaghetti and meatballs, beef brisket, goulash, and oxtail stew (depending on what day of the week you visit). They pile high their hand-carved corned beef, roast beef, and pastrami, and serve them with their famous potato pancakes. If you like your roast beef sandwich rare get there early; it goes quickly, especially on Saturdays. Come in from the Chicago winter weather and enjoy Manny's Matzo Ball Soup, which will rival your bubbe's. In true cafeteria style, Manny's also has vanilla, chocolate, or rice pudding; brownies and cookies; and their famous caramel cake for dessert.

NOTABLE

Frances' Restaurant and Delicatessen
Lincoln Park
2552 North Clark Street
(773) 248-4580
$

After a long night of barhopping along Halsted Street or Lincoln Avenue, a popular hangover remedy on a Saturday or Sunday morning might be an omelet from Frances' Restaurant and Delicatessen. Or choose from their list of creative hot or cold sandwiches named after popular locations around Lincoln Park.

Gene's Sausage Shop and Deli
Craigin
5330 West Belmont Avenue
(312) 777-6322
$

Nearly everything at Gene's Sausage Shop and Deli is homemade. The shop is well known for its variety of European-style sausages. The small retail area sells imported European chocolates and other specialties.

Wikström's Delicatessen
Andersonville
5247 North Clark Street
(773) 275-6100
$$

Perhaps the nation's largest Scandinavian food shop, Wikström's Delicatessen has been operated by Ingvar and Alfhild Wikström for forty years. Wikström's homemade foods are recipes passed down from Ingvar's mother and his own creations. Ingvar is famous for his Swedish meatballs and his house-cured herring, which is now trademarked as Herr Ing's Herring. Big sellers are the freshly baked limpa bread, a grand selection of cheeses, Swedish brown beans, deli salads, and creamy almond rice pudding. Wikström's is known not only to the Scandinavian community, but to a large and multiethnic group of customers.

FAMILY-FRIENDLY DINING

Slow Food passionately believes that our children are our greatest asset in changing the present food system, outmoded and unsustainable, for the better. They have the right to the best in food quality, taste, nuturitional value, and safety. Through various educational avenues Slow Food encourages children to think about where their food comes from, how it is grown, and what it looks, tastes, smells, and feels like. While the best place for children to learn is at the family dinner table, there are some amazing opportunities within Chicago for children to learn—from a visit to a local farmers' market to various child-friendly restaurants located right in your own backyard.

The Green City Market, located in Lincoln Park, hosts the only organic/sustainable market in the city. Held on Wednesdays from mid-May through the end of October from 7:00 A.M. to 1:00 P.M., this market is a great resource for children. Tours of the market are available for groups. Check out www.chicagogreencitymarket.org for a schedule of events.

The City Farm is an urban organic farm right in the middle of the city on the corner of Division Street and Clybourn Avenue. Kristine Greiber recognizes the importance of teaching children while they are young (you'll probably see her son, Soren, running in the fields), and she welcomes visiting tours. The City Farm will be creating a class schedule for the Green City Sprouts starting in 2004.

Other institutions that have outstanding programs for children include the Museum of Science and Industry, Peggy Notebaert Museum, John Deere Children's Zoo at the Lincoln Park Zoo, Garfield Park Conservatory, and the Chicago Botanical Gardens.

Eating out is a great way for children to experience other foods. **The Lucky Platter** (514 North Main Street, Evanston; 847-869-4064) is a casual, fun restaurant and has the best sweet potato fries on the North Shore. Good sturdy booths keep the young ones contained. Everything prepared at The Lucky Platter is made from scratch. Fifteen side dishes on the menu make it easy to order a mix-and-match meal for your child, from homemade mashed potatoes, luscious macaroni and cheese, vegetable sides (seasonal), sweet potato French fries, black beans, brown rice, and more.

Czerwone Jablusko (Red Apple Restaurant) has the most remarkable Polish buffet. There are seven to ten cold salads, including carrot and raisin salad; beets with horseradish; and potato, egg, tuna, and chicken salads. You'll also find seventeen to twenty-five hot dishes, including chicken, roast beef, Polish sausage, beef stroganoff, and corned beef. The dessert buffet could be a meal in itself with blintzes, cakes, cookies, ice cream, and hot apple fritters. Buffets can be a very handy setup when you're dining with children, as you can sit and eat right away. (No waiting for a waiter, no waiting for the food!) Children's meals are discounted according to the age of the child.

Wolfgang Puck's Café has a pizza bar for children, where they learn to make their pizza with a chef to guide them. The pizza chef sprinkles flour in front of them and gives them a big hunk of dough. Kids learn how to knead the dough and form the crust; the chef then patches up any holes before they add sauce and ingredients. The handmade pizza is placed in a wood-burning oven and kids can watch the flames dance around their creations. From dough to finished pizza takes about forty-five minutes. The kids' pizza bar is just $5.95 and includes a drink and dessert.

Interactivity wins favor with kids these days, and **Flat Top Grill** scores big in that department. Though many kids are reluctant to eat veggies at home, they love the do-it-yourself stir-fry at this restaurant. The concept is that you go through the fresh buffet line, which is loaded with twenty-two vegetable choices, seventeen sauce selections, and a variety of protein options from tofu to chicken to seafood. Add sauce and starch from rice to noodles and then hand your selections over to the stir-fry chef. You'll get a number that you take to your seat, and in a couple of minutes your creation comes to your table. Children love to see the final result. The buffet is a real bonus because kids can walk around; they don't have to stay in their seats the whole time. An added bonus is that a family of four can eat out for about $40.

**Czerwone Jablusko
(Red Apple Restaurant)
Avondale**
3121 North Milwaukee Avenue
(773) 588-5781
$

Other Location
6474 North Milwaukee Avenue,
    Chicago (Norwood Park);
(773) 763-3407

**Flat Top Grill
Lakeview**
3200 North Southport Avenue
(773) 665-8100
$

Other Locations
1000 West Washington Street,
    Chicago (West Town);
(312) 829-4800
7007 Church Street, Evanston;
(847) 570-0100

The Lucky Platter
514 North Main Street
Evanston
(847) 869-4064
$

Wolfgang Puck's Café
1701 Maple Avenue
Evanston
(847) 869-9653
$

FRENCH FRIES

As the deep-fried ubiquitous side accompanying many dishes, French fries are often overshadowed by whatever they sit next to. Yet some fries are good enough to stand on their own. The best fries are innately satisfying and make for the perfect comfort food. Here's a top-ten list (in alphabetical order) of places in the Greater Chicago area where French fries reign supreme.

Al's #1 Italian Beef
Little Italy
1079 West Taylor Street
(312) 226-4017

Al's opened in Little Italy back in 1938 and they make a mean Italian beef, but most regulars are equally fanatical about their fries. In fact, several loyalists implied that our list would be a sham if we failed to include Al's. Truth be told, Al's fries are killer: hand-cut, skin-on, and frankly a little too easy to gobble down. Remember to think S-l-o-w. For added zing, try mixing in some of their homemade *giardiniera*.

Athenian Room
Lincoln Park
807 West Webster Avenue
(773) 348-5155

This family-owned *taverna* has been around since 1972, serving their own brand of Greek-American hybrid specialties. Their fries have a fiercely loyal following because nothing else tastes quite like them: crispy plank fries smothered in a bath of olive oil, lemon, and red wine vinegar and topped with oregano, salt, and pepper. Their dense texture and piquant flavor leave a lasting impression.

Demon Dogs
Lincoln Park
944 West Fullerton Parkway
(773) 281-2001

A classic Chicago hot dog stand serving the masses under the Fullerton El. Demon Dogs is famous for its Vienna Beef hot dogs and fresh-cut, skin-on fries. Turnover is high, rendering the fries consistently fresh, hot, and crispy. They're served perfectly oversalted and overstuffed in brown paper bags. Watch as the bags turn magically transparent while absorbing the oil!

Gene and Jude's
2720 North River Road
River Grove
(708) 452-7634

This small family business has been around since 1952 and operates under the belief that you should do three things and do them well. Their particular three happen to be French fries, hot dogs, and tamales—the only items on their menu. It's a small operation, and the line is usually out the door. As you order you can see the fries being methodically cut and thrown into the deep fryer. They're generously salted, crispy, and golden brown on the outside with the perfect amount of tenderness inside.

Hopleaf Bar
Andersonville
5148 North Clark Street
(773) 334-9851

It is unofficially believed that fries (or *pommes frites*) are the national dish of Belgium. At Hopleaf, a casual European-style pub in Andersonville, they celebrate this concept with a Belgian-inspired menu and some two hundred Belgian brews. Treat yourself to some high-minded chat over a plate of *frites* and a complex, almost winelike, lambic ale. Hopleaf's fries are authentically prepared: blanched and doubly fried at both low and high temperatures, which turns them into crispy Flemish masterpieces. They are served with garlicky *aioli* and ketchup on the side.

mk
River North
868 North Franklin Street
(312) 482-9179

Slender and crispy, these *pommes frites* are served elegantly upright in a paper cone and accompanied by white truffle *aioli* for dipping. mk is an upscale restaurant, but simply ordering a cocktail and a side of fries at their lounge would perk up anyone's happy hour.

Parky's
329 North Harlem Avenue
Forest Park
(708) 366-3090

Parky's is a hot dog stand operating from an odd Brady Bunch–era orange frame-and-glass protuberance attached to a frame house on Harlem Avenue. Don't go there for the hot dogs, which are limp and unsatisfying. The fries are what really shine here. Hand-cut and fried to perfection—crispy on the outside, moist and with a hint of sweetness at their heart—they are served up in a brown paper bag speckled with grease spots. At first glance, a bagful seems too much for one person to polish off alone, but just try to stop eating them.

Superdawg
Norwood Park
6363 North Milwaukee Avenue
(773) 763-0660

Is it possible to experience true convivial pleasure in your car? You bet it is. At Superdawg, the last authentic drive-in in the city, the food tastes as good as the nostalgia feels. Since 1948 their fries have been originals: chubby, crinkle cut, crispy, and cooked to order. But once here, you might as well shoot for the classic triumvirate: cheeseburger, fries, and a milk shake (made with real ice cream—what a concept!). Superdawg is a feel-good place if there ever was one.

Twisted Spoke
West Town
501 North Ogden Avenue
(312) 666-1500

The Twisted Spoke may seem intimidating, with its metal facade and hard-core biker theme, but their menu soon reveals a softer side. In bold print it proclaims, "Each order receives the personal attention your mom would give a meal being prepared in her kitchen." That just-like-mom-used-to-make ideology sure shows in the quality of their French fries. No shortcuts here: Spuds are blanched a day in advance, chilled overnight, and then fried to order. One serving is a huge pile of potato perfection. They're about as meaty and satisfying as a fry can get. Up the ante by adding a cheese, chili, or sloppy joe topper.

The Wiener's Circle
Lincoln Park
2622 North Clark Street
(773) 477-7444

Your need for a late-night, postdrinking binge wouldn't be sated without a visit to The Wiener's Circle. But be forewarned: After midnight the place becomes a carnival of crass behavior. Prepare to be mocked and ridiculed as you place your order: The staff has a reputation for abusing the patrons. It's all part of their schtick, and anyway, you've come for the cheese fries. They are the stuff of legend: ooey, gooey, rich, and chewy. Just remember to take your abuse like you take your fries—with a grain of salt.

HAMBURGERS

Billy Goat Tavern
River North
430 North Michigan Avenue
(312) 222-1525
Open Sunday–Friday until 2:00 A.M., Saturday until 3:00 A.M.
$

People either love or hate the Billy Goat. The tavern was made famous as the inspiration for a John Belushi *Saturday Night Live* skit in the 1970s, because of how the cook said "Cheezborgor!" Though it has several locations now, the one really worth visiting is the original, beneath Michigan Avenue. Stop in to the dimly lit refuge from the Magnificent Mile for a drink and a burger, and soak up some of Chicago's history in newsprint; the walls are plastered with articles, many of which were written by long-time columnist Mike Royko, a former regular. The bar's special is the $4 Horny Goat, a strong blend of Bacardi Limon, 7-Up, and cranberry juice.

Try to order anything but a burger and you will be yelled at: "Cheezborgor! Cheezborgor!" If you order a single, you'll be pressured to make it a double- or triple-stacked burger. And don't bother asking for French fries; you'll be growled at, "No fries—chips!" Ordering here is not for the timid.

The requested patty is served plain on a kaiser roll wrapped in wax paper; you add your own toppings at the station just past the register. Two kinds of onions (chopped and ringed), pickles, and tomatoes are available, as well as ketchup, mustard, and mayo. The burgers themselves are thin and greasy, and the only cheese provided is American, but there's something about them that tastes better than it sounds. Perhaps it's the atmosphere, how very Chicago the underground (beneath the Tribune Building) Billy Goat feels, or the colorful company you may find yourself sharing a table or a piece of bar counter with.

If you're familiar with Cubs baseball history, you already know that the original owner of the restaurant, William Sianis, placed a curse on the team after its management stopped allowing Sianis to bring his pet billy goat (who always had his own ticket) to games. Things haven't changed much since Sianis's day: the Cubs still haven't won the World Series, and Sianis's nephew Sam now runs the place, which can be summed up by its slogan, "Butt in anytime."

Jury's
Lincoln Square
4337 North Lincoln Avenue
(773) 935-2255
$$

Given all the anxiety these days about eating rare meat (something that is fueled more by the failures of our mass food production and distribution system than any objective health concerns), Jury's strikes a blow for food freedom. Your server will ask you exactly how you want your burger cooked. If you ask for it rare, then you'll get a burger that is old-school rare.

Jury's has been around for almost twenty-five years, not always in the same neighborhood, but always a fixture on one stretch of Lincoln Avenue or another. It describes itself as a "classy neighborhood restaurant and bar," which it is, and more. They have a full and ambitious menu of sandwiches, pastas, seafood, pork or lamb chops, and at least three selections of USDA Choice steaks. But its reputation and longevity rest on that succulent burger, deservedly voted the best in Chicago in many a poll.

For what is essentially just a corner bar, Jury's also has a remarkable wine list, with more than a hundred bottles inventoried. Ever-smiling owner Pete Borkman prides himself on featuring vineyards from all over the world, with emphasis on wines he thinks provide outstanding character at great value.

Kevin's Hamburger Heaven
Bridgeport
554 West Pershing Road
(773) 924-5771
Open 24 hours
$

Situated in a run-down strip in the South Side Bridgeport neighborhood, between an Italian beef stand and another all-night diner, and across the street from a factory, Kevin's is a good place to get a cheap burger at any hour of the day or night. Be forewarned: You *will* mingle with the other patrons; the biggest booths seat two people, and most of the seating is counter space. However, the conversation here can be lively and great, if a bit surreal. Coffee is served in Styrofoam cups by a waitress who's been working here too long, and at night this twenty-four-hour diner uses a metal detector and requires you to pay before you eat. Even so, it's worth the trek for a simple but good burger.

Not much attention is paid to how the burgers are shaped; the cook barely forms them before throwing them on the griddle, but that adds to the texture: the edges of the burger are rough, just like the dining environment. While they're cooking, a lid is placed over the burgers so that they steam as well as fry. The menu says they're seasoned, and a tub of Lawry's seasoned salt near the grill gives away the secret ingredient. Customers are not asked how they want the burger cooked; everything here is medium.

The burger's juices seep out from the rough edges into the bun: This is pure greasy goodness. Plenty of pickles are served on the side, and mayo comes standard. If you order grilled onions they're skinny and plentiful, as are the fries. Malts and pies are reputed to be quite tasty as well, and the breakfasts are standard.

Note: There is another **Kevin's Hamburger Heaven** at 35th and Ashland, though a sign at the one on Pershing notifies customers that they are no longer associated.

L.T.'s Grill
Wicker Park
1800 North Wood Street
(312) 997-2400
Open for lunch Monday–Friday, for dinner Wednesday–Saturday,
    closed Sunday
$$

Recently opened in the space previously occupied by Munch, L.T.'s Grill serves one of the better burgers Chicago has to offer. The restaurant focuses on Southern cooking, offering dishes like catfish, jerk chicken, barbecue, and corn bread. Its environment is warm, with Southwestern decor and a stool-seated counter that creates an inviting place to pull up for a quick cup of locally roasted Intelligentsia coffee.

The Black Angus burger, well formed and weighing in at a whopping half pound (and an equally impressive $6 or $7), is what makes L.T.'s a destination. Like most of the other sandwiches offered, the burger can and should be ordered with Cajun spice. More of a light seasoning than a heavy heat-inducer, the Cajun spice option adds depth to the burger without overpowering or overshadowing the quality of the beef. The cook isn't afraid to let the flavor of the beef through; if you ask for a burger prepared rare, you'll get it.

If it's a cheeseburger you're in the mood for, L.T.'s offers five options: Havarti, mozzarella, blue, cheddar, and American. Bacon, sautéed mushrooms, and grilled onions are all offered as additional toppings, while lettuce, tomato, raw onion, and a crispy pickle spear are included. Staying true to the Southern style of the place, several choices of hot sauce are available on the table, but the traditional Chicago burger topping of mayonnaise is nowhere to be found. Dijon and yellow mustard are also provided on the side.

With the burger comes a choice of either spuds (home-style seasoned potatoes), potato salad, a Caesar salad, or a salad of mixed greens. The sweet balsamic vinaigrette dressing is a recommended accompaniment to this last salad, with chunks of fresh basil lurking in its depths.

The hours for L.T.'s Grill are not what might be expected, so call first to make sure it'll be open. Though it's not on any of Chicago's blossoming Restaurant Rows, L.T.'s Grill is worth the trip.

Pete Miller's
1557 Sherman Avenue
Evanston
(847) 328-0399
Open Monday–Thursday 4:30 P.M.–1:00 A.M., Friday–Sunday
  4:30 P.M.–3:00 A.M.
$$$

A decade-old Evanston steak house that opened another location in Wheeling, Pete Miller's offers steaks and jazz that Chicago is known for, as well as some pretty good seafood. Named for Harold "Pete" Miller, a former Marine who appreciated a quality steak, the restaurant cultivates its atmosphere as much as it does its aged steaks: port, billiards, live jazz, and cigars are all in steady rotation every night of the week. When it first opened, Pete Miller's upscale pricing seemed a bit out of place in downtown Evanston. But with the growth and redevelopment that the suburb has seen over the last five years or so, it fits in nicely. The clientele ranges from Northwestern University students seeking a good glass of wine to power diners and jazz aficionados.

While the steaks are worth trying, especially the bone-in fillet, the burgers here are excellent. Made with lightly seasoned prime beef by a chef who's not afraid to cook them rare, Pete Miller's burgers are consistently rated among Chicago's best. The burger is one of the more moderately priced items on the menu, and used to be a top seller when the restaurant was open for lunch. Each burger comes with a side of the vegetable of the day, which can be hit or miss, coleslaw, a pickle, and choice of potato: the fabulously strong garlic mashed potatoes, roasted rosemary red potatoes, or steak fries. If it's cheese you want on a burger, Pete Miller's offers a wide range, including provolone, Swiss, cheddar, American, and blue.

Other Location
412 North Milwaukee Avenue, Wheeling; (847) 243-3700

Twisted Spoke
West Town
501 North Ogden Avenue
(312) 666-1500
Open Sunday–Friday until 2:00 A.M., Saturday until 3:00 A.M.
$$

Twisted Spoke is a biker-themed diner, though a bit gimmicky and clean to feel like a real biker bar. Its crowd is an eclectic mix of yuppies, cops, neighborhood residents, and even a few bikers. The menu for their infamous Saturday-night Smut and Eggs, where patrons feast on strong coffee and big breakfasts while watching adult films, is also available, without the porn, on Saturday and Sunday mornings. A second location recently opened in Lakeview.

At Twisted Spoke, the Fat Boy Burger ($7.75) is described as a half pound of "heaven-sent bovinity." Reach for the extra napkins next to the beer-bottle salt and pepper shakers: It's a juicy burger, even when ordered well-done. This isn't the place to go if you want it rare, because they won't let it keep much pink, but it's still flavorful and retains juice. The meat's seasoning is present but mild; bacon adds a nice dimension of flavor. Other additional toppings include grilled onions (and lots of them), barbecue sauce (which is more tangy than smoky), Swiss cheese, and white cheddar. An interesting touch is that Twisted Spoke cuts their lettuce into a square, thus eliminating any extra lettuce spilling out over the burger's sides. The traditional bun is a thick, garlic-toasted egg bun, though rye is also available. If you're feeling famished the Double Fatty ($9.95) will provide you with a double burger, totaling a whole pound of meat, though there is a charge for sharing the burger. The fries are slightly sweet and plentiful.

A rooftop seating area is available in the warmer months, and counter seating at the bar is available year-round. Mixed drinks are served in pint glasses, and the bourbon selection is better than most restaurants in this price range; they even have Jim Beam on tap. Street parking is easy to come by, as the neighborhood hasn't been too developed yet.

NOTABLE

Athenian Room
See Greek, p. 77.

Burger Baron
West Town
1381 West Grand Avenue
(312) 733-3285
$

This brightly lit, yellow-hued burger joint has an expansive menu with an inclusive sandwich list. Everything from a patty melt to a Philly cheese-steak, gyros, Reubens, fillet of fish, grilled chicken, tuna steak sandwich, and even veggie burgers are offered here. Though the atmosphere is fast-food and the booths aren't very comfortable, everything is cooked to order and attention is paid to detail. The place has a blue-collar feel to it, and sells bottles of domestic beer to wash down the grease.

Burgers can be ordered by the quarter or half pound and are slow-cooked over a fire until they are done as requested, from medium-rare to well-done. The meat itself is a bit salty, but mostly unaccompanied by any seasoning. "Everything" encompasses lettuce, tomato, onion, and pickle, which are placed beneath the burger, not on top of it, and the bun is toasted. Available variations include freshly grilled mushrooms, bacon, and chiles.

Earwax Café
See Vegetarian, p. 181.

Top Notch Beefburger
Beverly
2116 West 95th Street
(773) 445-7218
Closed Sunday
$

Located in the South Side neighborhood of Beverly, Top Notch has been around since 1942, with the Soulian family serving up fresh burgers that haven't changed much since the restaurant's opening. The place has a standard grill feel to it, but it's the burgers that keep patrons coming back.

Available in basic, deluxe, and king-size versions, the burgers are prepared on the spot from fresh-ground round steak. The burgers are available in quarter-pound, half-pound, and three-quarter-pound sizes, the base model being "basic." Making a burger deluxe adds lettuce, tomato,

mayo, pickles, and "pre–World War II–style" fries. If you want cheese on that, your choices are American, Swiss, Monterey Jack, jalapeño Jack, and mozzarella, generously piled on.

Top Notch also offers three specialty king-size (half-pound) burgers. The Western Burger includes bacon and cheese, while the Mexican offers guacamole and cheese to the mix. The Italian Burger is a twist on a pizza burger, adding marinara and cheese. Turkey burgers are nicely seasoned, and chicken and fish sandwiches are also available.

HOT DOGS

The Chicago hot dog ranks right up there with Italian beef and deep-dish pizza as one of the city's trademark foods. What makes it different from hot dogs anywhere else in the country? Well, for one thing, there is the sheer pedigree of the Chicago dog, which was introduced by two young immigrants from Austria-Hungary at the 1893 Chicago World's Fair and Columbian Exposition. Today, the Vienna Beef Company (see "Made in Chicago," p. 326) still produces the classic natural-casing hot dogs that the city is known for, though unfortunately its future is anything but certain. (If there isn't one already, there needs to be a "Save Vienna Beef" movement.)

Vienna dogs give that satisfying *snap* when you bite into them. The majority of people probably prefer steamed dogs, but char-grilling has its adherents as well; some hot dog stands even offer a choice of cooking method.

The classic Chicago dog is served on a steamed poppy-seed bun, typically one from the S. Rosen bakery. The trick is warming the bun but not making it waterlogged; you need a pretty substantial bun to hold all of "the works" that accompany a piled-high Chicago dog.

Another crucial point: no self-respecting Chicagoan would think of using ketchup as a condiment (save it for your meatloaf sandwich!). And hold the sauerkraut, too, unless you're having a Polish sausage, which is a very different thing.

There are seven traditional, almost mystical, toppings appropriate for the Chicago hot dog: yellow mustard, emerald green relish, freshly chopped onion, fresh tomato slices, "sport" peppers (small, green, and mildly hot), a pickle spear, and celery salt (which adds a lot, and is a dash of sheer inspiration). When you ask for one of these beauties, don't ask for "the works" but, as they say in Chicago, "Run it through the garden!"

Finally, the Chicago hot dog is almost naked without a side order of French fries, and many of the hot dog places below make killer ones (see also "French Fries," p. 227). Whether you prefer simply a sprinkling of salt or celery salt on your hand-cut fries or an order of cheese fries, Chicago's hot dog shacks are among the best places in the city to get them.

What follows is a list of some of the top hot dog venues in the city and surrounding suburbs.

Byron's Hot Dog Haus
Wrigleyville
1017 West Irving Park Road
(773) 281-7474

At Byron's the hot dogs have a whole salad on top. With a large selection of toppings, including several kinds of peppers, and original concoctions

as well as the standards, Byron's hot dogs will satisfy anyone with a craving for good fast food. Portions are generous, while prices are low.

Other Locations
680 North Halsted Street, Chicago (River North);
   (312) 738-0968
1701 West Lawrence Street, Chicago (Ravenswood);
   (773) 271-0900

Fluky's
West Rogers Park
6821 North Western Avenue
(773) 274-3652

A venerable hot dog stand that rates highly with its loyal clientele. You'll get the full Chicago experience here: poppy-seed bun, Vienna Beef natural-casing hot dog, and the seven classic condiments.

Gene and Jude's
2720 North River Road
River Grove
(708) 452-7634

True to tradition, you won't find ketchup among the condiments at Gene and Jude's, nor are there poppy seeds on the buns. What you will find are steamed buns, Idaho potatoes that are fresh cut just before they are fried, and skinny Vienna Beef hot dogs with a good snap. Your only choices for dogs will be single or double. Order a double; it's worth it.

Gold Coast Dogs
River North
159 North Wabash Avenue
(312) 917-1677

In this unassuming space shared with a Church's Fried Chicken (Slow Food meets fast food), belly up to the counter and get ready to enjoy a legendary Chicago hot dog. Served freshly char-grilled or steamed, these classic franks provide the juicy, succulent trademark "snap" that hot dog lovers look for. For an added treat, order one of Gold Coast's thick and delicious milkshakes to wash down your dog.

Janson's/Snyder's Red Hots
Beverly
9900 South Western Avenue
(773) 238-3612

A Southwest Side institution. Be sure to check out the chili dogs at this classic drive-in.

Little Louie's
1342 North Shermer
Northbrook
(847) 498-1033

Don't even think of asking for ketchup on your hot dog here, or you just might get kicked out. But this is a great place to get a classic Vienna Beef hot dog and an order of fresh-cut fries.

Poochie's
3832 Dempster Street
Skokie
(847) 673-0100

Poochie's serves its char-grilled or steamed hot dogs to a worshipful, almost cultlike following.

Portillo's Hot Dogs
River North
100 West Ontario Street
(312) 587-8910

Dick Portillo opened The Dog House in a trailer back in 1963, and from those humble beginnings Portillo's has grown into a big, successful business, with twenty-seven locations throughout the city and $160 million in annual sales.

While purists might scoff at the chain-restaurant feel, the dogs are still awfully good here. Recently Portillo's canceled their contract with local Vienna Beef, which set dedicated local foodies to grumbling.

Superdawg Drive-In
Norwood Park
6363 North Milwaukee Avenue
(773) 763-0660

A colorful neighborhood favorite, Superdawg is a throwback to the 1950s, when carhops actually brought your dogs and shakes out to the car. No regular-size dogs here—just Superdawgs, big and loaded with all the trimmings, including pickled tomatoes and brilliant emerald green relish. Other specialties include shakes, malts, the root beer floats known locally as "black cows" or "brown cows," and onion chips—small pieces of onion fried like rings.

Vienna Beef Factory Store & Deli
Lincoln Park
2501 North Damen Avenue
(773) 235-6652
Open 9:00 A.M.–4:30 P.M. weekdays, Saturday 9:00 A.M.–1:00 P.M.,
    closed Sunday

In Chicago, Vienna Beef is the gold standard against which all other hot dogs are weighed. In fact, many of the best hot dog stands in town proudly feature the Vienna Beef logo on their menu signs. The dogs don't get any fresher than at this cafeteria on the site of the factory which churns out the cured meats that carry the revered Vienna Beef label—hot dogs, Polishes, corned beef, pastrami, Italian beef, and salami. You can enjoy a filling meal side by side with factory workers on break. Everything from hot dogs to chicken noodle soup to jumbo chocolate chip cookies is served over the counter for lunch or by the pound for take-out. Hot dogs are served boiled, just like at the ballpark.

The Wiener's Circle
Lincoln Park
2622 North Clark Street
(773) 477-7444

For great char-grilled hot dogs, lots of attitude, and a crazy late-night scene, The Wiener's Circle is the hands-down winner. If you show up after 2:00 A.M., be prepared for lots of, um, colorful language that is routinely tossed around by the staff. The Wiener's Circle also has terrific cheese fries (fresh cut and skin on).

ITALIAN BEEF

Chicago is Italian beef country, complete with its own language. Whether you like it juicy or dry, with or without peppers, sweet or hot, Italian beef sandwiches rank right up there with pan pizza as a critical dish in this town's food history. As the *Encyclopedia of American Food and Drink* describes, an Italian beef stand is "an inexpensive restaurant or street-side stand selling sliced beef in a spicy gravy." The reference book goes on to say that Chicago is the epicenter of this Midwest sandwich phenomenon. Oddly, the name *Italian* merely refers to "some vague idea of how Italians would serve their beef"—highly seasoned, that is, though no such dish actually exists in Italy. But Italy's loss is Chicago's gain, as evidenced by the plethora of travel-worthy Italian beef shops located throughout the city and suburbs.

Order a "combo" and you'll receive a hoagie-size piece of crusty Italian bread stuffed with thinly sliced beef, fennel-rich Italian sausage, and sautéed sweet bell peppers, or spicy hot pepper and oil *giardiniera*, soaked with salty, savory juice.

Al's #1 Italian Beef
Little Italy
1079 West Taylor Street
(312) 226-4017
River North
169 West Ontario Street
(312) 943-3222

Al Ferreri, along with his sister Frances Pacelli and brother-in-law Chris Pacelli, founded the humble Al's Beef in 1938. Today some call it number one, while others give mixed reviews on quality and value since the franchise rights were sold several years ago. But you can't knock the delicious, very thinly sliced, and uniquely seasoned homemade beef. Sit outside the Ontario Street location and enjoy some late-night people watching. For a less touristy locale, try Taylor Street and check out the Little Italy neighborhood. Want it juicy? Order it "dipped."

Buona Beef
6745 West Roosevelt Road
Berwyn
(708) 749-2555

The name says it all—Buona Beef is good beef. Founded in 1980 by Joe Buonavolanto and his sons, Buona Beef has grown to more than ten locations in the city and suburbs, including a vibrant catering operation and the Joey Buona Pizzeria Grille located at 162 East Superior Street in downtown Chicago. Some argue that the expansion has stripped the chainlike locations of some charm and quality, but the original Berwyn location still offers a good dose of down-home Chicago personality and a nicely garlicky beef sandwich, plus great hot dogs, burgers, sausage, steak sandwiches, and salads, in addition to the signature beef.

Other Locations
Buona Beef has more than ten other locations in the Chicago suburbs.

Carm's Beef & Italian Ice
Little Italy
1057 West Polk Street
(312) 738-1046

This true Little Italy beef shop has stood the test of time; it's been in business since 1926, when it began as part of Fontano Foods grocery (now located across the street). It was in the mid-1960s that Carm's separated from Fontano's and started focusing on serving the perfect Italian beef. The crowd is a great mix of old and new: longtime residents, new locals, and students from the nearby University of Illinois. While the beef may not be up to the standard of others, knowledgeable fans flock from April through September for the real, homemade Italian ice.

Johnnie's Beef
7500 West North Avenue
Elmwood Park
(708) 452-6000

If you want the real deal, Johnnie's is the place, gold-chained Italian staff and all. The North Avenue location west of Harlem has all the character, but you can still get the to-die-for beef sandwiches and Italian ice at the newer, neon-signed location in northwest suburban Arlington Heights. The Combo with beef and sausage is a favorite, as are the pepper-and-egg sandwiches, especially on Friday nights during Lent, when Catholics abstain from eating meat. Don't leave without a piled-high cup of Italian ice (or lemonade, as it's called). The creamy yet icy consistency is nothing short of a culinary miracle. Just don't try keeping it in your home freezer—it's never the same as it is fresh.

Other Location
1935 South Arlington Heights Road, Arlington Heights; (847) 357-8100

Max's Italian Beef
Rosehill
5754 North Western Avenue
(773) 989-8200

Chicago foodies in the know rave about Max's excellent beef, tasty *giardiniera*, and French fries (try them with chili). You can even get an order of the nearly impossible-to-find "broasted" chicken. A few tables are available for dining in, plus there's a room-wrapping counter for the diehards who believe the beef tastes better when you're standing up.

Mr. Beef
River North
666 North Orleans Street
(312) 337-8500

Comedian and talk-show host Jay Leno made this cozy beef joint famous when he named it his favorite place to eat in Chicago. Don't expect seats; buy your beef to go or stand and eat at the counters that wrap around the room. Standing makes it easier to maneuver the pleasantly soggy, juicy beef. And as if Leno's praise wasn't enough to draw a crowd, Mr. Beef was featured a few years back in an ad campaign for the Chevy Cavalier. You can even meet the guy from the commercial, Jerry Pontarelli, behind the counter.

Portillo's Hot Dogs
River North
100 West Ontario Street
(312) 587-8910

Founded by Dick Portillo in 1963 in a small trailer with no running water, this chain now boasts five different restaurant concepts with forty-plus units. And although the thoughtfully designed, manicured units don't feel very "old Chicago," Portillo's still manages to turn out quality beef with great grilled sweet peppers and tangy "sport" peppers for added heat. Want a modern spin? Try the pleasantly messy beef-and-cheese croissant with real melted cheddar. Plus you can get a great Chicago-style hot dog or grilled Polish sausage while you're at it. The service here gives new meaning to the term "sense of urgency"; uniformed staff actually walk the drive-up line to speed things along during the lunch rush.

Other Locations
Portillo's has more than twenty other locations in the Chicago suburbs.

LATE-NIGHT DINING

Like many great cities, Chicago has a plethora of late-night dining options all over town. Whether you are craving Chicago-style deep-dish pizza or a classic Chicago hot dog, you can get it in the wee hours of the morning. The listing below is just a smattering of the choices available to you, which range from Hopperesque diners to slick martini lounges with pulsing beats and sophisticated food.

The Diner Grill
North Center
1635 West Irving Park Road
(773) 248-2030
Open 24 hours
$

A late-night classic on the North Side, The Diner is an original streetcar diner built in 1934. You've got to try the Slinger: two cheeseburger patties with chile and eggs. Hey, it was good enough to merit a mention in *Food & Wine*, so don't knock it until you try it. Ask if you can watch the video full of patrons in various states of sobriety and/or insanity on the small television. Full of regulars (and irregulars), The Diner should be your last stop after closing time at the many neighborhood bars.

Iggy's
Wicker Park/Bucktown
1840 West North Avenue
(312) 829-4449
Open Monday–Friday 7:00 P.M.–4:00 A.M., Saturday 7:00 P.M.–
    5:00 A.M., Sunday 8:00 P.M.–2:00 A.M.
$$

A hip lounge/restaurant, Iggy's is for those who would rather have something besides a late-night burger or burrito. An upscale menu and lethal martinis bring a boisterous crowd at all hours. A great outdoor courtyard is available for the few short months when it is tolerable to eat outside in Chicago. And no, there is no Iggy; please don't ask the staff if there is.

Korean Restaurant
Ravenswood
2659 West Lawrence Avenue
(773) 878-2095
Open 24 hours
$

At the unimaginatively named Korean Restaurant, no matter what the day or hour you can satisfy your *kimchi* craving. You also get a plethora of

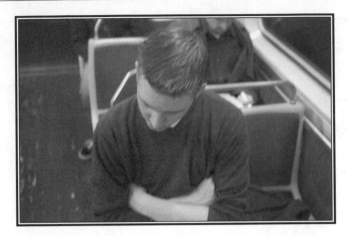

panchan, or small plates including the aforementioned *kimchi*. This is a great place to bring a group of people late at night.

La Pasadita
Noble Square
1140 North Ashland Avenue
(773) 384-6537
Open 9:30 A.M.–1:30 A.M.
$

THE BEST TACOS IN TOWN says the sign outside La Pasadita, and it's hard to argue based on price and flavor. No sour cream, lettuce, tomato, or other filler. Choose your meat and you get a taco that is all killer, no filler, with optional cilantro, cheese, and chopped onion. The fiery green tableside salsa is the perfect complement. Part of a mini-empire, there are no fewer than *three* La Pasaditas within one block on Ashland just south of Division (see full entry in Mexican, p. 131).

Zaiqa
River North
858 North Orleans Street
(312) 280-1652
Open 24 hours
$

Zaiqa translates to "taste" and is frequented mainly by Indian and Pakistani cab drivers; the lot is full of parked taxis. The room is thick with smoke, atmosphere, and lively conversation. I had to employ the "point" method to order my food, and ended up with some tasty chicken, flatbread, and a mountain of rice for a pittance. Located practically in Cabrini Green, the infamous Chicago housing project, gentrification and condos, condos, condos are changing the demographics of this neighborhood.

PIZZA

What is Chicago-style pizza? We have four competing pizza styles in Chicago: deep dish (which is thick-crusted and often requires a knife and fork), stuffed (which is similar to a pie with two layers of crust), Italian-style thin-crust, and wood-oven thin-crust pizza, a newcomer on the scene. But the overwhelming favorite and the type most recognized as Chicago style is definitely the deep-dish pizza.

Deep-dish pizza is to Chicago what Cajun food is to New Orleans. There are more than two thousand pizzerias in Chicago, most of them serving deep-dish and many of them offshoots of the original Pizzeria Uno, where back in 1943 Ike Sewell and Riz Ricardo invented the Chicago-style deep-dish pizza.

Deep-dish pizza is usually eaten with a knife and fork rather than the hands because it is so thick and heavy. In preparation, the dough is raised high on the sides of seasoned deep-dish pans. Cheese is placed directly on top of the dough, and toppings are then added. Next is more cheese, followed by a chunky tomato sauce and a light sprinkling of grated Parmesan.

Since deep-dish pizza is so dense, it takes much longer to bake than a typical thin-crust pizza, which might be in and out of a red-hot pizza oven in minutes. Be prepared to wait at least thirty-five to forty-five minutes for a classic deep-dish pie. For the authentic stuff, the anticipation is all part of the experience.

In 1974 Rocco Palese of Nancy's further refined the deep-dish style by introducing the stuffed pizza. This adds a second thin layer of dough above the cheese and below the other toppings, creating a somewhat firmer pie that is capable of holding even more cheese.

Thin-crust pizza still has a loyal, albeit small, following in certain neighborhoods. In addition to Italian-style thin-crust, lately we have seen the emergence of several new establishments that bake their pizzas in wood-burning ovens.

DEEP-DISH PIZZA

The Art of Pizza
Lakeview
3033 North Ashland Avenue
(773) 327-5600
$

This pizzeria won the *Chicago Tribune* prize for best spinach-mushroom pan pizza. It has a great flavorful crust, fresh ingredients, and winning taste. The dining area is limited, so take-out might be preferred.

Lou Malnati's
Lincoln Park
958 West Wrightwood Avenue
(773) 832-4030
$

Malnati's serves classic Chicago-style deep-dish pizza. A growing favorite is the butter-crust sausage, served in their very comfortable dining room. Take-out and delivery are also available.

Old World Pizza
7230 West North Avenue
Elmwood Park
(708) 456-3000
$$

When it comes to deep-dish pizza, Old World Pizza is the deepest of the deep. In some respects it is very similar to stuffed pizza without the second crust. This pizza has won several awards because of its zesty tomato sauce, tasty and wonderfully textured crust, and its delicious fennel-flavored sausage. It is also the best value for deep-dish in the Chicago area, and has a friendly staff. Take-out and delivery are popular, as the dining area is very comfortable but small, and does not have a liquor license.

Pequods
Lincoln Park
2207 North Clybourn Avenue
(773) 327-1512
$

The specialty at Pequods is caramelized cheese deep-dish pizza. Try the fennel-scented sausage and mushroom pie—it's terrific. The dining room has a lively bar and a friendly atmosphere, frequented by people of all ages.

Pizzeria Due
River North
619 North Wabash Avenue
(312) 943-2400
$

All things considered, this is the all-around favorite spot for deep-dish pizza in Chicago. Pizzeria Due, which originally opened to accommodate the overflow crowds from its sister restaurant, Pizzeria Uno, has certainly come into its own. The deep-dish pies are extraordinary, with excellent crust, sausage, and fresh tomato toppings. You order as you enter, before being seated, because a specialty deep-dish pizza takes about forty-five minutes to cook. For a full meal it would be wise to plan on only two or three slices of the thick and cheesy Chicago-style pie. Unless you're really hungry, skip the salad or appetizer and postpone dessert (probably to another day).

Due attracts a loyal following of Chicagoans taking a lunch break from shopping on Michigan Avenue, local professionals, hotel patrons, and conventioneers. It also draws media and sports celebrities. Dining here is truly an enjoyable experience. Crowded, lively, and touristy, this pizzeria is a must-visit destination when you're visiting Chicago.

Pizzeria Uno
River North
29 East Ohio Street
(312) 321-1000
$

The original restaurant where the deep-dish pizza was born back in 1943, Pizzeria Uno is a historic place and still thriving. Uno's dining room exudes old-fashioned charm, with a vintage bar and paneled walls. It is smaller than its sister restaurant, Pizzeria Due, and not as lavish, but Uno serves the same great pizza.

STUFFED PIZZA

Bacino's
Lincoln Park
2204 North Lincoln Avenue
(773) 472-7400
$

The heart-healthy special made with delicately flavored spinach and low-fat mozzarella is the favorite here. If you're dining alone try the unique low-cost Bambino individual-size pizza. The dining room is very accommodating, but if you are in a hurry take advantage of their speedy delivery service.

Other Locations
75 East Wacker Drive, Chicago (Loop); (312) 263-0070
118 South Clinton Street, Chicago (South Loop); (312) 876-1188
1001 West Belmont Avenue, Chicago (Lakeview); (773) 404-0111

Edwardo's Natural Pizza
South Loop
521 South Dearborn Street
(312) 939-3366
$

Don't let the "natural" fool you—this is great stuffed pizza. Look for a thick, dense cheese filling packed with your favorite toppings and stuffed between two thin crusts. Edwardo's also offers a full dinner menu.

Giordano's
Lakeview
1040 West Belmont Avenue
(773) 327-1200
$

The *New York Times* has proclaimed that Giordano's serves "The Ultimate Pizza." *Chicago Magazine* has called it best in the city, and *Food Industry News* has awarded it their coveted Silver Platter Award. These accolades are well deserved, as it is truly difficult to find a better stuffed pizza than at Giordano's.

Giordano's has successfully modernized the concept by producing a lighter product with a tasty crust and a beautifully flavored fresh tomato topping. This has been achieved by limiting the amount of tomato topping and properly balancing the amount of cheese and filling. Their spinach-and-mushroom pie has consistently been the biggest seller here. The dining area is large and comfortable, and has a full Italian menu; however, most patrons seem to prefer take-out or delivery.

Nancy's
Lakeview
2930 North Broadway
(773) 883-1977
$

Nancy's is where the stuffed pizza was born. They are best known for their spinach pie and for a delicious newcomer, the stuffed Chicken Cacciatore Pizza. The dining area decor is somewhat outdated, but it is worth the trip to sample the original.

ITALIAN-STYLE THIN-CRUST PIZZA

Aurelio's Pizza
18162 Harwood Avenue
Homewood
(708) 798-8050
$

The Aurelio family still owns and operates the original flagship restaurant that was founded by Joe Aurelio back in 1959, and which is located in Homewood's refurbished downtown area. Although a full Italian menu is available, the specialty of the house is Chicago-style thin-crust pizza, with a sauce made from a family recipe that has not changed in over 43 years. Aurelio's uses only the freshest cheeses, meats, and vegetables for its toppings.

Aurelio's remains "the" place to go for pizza on Chicago's south side, and its newer locations are expected to uphold the original restaurant's high standards for quality and value.

Other Locations
Aurelio's has several other locations, including 506 West Harrison Street, Chicago (West Loop Gate); (312) 994-2000.

O'Fame
Lincoln Park
750 West Webster Avenue
(773) 929-5111
$

The name *O'Fame* is presumably a play on an Italian phrase that means, "I'm hungry," and if you are hungry O'Fame will indeed satisfy you. There are many variations of thin-crust pizza in Chicago, but this is by far the best pizza of its type that you can get in the city. Even when it's delivered to your home the pizza is delicious and very fresh. With a tasty light tomato sauce and a hint of garlic, this is pure pizza pleasure. Mushrooms, chopped green olives, and onions are an outstanding combo.

O'Fame has a comfortable, relaxed dining room with large windows looking out onto the bustling corner of Webster and Halsted streets. The service is friendly and quite capable, and they offer a full Italian dinner menu.

Located in the heart of Lincoln Park, O'Fame has been family-operated for more than fifteen years. The Italian restaurant draws crowds of locals, theatergoers (with tickets for nearby Steppenwolf and Royal George productions), as well as out-of-towners. Valet parking is available and advisable.

Pizza Metro
Wicker Park
1707 West Division Street
(773) 278-1753
Open until 4:00 A.M. on Friday and Saturday
$

Metro serves wonderful classic Italian square-cut thin-crust pizza, with a very light tomato presence. The dining area is very small and dinerlike, and does not have a liquor license; as a result, take-out is popular.

WOOD-OVEN THIN-CRUST PIZZA

Piece
Bucktown/Wicker Park
1927 West North Avenue
(773) 772-4422
$$

Lately many Chicagoans frequent Piece because cast members from MTV's *The Real World: Chicago* worked here during filming, but the real reason to visit this hip Wicker Park pizzeria is to try the tasty East Coast–style pies. An exposed kitchen behind the 5,800-square-foot dining room lets diners view the dough being tossed, topped, and cooked in a wood-fired brick oven. Quite the opposite of Chicago-style deep-dish pizza, Piece's flat pies are modeled after those served at Sally's, the legendary pizzeria in New Haven, Connecticut (though Sally's uses a coal-fired oven, which produces quite a different crust).

Deep-dish fans may scoff, but Piece's hand-formed pies have made believers out of many Chicago pizza fans. The free-form, eat-off-the-baking-sheet pizzas come in plain (tomato sauce, Parmesan, and garlic), white (olive oil, garlic, and mozzarella), or traditional red with numerous conventional topping options, as well as more unusual items such as clams and broccoli rabe. And for the thirsty, house-brewed beers are a definite plus.

Wicker Park patrons, mostly in their twenties and thirties, converge at this hip spot, which is generally crowded, though it occupies a vast former garage. With its faux concrete floor, multilevel seating, skylit ceiling, and two sunken lounge areas, this pizzeria's decor is definitely cooler than most. Delivery and take-out are also available.

Pizza D.O.C.

Lincoln Square
2251 West Lawrence Avenue
(773) 784-8777
$

Named for the place-of-origin system for Italian wines (*Denominazione di Origine Controllata*), D.O.C.'s specialty is thin-crust pizza similar to Piece's, with very flavorful combinations. The dining room is tastefully decorated and has a bustling, social, family atmosphere. It also has a complete Italian dinner menu.

Convito Italiano
1515 Sheridan Road (Plaza del Lago)
Wilmette
(847) 251-3654
$$

Convito Italiano owner Nancy Brussat lived in Europe during the 1970s and fell in love with Italy. She learned to cook classic Italian dishes from a friend who lived there as well, using fresh, wonderful local ingredients.

When she returned Stateside, she was dismayed, according to her daughter Candace Warner, "that no one here knew what pesto was, or how different fresh Parmesan was" from the pregrated stuff. Her mission became to educate Midwestern Americans about real Italian food.

The first Convito, which opened in 1980 just down Sheridan Road from its current location, was a small retail shop selling Italian foods and wines. In 1982 a larger space at the Plaza Del Lago became available, and she opened her trattoria-style restaurant, which also includes a sizable deli with delicious prepared foods for take-out, plus an excellent selection of Italian and other imported dry goods, an extensive array of artisanal cheeses, and one of Chicagoland's largest selections of Italian wine.

Convito is a charming, well-managed neighborhood restaurant—a great place to meet friends for lunch before shopping the plaza, as well as a great take-out destination when you want good Italian food without a lot of fuss. The main menu, which changes twice a year, includes notations indicating the region of Italy from which the recipe originated. Overseeing the kitchen is Edmund Beberdick, who was sous chef at Convito from 1984 to 1991 and who recently returned to become head chef. He provides an additional menu of weekly specials to take advantage of fresh produce and other seasonal items.

Fox & Obel
Streeterville
401 East Illinois Street
(312) 379-0143
$$–$$$

Fox & Obel is a gourmet grocery store that excels in food to go. There are sixty to seventy choices of prepared foods in the attractively presented cases. Perennial favorites include crab cakes, ahi tuna, sun-dried tomato ziti, herb-encrusted beef tenderloin, truffled mashed potatoes, and chopped liver ("made the old-fashioned way with chicken liver, schmaltz, and love"). Smoked fish from salmon to rainbow trout and diver sea scallops, plus a huge array of common and hard-to-find charcuterie, are also

available. Easy-to-nibble goods, many with Asian or Mexican flavors (potstickers, vegetable spring rolls, tamales, quesadillas with mango salsa), are perfect for picnics or cocktail parties.

Vegetarians will find plenty of reasons to be happy here too, with roasted seasonal vegetables, their famous mac and cheese, and bean and grain salads. Salads such as spinach and mixed baby greens with house-made dressings, and sushi made daily on the premises are other attractive options.

Fox & Obel strives to source from local producers. Some products are made with organic or free-range ingredients, and the produce and soups change seasonally. All take-out dishes are made on the premises, as are their awesome breads. The bread makers arrive at 4:00 A.M. to start preparing the twenty-five or so selections, such as baguettes (and mini baguettes perfect for one or two people—a great idea!), ciabatta, cracked wheat, semolina, olive, and several varieties of rolls.

Large vats of olives entice you, and the cheese department is top-notch—a destination in itself for Chicago-area cheese lovers. Fox & Obel's knowledgeable cheesemongers stand ready to give you a taste of whatever you wish to help you find just the right flavor and texture.

Sweets—chocolate-chip cookie lovers must try their version—are another specialty. In addition to cookies, small and large cakes, tarts, and pies are beautifully displayed. Vosges chocolate truffles, angel food cake muffins, brownies, scones, and more will tempt you.

Because Fox & Obel is a grocery store, you can round out your meal with a nice assortment of produce—much of which is organic and may include some unusual and fun-to-try exotic fruits. Their decent wine department features selections from around the world and has a good assortment of half-bottles.

Freddy's Pizza
1600 South 61st Avenue
Cicero
(708) 863-9289
Closed Sunday
$

Freddy's is a simple corner grocery store/pizzeria, which from the street appears indistinguishable from a hundred other corner groceries scattered throughout the city. Undistinguished Freddy's is not, however, as nowhere else in the city are you likely to find more of the vibrancy and flavor of Italy packed into such a tiny space. In a space that's smaller than five hundred square feet, owners Guiseppe Quercia (a.k.a. Joe) and his wife, Ann Marie, manage to pack an astonishing variety of fresh foodstuffs made lovingly by their hands every day.

The best time to go is around noon, when their little store could be the liveliest place in Cicero. A steady stream of people crowd in to get a look at the hand-printed menu tacked on the shelf behind the counter, and to smell and gape at the array of prepared foods in their *tavola fredda*. There will always be a sheet pizza coming out of the oven, along with calzone, stromboli, and *panzerotti*, but you will also find a marinated seafood salad, mussels *alla marinara*, rigatoni in a Bolognese sauce, grilled and marinated peppers, marinated artichokes (as well as eggplant, mushrooms, or olives), *spaghetti al aglio e olio*, chicken Vesuvio, *peperoni ripieni*, breaded chicken or pork tenderloin ready for sandwiching, *arancini* (rice and cheese balls), and a specialty from Joe's hometown of Cimitile di Nola just outside of Naples, *i supplì al telefono* (deep-fried rice and cheese balls). For dessert there is always gelato or Italian ice, made throughout the day and on the premises.

Meat, cheese, and vegetable lasagnas are made everyday. On weekends and holidays they make fresh pasta. Otherwise, in the freezer case you'll find their duck, artichoke, shellfish, portobello mushroom, cheese, or meat ravioli, as well as three kinds of gnocchi and two varieties of cavatelli. They will make to order any sauces to go, if requested ahead of time.

Guiseppe makes his own prosciutto, capicola, *soppressata*, and *salamini*. Ann Marie makes at least ten different kinds of bread every day, including focaccia, *rimini*, and a small pepperoni-studded bun. If you're lucky enough to be there at the end of the day when there are a few unsold loaves, she oftentimes gives them away.

As for the name Freddy's, that's what it was called when thirteen-year-old Joe—who spoke no English—found a job here making pizza and Italian ice for the original owner. Five years later he bought the store, and as Ann Marie says, "Why change the name if the business is good?"

Sultan's Market
Wicker Park
2057 West North Avenue
(773) 235-3072
$

The last few years have seen Sultan's Market evolve from a Middle Eastern– and Asian-oriented convenience store with a deli counter in the back to a full Middle Eastern restaurant, lacking only table service. Shelves of dry goods were cleared aside to make room for a generous salad bar, with offerings like stuffed eggplant, *dolmas*, roasted mushrooms, and char-grilled chicken. Though deli sandwiches are still offered, the menu is focused on more traditional Turkish items, starting with spinach pie, *fettia* (egg bread topped with cheese and then baked and covered in hot sauce), and some of the best baba ghanoush in Chicago.

Located in the heart of Wicker Park, Sultan's Market knows its clientele, and designates which menu items are vegan or vegetarian. Run by the Ramlis, a mother-and-son team from Jordan, Sultan's Market seems more interested in feeding the neighborhood with good, healthy fare than charging the more expensive prices they could get away with. The lentil soup (made with Grandma Zarifa's recipe) is sold for $2 or $3 depending on size, and comes with a side of pita. They do not make their own pita bread in-house, but everything else is fresh. The falafel sandwiches are excellent: delicately spiced yellow falafel made ahead of time and served cold. Though the cold falafel may take some customers by surprise, any doubts are erased upon consumption. Their Jerusalem salad and hummus are the perfect complements to the sandwich. For meat lovers, Sultan's Market prepares lamb *kefta* with roasted tomatoes and onions, as well as chicken *shawerma*. When ordered as a "dinner," they are accompanied by curried basmati rice.

Turkish delight, baklava, and *halvah* are all offered for dessert, as well as candied pistachios, wafer cookies, candied tamarind, and other packaged confections. A wide assortment of beverages is available, including mango, guava, and tamarind nectar.

Sultan's market recently added a delivery service, and will deliver any of their market items along with food. Catering is also available.

Trotter's to Go
Lincoln Park
1337 West Fullerton Avenue
(773) 868-6510
$$

Although it's located in a ubiquitous strip mall, squeezed in between a UPS office and a dry cleaner, make no mistake: Charlie Trotter has made no compromises on his take-out cuisine.

The renowned chef made his reputation serving long, unhurried dinners. Trotter's to Go serves the chronologically challenged. It's not exactly the same as if you pulled the car up to his legendary Lincoln Park restaurant and asked for a meal to go, but the quality and flavor combinations are all there. They use fresh, seasonally changing organic products, and almost everything is made on the premises. Selections include spitroasted and slow-braised meats, fish, and seafood, and grain and vegetable sides. Entrée choices might include Lavender-Glazed Free-Range Chicken, Peekytoe Crab Cakes with Seasonal Fruit Salsa, Pineapple-

Chipotle Baby-Back Ribs, or Ahi Tuna Poke (sashimi-grade tuna, cubed and marinated in garlic, sesame oil, chili paste, and soy sauce). Sides or vegetarian entrées include Brussels sprouts with apple cider reduction, cremini mushroom salad with pecorino, braised daikon with organic soy and lemon, Israeli couscous with black mission figs and edamame, or Chinese long beans tossed with hoisin sauce.

Sandwiches aren't your normal deli fare: They feature ingredients like roasted turkey, Brie, Fuji apples, and celery remoulade; Dungeness crab with spicy fennel; and beef tenderloin with Bermuda onions, Stilton, and watercress. Bread and desserts are excellent and always fresh.

Decorated with stylish contemporary art, the high-ceiled, brightly lit shop looks like a stage where good living has the starring role. The pre-pared foods are stage right; next are boxed and canned goods such as Sarabeth's Spreadable Fruit, Cherith Valley Mixed Vegetables, and Café Fanny (as in Chez Panisse) Organic Granola. Around the corner are exotic pasta sauces (eggplant, fennel, and puttanesca), as well as innova-tive condiments, elegant truffles, and wines and cheeses. The wines, which come with descriptions of foods they complement, are available by the bottle and half-bottle.

All this comes at a price. Entrées hover around the $20.00 mark, salads range from $9.95 to $14.95, and a sandwich will set you back $6.95.

NOTABLE

Foodstuffs
2106 Central Street
Evanston
(847) 328-7704
$$

This attractive, upscale take-out food market has a huge selection of breads, many made on the premises. Made-to-order and prewrapped sandwiches are available with a multitude of ingredients. House-made soups (butter-nut squash, chicken noodle, sirloin chili), as well as chicken and veal stocks, can be purchased frozen, refrigerated, or hot. An appetizing selection of sal-ads and entrées changes daily. Complete your meal with a selection from their collection of cheeses, cookies, pastries, and fresh fruit.

Other Locations
338 Park Avenue, Glencoe; (847) 835-5105
255 Westminster, Lake Forest; (847) 234-6600
1456 Waukegan Road, Glenview; (847) 832-9999

Malabar Catering and Carryout
Albany Park
3519 West Montrose Avenue
(773) 588-0304
Take-out only
$

Slow Food emphasizes traditional, authentic food served in a spirit of conviviality. Frequently this means home-cooked, not restaurant, food, yet ordering a full meal for friends from Malabar Catering can achieve some of the same Slow effects, with the added bonus of introducing your guests to an unusual regional style of Indian food.

Strictly take-out and accepting orders *only* in advance (fortunately, the staff speaks excellent English), Malabar cooks up the food of Kerala, a coastal region in Southern India known for its spice fields. Kerala has a population of Syrian Christians, and Keralan food features beef, duck, and plenty of seafood as well more typical southern Indian dishes like *vada*, the fried lentil doughnuts. Malabar Catering can help you set up a menu that is well balanced between flavors and textures.

Middle Eastern Bakery
Andersonville
1512 West Foster Avenue
(773) 561-2224
$

More of a grocery than a restaurant, Andersonville's Middle Eastern Bakery boasts an excellent deli counter in back that keeps patrons returning for more. A falafel sandwich is just over $2.00, or you can purchase a bag of a dozen fresh falafel balls for $2.50. They offer an assortment of variations on spinach pies; besides the traditional there are spinach-and-cheese pies, as well as lamb, chicken, eggplant, artichoke, and other combinations thereof.

The deli also sells trays of baklava, *dolmas* by the dozen, pickled vegetables, olives, and soups. Several nearby refrigerated cases offer many different kinds of soups, as well as a half-dozen variations on hummus: garlic, roasted red pepper, olive, and so on. Other sides, like Moroccan eggplant salad, tabbouleh, and baba ghanoush, are worth stocking up on. In addition, you'll find plenty of bulk goods: dried fruits, nuts, and candies, plus Mediterranean dry and canned goods.

Urban Epicure
Andersonville
1512 West Berwyn Avenue
(773) 296-3663
$

Sporting an attractive and, yes, urban feel, Urban Epicure offers an enticing selection of six or seven main dishes (Cumin-Rubbed Pork Chops with Kumquat-Garlic Jam, Cornish hens stuffed with tabbouleh, or seasonal-vegetable lasagna), another half-dozen or so side dishes (roasted Brussels sprouts are a customer favorite), and still more soups, salads, and sandwiches. A small but well-chosen cheese selection, Red Hen bakery breads, and an assortment of gourmet packaged goods rounds out the selection.

Urban Fridge
Lincoln Park
2679 North Lincoln Avenue
(773) 244-6568
$-$$

The perfect place for busy families and individuals to pop in and grab dinner from their prepackaged and ready-to-go items. Urban Fridge offers a large selection of seasonal soups and fresh salads, appetizers, and house-made breads, side dishes, sandwiches, and main courses. Many are accented with Asian, Latin, or Mediterranean flavors, but you'll find some good basics like meatloaf and roast chicken too. Parents will appreciate the selections designed (and priced) for kids. All items are priced for individual or family servings.

WINE BARS

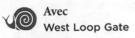

Avec
West Loop Gate

615 West Randolph Street
(312) 377-2002
$

On his honeymoon trip to Switzerland, Avec owner Paul Kahan and his new bride stayed up till the wee hours eating local foods with townspeople. This experience opened his eyes to enjoying foods that are unique to a place, and to the notion that who you eat with can be just as important, if not more important, than the food itself.

Thus was born his idea to create a place to enjoy "peasant-style" foods and wines. Avec is a tiny place—a long, narrow, cedar-lined room with five communal tables each seating eight or ten, separated by a narrow aisle from the bar spanning the length of the room. While you'll probably make new friends among those you're sharing the table with—as you ask which wine they ordered, or what that fabulous-smelling dish is—conversation can be challenging in this loud, boisterous room.

No New World wines have conquered Avec; the focus here is on southern France, Italy, Spain, and Portugal—the "sun-drenched wine regions," as the wine director calls them. There are more than thirty-five available by the glass, and seventy-plus bottles of these robust rustic wines. Wines by the glass are actually 250 ml pours (one-third of a bottle) served in delightful little pitchers. The thinking behind the 250 ml servings (which are priced no more than one regular glass would be at other places) was that patrons could share with their companion, or perhaps have a different wine with each dish. Avec's philosophy is to encourage people to share and try new things.

As with Kahan's next-door restaurant, Blackbird, Avec uses local purveyors and organic produce, meats, and eggs when possible. Menu items are designed using whatever is in season. Environmentally conscious, Avec lets nothing go to waste. Poultry bits from Blackbird are turned into amazing sausages by Koren Grieveson, Avec's talented chef. (A dozen or so varieties of house-made *salumi*, a specialty of theirs, are offered daily.) Even the little wooden serving boards are actually recycled scraps from the building material used on the walls.

Other foods include a nice selection of small plates such as a salad of organic roast beets, bean crostini with wild arugula, duck confit with black mission figs, and pan-fried sardines. There are a few "large plates," which may include a poached fish stew; *pissaladière* with caramelized onions, anchovies, and Niçoise olives; and pork shoulder with sofrito and green chiles. In keeping with the Old World wine focus, cheese selections are also from Italy, Spain, France, and Portugal (three selections for $12).

Some French-inspired desserts tempt the sweet tooth—apple galette, chocolate sorbet, and roasted figs with honey-lavender ice cream.

Bin 36
River North
339 North Dearborn Street
(312) 755-9463
$$

Bin 36 is a large, hip, modern space in the House of Blues hotel and concert hall complex. The two-story light and airy room is accented with tomato-soup-orange drapes and touches of gold. Metal chairs/bar stools complete the decor, but can become uncomfortable if you linger in them too long; the few upholstered couches offer an alternative. Expansive windows look out onto the vibrant River North scene.

Surrounded by a number of large hotels, Bin 36 doesn't have a neighborhood feel—rather, it's more chic and eclectic. Take a seat at the large, oval, zinc-topped bar. Wines are offered by the glass ($6.50 to $13.75) or taste (about $3.00) or in flights ($13.00 to $16.00). You'll get four 2.5-ounce selections per flight. Flights change seasonally, but also at the whim of the owners, who taste new wines daily. Special $10.00 flights are available on Sundays from 2:00 P.M. to closing.

Descriptions are opinionated and evocative: "Plain old lip-smackin' good," "What a delicious mouthfeel of dark fruit and bittersweet chocolate," and, "So voluptuous that it's bursting at the seams." These people love wine.

The wine-by-the-bottle book, made even more substantial by its metal jacket, is twenty pages of half-bottles, standards, and magnums. Each varietal has helpful explanatory text (mostly straightforward and serious, though they tell us that "Red Burgundy = Ella Fitzgerald," and go on with a poetic paragraph comparing the two).

The bar area has tables and booths for smaller or lighter meals, though the full restaurant menu is also available in the more casual area. The tavern menu is more extensive than at many wine bars. Small plates are interesting salads (peekytoe crab salad, heirloom apple salad), duck pate, raw oysters, clams, and pan-roasted mussels ($7.00 to $12.00). Large plates range from a burger to a peppercorn-crusted swordfish and a calzone filled with fennel sausage, oven-dried tomatoes, ricotta, and arugula.

The front of the house is a shop with many bottles for purchase (perfect if you've got to have that wonderful wine you just tasted—though they usually can be found elsewhere for a few dollars less). Also for sale are books on wine and cheese, colorful dishes, glassware, cheese servers, and many other fun toys for wine and food lovers.

Bin 36 has an ongoing calendar of special wine tastings, classes, and vintner dinner parties. A full bar and beer are also available.

Other Location
275 Parkway Drive, Lincolnshire; (847) 808-9463

Enoteca Piattini
Lincoln Park
934 West Webster Avenue
(773) 281-3898
$$

The El train running regularly just outside the windows gives a rumbling Chicago flavor to this candlelit, relaxed spot. The owners sought to give Chicagoans tired of gigantic plates of pasta a casual place to "enjoy wine and food, a little at a time." *Piattini* means "little plates" in Italian, and you'll find an enticing selection of reasonably priced salads and other appetizer-style dishes such as calamari, stuffed artichokes, and olives and cheeses. Pasta, lamb, chicken, and beef plates are a little more substantial, but still smaller and more manageable than the usual oversize restaurant meals. All dishes are designed to be shared with your companions. The restaurant uses local producers whenever possible, such as for their bread (which is served with complimentary olive tapenade) and ice cream. Other desserts are made in-house.

There are thirty or so wines by the glass, several thoughtful flights, and more than two hundred bottles to choose from. The world's major wine-growing regions from France, Italy, and Spain to Australia, Argentina, and the United States are all represented here. Bottles are priced from $25 to around $100 (for a couple Brunellos), with most in the affordable mid-$20s to mid-$40s range. Befitting the provenance of Enoteca Piattini, the list is weighted toward Italian selections. You'll find wines from Tuscany, Umbria, Piedmont, Veneto, Molise, Puglia, Sicily, and Emilia-Romagna. All wines are accompanied by short but helpful descriptions.

Enoteca Piattini is a comfortable, neighborhood place, with brick walls, upholstered banquettes, wood chairs, tile floors, and a gas fireplace. They offer occasional special events, such as winemaker's dinners, where the food is served family-style and priced moderately ($48 for five courses with wine). Beer, port, mixed drinks, and a nice selection of Italian liqueurs are available as well.

Pops for Champagne
Lakeview
2934 North Sheffield Avenue
(773) 472-1000
$$

Open since 1982, Pops is a Chicago classic—a perfect place for a romantic evening, or an elegant place to impress a client. The dark wood walls, the vaulted ceiling painted with clouds, and the dim lights and candlelight give a dreamy and sophisticated feel to the intimate room. The focal point of the room is the raised stage, where live jazz is featured nightly. Long-established and respected musicians play Pops, where there is a $6 cover Tuesday through Thursday, $12 on Fridays and Saturdays, and no cover on Sundays and Mondays (check their Web site for the schedule). Choose a seat by the large front windows to view the charming Lincoln Park neighborhood. A fireplace adds warmth in winter, and the outdoor garden area is a nice alternative in summer.

Pops for Champagne focuses on—you guessed it—champagne. Choose a flight of three out of nine possibilities, a glass ($11 to $18), or a 2.5-ounce taste. Dozens of bubblies by the bottle (as well as half-bottles or magnums, for those really big celebrations) are also available. Most selections are true champagnes, but there are also sparkling wines from California, Spain, and Italy. Good champagne and sparkling wines don't come cheap, but Pops's markup isn't bad, and there are selections in the

$20 and $30 range. Pops also has red and white wines by the glass and bottle. The selection of these is smaller, but has solid choices from the United States, Italy, and Germany, as well as New Zealand and Argentina. Dessert wines, cocktails, and beer are also offered.

The food choices are limited to appetizers, cheeses, and desserts. It is mostly traditional Old World fare designed to complement champagne: caviar, smoked salmon tartare, crab cakes, a charcuterie plate, and a mushroom tart. Cheese selections are predominantly Midwestern, coming from Wisconsin, Michigan, and Colorado. Desserts include chocolate fondue, apple tart, or a plate of cookies.

Cigars are also offered on the menu, and smoking them is permitted in the room "unless it offends other guests," as the menu says.

Other Location
214 Greenbay Road, Highwood; (847) 266-1313

The Tasting Room
West Loop Gate
1415 West Randolph Street
(312) 942-1313
$$

The Tasting Room offers wines from plenty of lesser-known producers, which provides a fine opportunity to try something really different. The menu lists an extensive number of red, white, and bubbly flights ($13 to $22), which change regularly and may be organized by Bubbly, Best of Bott (Alsatian wine), many shades of white, Bordeaux Blitz, Cabs, Pleasures of Piedmont, and several dessert wine flights. Five additional pages present an array of whites and reds by the glass, bottle, and taste. Some by-the-glass selections can get on the pricey side (up to $25 for an Australian cabernet), but here's your chance to taste some extraordinary wines without buying a bottle. Bottles come in price ranges for all budgets. Also available are dessert wines, spirits, and some unusual beers.

The food is innovative and mostly hits the mark. Choices may include small thin-crust pizzas, warm crab-and-artichoke dip with house-made wontons, Moroccan chicken salad, and zucchini cakes ($5 to $8). Seafood and charcuterie are offered in flights. The Tasting Room has a large cheese selection, which can be ordered in individual tastings or a selection of three by type (goat's, cow's, sheep's, or cheddars). Two degustation menus ($45 for four courses and $55 for five courses) are paired with the appropriate wines. An enticing selection of desserts is available; the chocolate fondue is especially fun with a group or a date.

The place has a cozy feel on two floors, and is popular with the after-work and after-dinner crowds. With exposed brick walls, dim lighting and candles, and comfy couches and chairs, it's ideal for just hanging out with friends or a sweetheart. The second-floor windows afford a wonderful view of the Chicago skyline. Next door is a companion wine shop, Randolph Wine Cellars (see p. 343), for further wine exploration.

Webster's Wine Bar
Lincoln Park
1480 West Webster Avenue
(773) 868-0608
$

Each month Webster's showcases a different grape varietal or wine region—perhaps Portugal, northern France, Austria, or the Pacific Northwest—and offers four choices of wine by the two-ounce taste or the glass or bottle. The opening pages of the menu will tell you all about that featured region, providing an education for the mind as well as the palate. Thirty-odd other wines by glass are divided into categories like Cabernet and Merlot, Euro Classics, Pinot Noir, Spicy Reds, Bubbly, Chardonnay, Aromatic Whites, and Classic Whites, with, on average, three selections each ($5.50 to $9.00).

Next up in Webster's enjoyable wine book are twenty pages of wines from all over the world by the bottle ($28 and up), which should keep you busy and encourage discussion with your companions and the friendly and helpful staff. The folks at Webster's insist on serving handcrafted selections from predominantly family-owned wineries.

Special events are numerous and entertaining. They have monthly classes, which are in-depth, and special Wednesday-night tastings where they showcase approximately fifteen wines from regions such as the Willamette Valley, Champagne, or Chile, along with appetizers and cheese. On Mondays there is live music with no cover charge.

The small but satisfying food menu changes seasonally. Possibilities include house-made soups, salads, gourmet pizzas, and simple pastas ($7 to $10). They aim to focus on an all-American cheese selection, but will offer whatever fits best with featured wines. Several desserts, dessert wines, and cordials are also available.

The atmosphere is comfortable, dark, and candlelit. It's popular with the twenty-somethings who have discovered the pleasures of wine, but you'll see all ages and types here. Seating is at a comfortable bar, small table groupings, and a few couches and oversize chairs. The front room features large windows perfect for watching the street scene or the snowfall. The back room is decorated with old wine bottles and books on floor-to-ceiling shelves, like a welcoming study. There's even a free parking lot, and in this Lincoln Park neighborhood, that's reason enough to go there.

NOTABLE

404 Wine Bar
Lakeview
2852 North Southport Avenue
(773) 404-5886
$

Don't be put off by having to walk through Jack's (a noisy, more typical bar complete with pool table, the game on TV, and video games) to get to the 404 Wine Bar. It's quieter, with soft pumpkin-colored walls, candlelight, and fireplaces. The bar menu consists of light appetizers (Brie, *bruschetta*, wontons), pizzas, and desserts (chocolate cake, cheesecake, raspberry ice cream). There are fifteen to twenty by-the-glass selections each for reds and whites, plus dessert wines and champagne by the glass ($5.75 to $9.00), and forty-plus choices by the bottle from the United States, Spain, France, Italy, and Australia. Each month sees a featured wine flight (pinot grigio and pinot noir, for instance) where they offer two-ounce tastings of three choices.

PART THREE

FOOD SHOPS, MARKETS & PRODUCERS

BREAD BAKERIES

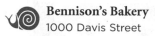 **Bennison's Bakery**
1000 Davis Street
Evanston
(847) 328-3854

Who says you can't teach an old dog new tricks? In operation since 1938, Bennison's Bakery in Evanston has recently become a leading producer of organic artisanal breads in the Chicagoland area. Owned since 1967 by the Downer family, Bennison's has always prided itself on its "excessive usage of cream, butter, fresh buttermilk, and fresh broken eggs." This commitment to quality ingredients prompted the bakery's recent decision to produce organic baked goods for the local farmers' markets. Setting up their tent for the first time in 2003, Bennison's sold croissants, *pain au chocolat*, ciabatta, and several varieties of sourdough breads at Chicago's Green City Market. During the weeks of the market's season, Bennison's rotated in other types of breads including olive, fennel, Asiago-garlic, and the very popular apple cider bread in the fall.

All of Bennison's breads are long fermented, each requiring about thirty-six hours from start to finish, and are baked in an Italian brick oven. Following up on their success at the market, Bennison's has begun offering these organic breadstuffs in their Evanston location.

Fox & Obel
Streeterville
401 East Illinois Street
(312) 410-7301

This 22,000-square-foot premium food market and café also offers exceptional, beautiful, fresh breads. The wonderful variety of hand-shaped organic-flour breads are a treat both for the eyes and the palate.

Pamela Fitzpatrick, the creative force behind the bakery, is inspired by "the beauty of the hands that make bread" and bread's connection to world history as an ancient food source. Fitzpatrick started her baking career working with Nancy Silverton at La Brea Bakery in Los Angeles. Upon moving to New York she consulted with many well-respected bakeries, notably Amy's Breads, Eli's Manhattan, and The Vinegar Factory.

The exceptional selection of artisanal breads includes the popular Daily Bread (a multigrain rustic semolina), their superb French baguette, and the Sicilian Italian Sun (a traditional Sicilian semolina bread with golden raisins and fennel seeds, rolled in cornmeal). Equally impressive are the light and dangerously addictive buttermilk-baked crackers with butter, shallots, Parmesan cheese, and herbs, and Fitzpatrick's raisin-nut bread packed with pecans, walnuts, pistachios, raisins, and dried apricots.

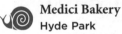 **Medici Bakery**
Hyde Park

1327 East 57th Street
(773) 667-7394

Like a child prodigy with talent beyond its years, the excellence of Medici Bakery belies its youth. Medici opened in June 2003 as an adjunct to Hyde Park's Medici on 57th, a pizza-and-burger restaurant popular among University of Chicago students. The driving force behind the bakery is Lauren Bushnell, herself a 1995 U of C graduate and former math teacher. A young bakery catering to a young clientele, Medici has begun to make its mark on the Chicago bread market.

Medici refers to itself as a "small-scale community-oriented bakery" offering naturally leavened breads produced with the highest-quality ingredients. The bakery uses artisanal techniques, including long fermentation and multiple builds to create layers of flavor. Medici bakes on a daily schedule, but also offers some of its more popular loaves everyday. Particularly appealing is the ciabatta, salt-coated and crusty with a web-like interior. Other standouts include the seeded baguette and the challah, a recipe taught to Bushnell by her home economics teacher.

Spartan in decor, Medici has just a few tables, clearly focusing its attention and energies on the ovens' output. In this setting customers can enjoy the breads and other items offered by Medici, which include bagels, biscuits, muffins, *conchas* (sweet Mexican rolls with streusel topping), and some sweet options.

Red Hen Bread
Wicker Park
1623 North Milwaukee Avenue
(773) 342-6823

While Nancy Carey did not start out as a trained baker, she has taken her artistic training as a graduate of the Art Institute of Chicago and applied it to artisanal breadmaking.

Red Hen offers more than varieties of high-quality bread each day. Favorites are multigrain, Italian roasted garlic ring, and chocolate bread consisting of bittersweet chocolate dough with semisweet chocolate chunks—perfect for French toast, bread pudding, or just eaten with jam. There's also the Ami de Fromage; as its name implies, a great "friend for cheese" and wine. It's well worth trying all varieties and finding your own favorites.

Sandwiches served on a roll or "between the bread" and pastries are also available and can be consumed on the premises, where there is limited seating.

Other Location
500 West Diversey Parkway, Chicago (Lakeview); (773) 248-6025

NOTABLE

Argo, Inc. Georgian Bakery
West Rogers Park
2812 West Devon Avenue
(773) 764-6322

Georgian-style breads and pastries are baked against the side of the large, imported brick beehive-shaped oven (according to the owners, the only one like it in the country) that sits near the front of this small storefront bakery. The entire bread-making process, from baker preparation to hand molding and baking, is on view.

Only two forms of bread are made here—the very large, round, slightly raised Georgian-style flatbread, and an elongated bialy-shaped version called *shoti*.

Several pastries are also available. The most popular is *hachapuri*, a puff pastry filled with a combination of feta, farmer's, and mozzarella cheeses to approximate the flavor of a Georgian cheese that is not available in the United States.

Bombon Bakery
See Pastries & Baked Goods, p. 332.

Breadsmith
Old Town
1710 North Wells Street
(312) 642-5858

Breadsmith offers a large selection of handmade breads on a daily and a weekly basis. In addition, every day of the month they make one or two specialty breads, including gluten-free products.

Calendars listing the availability of the various breads can be found online and at the store. Be sure to try their Asiago cheese sourdough with Tuscan herbs, or the unusual sauerkraut rye.

CHICAGO'S OWN

The city of Chicago has been the birthplace (or the launching pad) for various unique recipes. A few of these foods have since become a integral part of American culture, while others are locally famous and today can be found only in various establishments throughout the city.

During Chicago's famous World's Fair and Columbian Exposition of 1893, several now-familiar foods were introduced, including a popcorn, peanut, and molasses snack called Cracker Jax, a ready-mixed pancake flour called Aunt Jemima's Pancake Mix, and German sausages called Hot Dogs. At the end of the nineteenth century, when technology, convenience, and invention held the interest of the public, these products gained popularity and rose to national and international fame. The origins of these foods are not often associated with Chicago, yet they remain linked to its culinary history.

Of course, Chicago has several foods that embody local culture. Deep-dish pizza (see p. 247) has risen from a unique recipe to a city trademark, Italian beef (p. 242) has secured an honored place in the street-food culture of the city, and Chicago-style hot dogs (p. 238) rival those of other cities for creativity. But what about other dishes that originated in Chicago but never really made it out of the region? Here are a few of Chicago's very own local specialties.

The Original Rainbow Cone. Located near the southwest edge of the city, this ice cream shop has been around since 1926. The famed recipe

has five flavors developed by the original owner, Joe Sapp. A cone swirled high with colorful flavors includes chocolate, strawberry, pistachio, and vanilla-cherry-nut ice cream, plus orange sherbet. *Original Rainbow Cone, 9233 South Western Avenue, Chicago (Beverly); (773) 238-7075.*

For a unique Chicago-style Puerto Rican recipe, try a *jibarito* (literally, "little hillbilly") sandwich. Restaurant owner Juan Figueroa invented the fragrant, hot sandwich at his eatery in Humboldt Park in 1996 (see p. 32), after reading an article on *platanos* sandwiches in a Puerto Rican newspaper. Figueroa developed his own version using crispy, flattened, deep-fried plantains; these are used instead of bread and piled with juicy steak (or your choice of meat), as well as cheese, lettuce, tomato, mayonnaise, and a healthy dollop of garlic paste. Each *jibarito* is served with a side order of rice and beans. Today the *jibarito* can be found at most Puerto Rican restaurants in Chicago. For the original go to *Borinquen Restaurant, 1720 North California Avenue, Humboldt Park; (773) 227-6038.*

You know you're in Chicago if you find *Shrimp deJonge* on a menu. More than a hundred years ago the recipe was developed by the large deJonge family at their family restaurant in Chicago, and its fame spread throughout the region. Today you can find this classic sizzling dish in Chicago's more traditional restaurants. It consists of shrimp broiled with bread crumbs in a sauce of sherry, garlic, and butter. Places to go for *Shrimp deJonge* include Harry Caray's, Hugo's Frog Bar, Butterfield 8, and The Rosebud on Taylor.

—Lynn Peemoeller

Graham's Fine Chocolate and Ice Cream
302 South Third Street
Geneva
(630) 232-6655

It's a long way to Geneva from downtown Chicago, but worth the drive for Graham's alone. Nestled in a row of old homes converted to businesses, most with mom-and-pop owners, you'll find this delightful shop—though it may take you a while to actually get inside the door. On warm summer evenings and during Geneva's many street festivals, there is often a long, salivating line of people. You will be kept entertained, however, by watching the candy makers through the large glass front windows. They might be making fudge or perhaps dipping giant apples in various gooey coatings. But no matter how busy they might be, service is always efficient and friendly.

Graham's own mom and pop are Beckie and Bob Untiedt, whose business relationship blossomed into a marriage. They have been making chocolate for sixteen years. The shop features their own hand-rolled truffles, giant pecan *Skalies* (Swedish for "turtles," in keeping with Geneva's Swedish heritage), caramels, toffees, homemade ice cream, and other one-of-a-kind chocolate creations. They also have a nice selection of sugar-free—yet still decadent—chocolates.

Other Location
119 West Front Street, Wheaton; (630) 221-1199

Piron-Belgian Chocolatier
509 Main Street
Evanston
(847) 864-5504

Master chocolatier Robert Piron has chocolate in his veins. His Belgian parents instilled in him the taste for fine chocolate, which he now shares with those who enter his wonderful shop in Evanston. Trained in Antwerp under Renée Goossen, Piron introduced classic Belgian-style chocolates to the Chicago area twenty years ago. He uses only Callebaut, a fine Belgian brand of chocolate, along with fresh unsalted butter and cream to craft twenty-plus varieties of chocolates. Dark, milk, and white chocolate shells are filled with traditional flavors like hazelnut praline in the Fruit de Mer; bittersweet chocolate ganache is flavored with cognac in the Lion. The marzipan is exceptional and comes in both a traditional style and one enhanced with orange peel, while the Morello wild cherries soaked in brandy and covered in dark chocolate will forever change your idea of chocolate-covered cherries. Chocolate-covered ginger is not too sweet and wonderfully tender and spicy.

Everything is made by hand in the shop, and the smell of melting chocolate is one of the first things you notice upon entering. The staff is very helpful and wraps each order, even if it is just a couple pieces, in a beautiful gold box tied with ribbon. Every morsel is a treat for the soul.

Vosges Haut-Chocolat
River North
520 North Michigan Avenue
(312) 644-9450

Walking into this jewel box of a shop you cannot help but wonder if you have wandered into an exclusive clothing store. This idea vanishes once you taste the chocolate, but Voges Haut-Chocolat is anything but the traditional chocolate shop. Owner and chocolatier Katrina Markoff has created a fantasyland for chocolate lovers, one where you can discover flavor combinations found nowhere else.

Markoff learned to make chocolates at Le Cordon Bleu in Paris. She went on to work and travel throughout Europe, Southeast Asia, and Australia. This worldliness is reflected in the truffle flavorings. Her first creation was the Naga truffle, a blend of milk chocolate, coconut extract, and curry powder. This set the stage for even more challenging combinations. Other delicacies include dark chocolate flavored with ginger and wasabi, milk chocolate with chipotle peppers, and cinnamon—and even white chocolate with olive oil and kalamata olives. No promising flavor combination is left untried. A recent spring collection included truffles

flavored with kaffir lime, cardamom, and green tea. And Vosges just introduced a truffle with dark chocolate and Taleggio cheese that is so popular
the store cannot keep it in stock. These wonderful new confections appear
on a regular basis.

Along with the truffles you can indulge in sinfully rich hot chocolate in
three variations, and exotic candy bars. If the shopper in you is still not
satisfied there are also T-shirts as well as handbags printed with cocoa
bean pods.

Other Location
The Peninsula Hotel, 108 East Superior, Chicago (Streeterville);
   (312) 335-9858

NOTABLE

Blommer's
River North
600 West Kinzie Street
(312) 492-1336

Chicago is a city filled with wonderful smells, but nothing beats the smell
of chocolate that hits you when you leave the west end of the Merchandise
Mart, or after a tough workout at the East Bank Club. Blommer's
Chocolate Company is the nation's largest producer of bulk chocolate,
which you have probably eaten in the baked goods and candies throughout the city. Their retail shop is filled with chips and chunks of chocolate
that you can sample at will, but the smell alone is worth a visit.

Chicago Nut Company
Lakeview
843 West Belmont Avenue
(773) 871-4994

This family-owned business, founded in 1982, offers a huge variety of
fresh nuts and abundant candies and confections. Service is fast and
friendly.

Dulcelandia
Logan Square
3855 West Fullerton Avenue
(773) 235-7825

It's hard to miss Dulcelandia—its festive, piñata-stuffed windows are an eye-catching splash of color on an otherwise dreary strip of West Fullerton Avenue. Billing itself as "La Dulcería Mexicana," Dulcelandia is the place for one-stop shopping for traditional and contemporary Mexican candy sold in bulk and piñatas. For the curiosity seeker or just the homesick, interesting and tempting flavors abound, from tamarind to chile to coconut. The piñatas range from traditional donkeys to the latest in Japanese animé characters. This is also the place to shop for children's party favors—racing cars for the boys and miniature irons for the girls, or vice versa.

The Fudge Pot
Old Town
1532 North Wells Street
(312) 943-1777

If you yearn for the fudge shop you visited on a summer-vacation road trip to the Atlantic coast or Mackinaw Island, The Fudge Pot is the place for you. Located in Old Town since 1963, this landmark makes very good fudge and every imaginable form of molded chocolate, from your name rendered in milk chocolate to a human heart done in dark and white chocolate, which is framed and hanging by the entrance to the shop.

Long Grove Confectionery
333 Lexington Drive
Buffalo Grove
(847) 459-3100

From humble beginnings in an old-style red schoolhouse back in 1975, Long Grove Confectionery is now at home in an 85,000-square-foot manufacturing facility. However, their passion for chocolate remains the same. Probably best known for their Myrtle (fresh, salted, roasted pecans drenched in caramel and chocolate), giant peanut butter cups, and chocolate-covered strawberries, they also specialize in molded chocolates.

Margie's
West Bucktown
1960 North Western Avenue
(773) 384-1035

This family-owned business has been making handmade chocolates and marzipan since 1921. Walking into this shop is like stepping back in time. Along with the chocolates you'll find an old-fashioned soda fountain.

Marly's Chocolates
527 Davis Street
Evanston
(847) 328-3333

The marble display table filled with chocolates is the first thing you encounter when you enter the shop in Evanston. Chocolates from all over the world are lined up and labeled for your inspection. You can buy imported and domestic chocolates in addition to Marly's own homemade confections. Marly's truffles, a basic ganache with flavorings like blue cheese, goat cheese, and two types of curry, are more unique than exceptional. Gail Robinson opened the shop in 2002 and has not only brought together a beautiful selection of chocolates, but also has the best hot chocolate in the area. With either 63 or 73 percent cocoa content, it is heaven in a cup.

Moonstruck Chocolate Company
River North
320 North Michigan Avenue
(312) 696-1201

Moonstruck Chocolate Company combines the best of both worlds—a coffee shop with gourmet chocolates. The warm, relaxed environment is perfect for enjoying a cup of coffee or exceptional hot chocolate—try the Chocolate Truffle, with a yummy dessert or a piece of chocolate. The molded chocolates feature delicately light flavorings that include pear brandy, Earl Grey tea, and rum raisin.

Mr. Kite's
Gold Coast
1153 North State Street
(312) 664-7270

A tiny shop filled to the brim with chocolate-covered snacks and candies, this stop may satisfy a sweet tooth after a night of fun on Rush Street. Mr. Kite himself watches over the dispensing of chocolate-covered almost anything—Oreos, graham crackers, marshmallows, and pretzels—along with truffles, bark, and toffee.

Nuts on Clark
Wrigleyville
3830 North Clark Street
(773) 549-6622

This family-run business is infamous for its wacky ambience and its diverse line of good, affordable, fresh nut products. Several satellite locations can be found throughout Chicago.

Rahmig's House of Fine Chocolates
Lakeview
3109 North Broadway
(773) 525-5700

The House of Fine Chocolates has created high-quality chocolates and specialty cakes for more than fifty years in the East Lakeview neighborhood. Husband-and-wife team Michael and Karen Mech personally design cakes for weddings and every other occasion. The photos on their Web site attest to the artistry that goes into each cake. Their signature cake is an awning stripe of alternating white and dark chocolate panels, trimmed in fudge, with chocolate roses and chocolate sticks.

The House of Fine Chocolates makes molded chocolate Santas and Easter bunnies for the holidays, as well as handmade chocolates that are available year-round. But chocolate is not all that the House of Fine Chocolates is about; their butter cookies are melt-in-your-mouth gems.

Ricci & Company
River North
162 West Superior Street
(312) 787-7660

Since 1919 the family-owned Ricci & Company has offered diverse, quality nuts and sweets at an impressive value. Freshness and flavor are their hallmarks.

Windy City Sweets
Lakeview
3308 North Broadway
(773) 477-6100

This neighborhood shop offers excellent customer service for those seeking an extensive variety of dried fruits and nuts in bulk. Rapid turnover ensures freshness.

DAIRY & CHEESE

The Cheese People
(773) 269-2033

Available at farmers' markets in the following communities: Barrington, Chesterton (Indiana), Deerfield, Elmhurst, Hinsdale, Lake Bluff, Libertyville, Northfield, Oak Park, Park Ridge, Schaumburg, Skokie, Wheaton, and Wilmette.

Sold at farmers' markets throughout the Greater Chicago area, The Cheese People's products are a delicious, seasonal treat. Jon and Sarah Hanchett, a husband-and-wife team—work with small cheese makers in southwest Wisconsin's Hill Country to come up with about forty custom-made cheeses. The Cheese People hand chop fresh herbs and prepare other ingredients—like applewood for creating the mellow, smoky flavor of its Gouda—which then are provided to the individual cheese makers. The Hanchetts have sought out a dozen or so family-owned producers (a rarity in this day and age) who specialize in traditionally made cheeses. Many of their cheese recipes have been been handed down from generation to generation and are still being made by the same family. The Cheese People then pair these craft-made cheeses with their own original recipes to create interesting flavor combinations: Chipotle Cheddar, Tex Mex Monterey Jack, Fresh Herb Basil Brie, Fresh Dill Brie, and more. Their Brie with Blue is a stunning creation: a triple-crème Brie layered with blue cheese and honey. Pick up a sack of their fresh cheese curds for the kids, or simply for munching on the way home from the market.

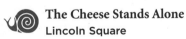

The Cheese Stands Alone
Lincoln Square
4547 North Western Avenue
(773) 293-3870

Sarah Parker says she and her husband, Matt, started this little gem of a shop for selfish reasons: They love cheese and wanted a neighborhood cheese store. "There's nothing like that in Chicago. In Paris there's one in every neighborhood," she says. The Cheese Stands Alone carries a staggering variety of cheeses, many from small artisanal makers. At any given time, the counter is stocked with 130 to 140 varieties of cheese. The biggest sellers are the soft, creamy cheeses of France, but the Parkers love the artisanal cheeses from America, most of which are made in California, Vermont, and Wisconsin. Prices on these can range up to $35 a pound, but Sarah points out that these artisanal cheeses come from small makers who have honed their craft, often by studying overseas. Among her favorites of these artisanal cheeses is Three Sisters Serena, made by a twenty-two-year-old California woman, and Carr Valley Cardona, which with its rind made from cocoa is one of the more unusual cheeses that comes from Wisconsin.

Despite the store's name, the cheese doesn't exactly stand alone. The store carries fresh baguettes and a few specialty meats, such as prosciutto and Serrano ham, along with a few other gourmet items.

Oberweis Dairy
951 Ice Cream Drive, "Sweet" One
North Aurora
(630) 801-6100

Oberweis got its start when family patriarch Peter J. Oberweis's cows began producing too much milk for his family to drink. He began selling some of it to his neighbors in the then-small town of Aurora. Several years later, in 1927, the dairy maker began delivering milk door-to-door, a tradition that continues to this day.

The family-owned Oberweis Dairy now sells its products in stores throughout the Chicago area, and through home delivery. Glass-bottled, BGH-free milk is its signature item. Try the skim milk, which is so tasty you'd swear it was 2 percent. Kids rave about the chocolate milk. Oberweis also sells butter, cream, eggs, cheese, yogurt, ice cream, and nondairy items like meat and bottled beverages.

Other Locations
For a list of all of Oberweis Dairy's Chicago-area locations, go to
www.oberweisdairy.com/alllocations.asp

Taste
Bucktown
1922 West North Avenue
(773) 276-8000

This cheese-and-wine shop carries a small but notable selection of artisanal and farmstead cheeses, which owner Rodney Alex fondly calls "stinky cheeses." Alex opened Rushmore in 2000 (see p. 24), later selling his stake in the restaurant to pursue his passion for wine and cheese. Taste focuses on small American producers, with an eye toward freshness. At any time, there are between thirty and fifty kinds of cheese. The inventory changes frequently, so if you see something you like grab it fast. This store is high on taste but low on pretense. The workers bring a delight for wine (mostly from the Pacific Northwest) and cheese as well as a passion for education, and freely offer samples. Taste also holds a number of special events. Log onto www.juicywine.com for information on upcoming events or to get on their e-mail list.

NOTABLE

Binny's
River North
213 West Grand Avenue
(312) 332-0012

Visit Binny's River North location for one of this chain's largest cheese counters. The eccentric gentleman behind the counter is charming and knowledgeable.

Convito Italiano
1515 Sheridan Road
Wilmette
(847) 251-3654

For more than twenty years, Convito—which means "banquet" in Italian—has sold Italian wines and more than a hundred kinds of cheese.

Foodstuffs
338 Park Avenue
Glencoe
(847) 835-5105

Foodstuffs features an interesting selection of cheeses, meats, seafood, wines, breads, and pastries. They also have locations in Glenview, Evanston, and Lake Forest.

Fromage and Company
405 North Main Street
Glen Ellyn
(630) 469-7100

This Glen Ellyn gourmet shop stocks quite a few artisanal cheeses from small American producers.

Sam's Wines & Spirits
Goose Island
1720 North Marcey Street
(866) 726-7946

From the Indiana-made Capriole Banon to the Spanish El Suspiro de Cabra, this store sports a large selection of both domestic and international cheeses. Some, including Cow Girl Creamery's Mt. Tam, are handmade organic cheeses.

Schaefer's
9965 Gross Point Road
Skokie
(847) 673-5711

Schaefer's features a variety of gourmet cheeses and also sells a small but distinguished selection of wines.

Whole Foods Market
Lakeview
3300 North Ashland Avenue
(773) 244-4200

If you're looking for knowledgeable and helpful cheesemongers, visit the Whole Foods store near Ashland and Belmont. However, every store of this natural grocery chain offers a dependably good selection of cheeses from around the world.

ETHNIC & SPECIALTY MARKETS

ETHNIC MARKETS

AFRICAN

Abyssinia Market   *(Ethiopian)*
Edgewater
5842 North Broadway
(773) 271-7133

Highlights include a selection of *injera* (teff flatbreads) cooked by at least a half dozen Chicago chefs (only $1.50 per packet). A variety of Ethiopian spices, herbs, and other ingredients are also available.

Chika International Food Market
6350 South Cass Road
Westmont
(630) 435-0899
522 East Boughton Road
Bolingbrook
(630) 739-7799

Both stores are well stocked with a variety of African foods and various African cosmetics. Chika has the largest line of Ghanaian products in the Greater Chicago area.

Homeland Food Market
Edgewater
6046 North Broadway
(773) 973-1445

Homeland is a light, bright store offering a wide range of dried and frozen fish and meats, assorted legumes, a variety of flours, and *dende* oil. Though scrupulously clean, the store is quite pungent due to the cumulative odors of its diverse products.

Makola African Super Market   *(Afro-Caribbean)*
Uptown
1017 West Wilson Avenue
(773) 878-3958

This very clean and fresh-smelling market houses an impressive diversity of African and Caribbean foods and products in a small space. Spices, meats, fish, fresh produce, and many dry goods fill the abundant shelves, racks, and refrigerated cases.

CHINESE

Best Food Products
Chinatown
2403 South Wentworth Avenue
(312) 808-8878

This shop specializes in live and fresh fish, seafood, and fresh meats. At a small counter in the front of the shop, they sell barbecued and roasted meats. The butcher counter has pork hocks, whole chickens, chicken feet, Chinese "bacon," lup cheong sausages, salted duck legs, ground pork, and rib racks. Candies, Asian snacks of all sorts, and bulk items like dried shrimp, scallops, and anchovies are also available.

Chinatown Market
Chinatown
2121 South Archer Avenue
(312) 881-0068

Chinatown Market features a large assortment of beautiful produce: miniature cucumbers, lemongrass, enoki mushrooms, fuzzy gourds, yams, and jicama. The pristine seafood counter dispenses razor clams, oysters both unshucked and shucked, live frogs, live eels, and clams. There are several fish tanks from which you can choose your own tilapia, catfish, or carp.

Mayflower Foods
Chinatown
2140 South Archer Avenue
(312) 326-7450

Mayflower carries a wide selection of dried seafoods, herbs, and fungi, all sold from glass jars by the pound. The store has a meat counter (with pressed duck and dried Chinese sausages), a live/fresh seafood counter, and a good produce section, where you can often find fresh lily bulbs, pea shoots, chayote, daikon radish, winter melon, Chinese chives, and burdock root.

Mayflower also has the widest assortment of fresh noodles in the area. These include *banh pho*, Shanghai, Hokkien, *bamee*, *shiritaki*, and rice

noodle sheets. The dried noodle selection includes *pancit, e-fu,* longevity noodles, ramen, bean thread, and rice stick noodles.

Richwell Market
South Loop
1835 South Canal Street
(312) 492-7015

Richwell Market houses an outpost of Chinatown's BBQ King House, as well as the bakery Café de Victoria. The cafe bakes a daily assortment of tarts, cakes, and breads, including egg custard tarts, coconut buns, as well as an ersatz "hot dog roll."

The barbecue shop sells barbecued meats by the pound as well as roast duck and pork and soy chicken.

The market has an impressive assortment of vinegars, cooking oils, cooking wines, sauces, marinades, and condiments. And the customer service counter doubles as a sort of Chinese apothecary, dispensing various tonics and herbal remedies.

See also "A Walk around Argyle Street" in Chinese, p. 46.

EASTERN EUROPEAN

A-J Meats   *(Lithuanian, Polish)*
3541 West 99th Street
Evergreen Park
(708) 422-4130
Closed Sunday and Monday

This third-generation family-owned store carries many items that are uniquely Lithuanian, such as the ready-made *kugelis* and bacon buns, and at Christmastime the dumplings used to make *shlisikai* or poppy-seed milk soup. An old-fashioned meat counter provides fresh prime meat, cut to order, and one can also get beef ground to order. The Plienis father-and-son team also make Lithuanian, Polish, and Italian sausage themselves. The array of Lithuanian and Polish items includes fried pastries, farmers cheese, sauces, a variety of sauerkrauts, and a full deli with sliced cured meats.

Three Sisters Delicatessen & Gift Shop (Russian)
West Rogers Park
2854 West Devon Avenue
(773) 973-1919

Whether shopping for a party or just picking up their favorite foods, Russians in the Chicago area head for the Three Sisters Delicatessen. Nondescript on the outside, this small, narrow store is packed with Russian and European favorites. Shoppers select items from the long wall of shelves, then stand in a single line to be waited on by one of the white-robed assistants behind the counters. You'll need to be patient, as shopping here may not be quick, but it is worth the wait. Regulars come for the smoked fish, herring, and caviar. There also is a large selection of salamis, sausages, bolognas, and cold cuts, and favorites like farmers' cheese, a mild feta cheese (*Odessa Brinzya*), Russian-style sour cream (*smetana*), and slab bacons.

GERMAN

Delicatessen Meyer
Lincoln Square
4750 North Lincoln Avenue
(773) 561-3377

Because it has so many different kinds of foods on offer—meats, cheeses, sweets, and wines—Delicatessen Meyer is unlike any shop one would find in Germany, where its wares would be spread across several different types of stores. That's about the only thing that's inauthentic about this *wunder* deli. From the uniforms to the fussy wrapping and the German spoken by staff and customers alike in a variety of accents, this is a decidedly Old World shopping experience.

Don't forget to take a number when you come in; they're often quite busy, especially on weekends.

INDIAN & PAKISTANI

Fresh Farms International Market
West Rogers Park
2626 West Devon Avenue
(773) 764-5757

This large clean market offers diverse, high-quality products (including produce) representing many diverse cultures, most notably Indian and Pakistani. Prices are excellent and the unusual varieties of produce are seemingly infinite.

Patel Brothers
West Rogers Park
2610 West Devon Avenue
(773) 262-7777

This well-organized store stocks the full range of ingredients for all types of Indian and Pakistani cuisine, starting with essential oils, flours, and rice, including the world-famous basmati. Almost an entire aisle is devoted to various dried legumes, or *dal*. Perhaps the one unifying thread of all the different regional cuisines is the extensive use of spices and seasonings, all of which you will find in abundance. Spices of all kinds and in all forms (whole, ground, powder) are stacked nearly floor to ceiling and well labeled in English. Prices are very reasonable and the offerings are fresh thanks to high turnover. Patel Brothers also carries an immense variety of condiments such as pickles, pastes, chutneys, and sauces.
See also "A Walk down Devon Avenue" in Indian & Pakistani, p. 89.

ITALIAN

Bari Foods
West Town
1120 West Grand Avenue
(312) 666-0730

This grocery store, butcher shop, and deli is famous for its submarine sandwiches and bottled *giardiniera*. People line up at lunchtime, waiting for sandwiches made to order using bread from D'Amato's bakery next door. Also, go for the fresh meats and imported cheeses.

Caputo's Market
2560 North Harlem Avenue
Elmwood Park
(708) 453-0155

Although Caputo's specializes in Italian foods, there are also grocery-store staples and an outstanding fruit and vegetable section, along with baked goods, prepared foods, and a full-service butcher.

Conte di Savoia
Little Italy
1438 West Taylor Street
(312) 666-3471

This well-stocked deli carries many imported goods, including meats and cheeses. Many items are made in-house, including the sausage, ravioli, pasta sauces, and desserts. Great bread, fresh sandwiches, and several kinds of marinated salads make this a popular place at lunchtime.

Gino's Italian Import Foods
Belmont Heights
3420-22 North Harlem Avenue
(773) 745-8310

Gino's sells a wide variety of specialty goods, including Italian ceramics and cookware. The prepared-foods counter at the back of the store has an excellent selection of cheeses, salamis, and homemade sausages.

Joseph's Food Mart
Irving Woods
8235 West Irving Park Road
(773) 625-0118

Joseph's sells prepared foods, cheeses, and homemade pastas and has a full-service butcher and fish counter. It's also an excellent source for imported dry goods such as pasta, *carnaroli* rice, and a huge selection of condiments.

Pasta Fresh
Belmont Heights
3418 North Harlem Avenue
(773) 745-5888

You can watch the pasta being made through the window separating the small retail area from the kitchen. In addition to the perfectly fresh, house-made pasta, there are a few excellent southern Italian prepared and fried goods like *arancini* and *panzerotti*.

Riviera Market
Belmont Heights
3220 North Harlem Avenue
(773) 637-4252

This small market is a good source for Italian newspapers and Italian soccer jerseys. The butcher counter features homemade sausage and a nice selection of cheeses, vegetables, and house-made deli meats. For a great sandwich, pick a roll out of the bread bin and hand it over the counter to the deli man.

JAPANESE

Mitsuwa Marketplace
100 East Algonquin Road
Arlington Heights
(847) 956-6699

Mitsuwa Marketplace is a little bit of Japan in suburban Arlington Heights. The marketplace encompasses a large Japanese grocery, a food court, and a collection of Japanese shops, including an outstanding bookstore, a housewares and gift shop, a liquor store featuring a large selection of sakes and Japanese beers, and a wonderful toy shop selling everything from wooden children's toys to collector Godzilla sets!

The grocery is sparkling clean and bright and features every kind of Japanese foodstuff imaginable. The food court comprises several counters selling high-quality and very reasonably priced boxed sushi combinations, several ramen and udon noodle options, and a variety of other traditional cooked dishes. Portions are generous and the food is served in bento boxes and Japanese bowls.

KOREAN

Chicago Food Corporation
Avondale
3333 North Kimball Avenue
(773) 478-5566

Located just off the Kennedy Expressway, this is the place to go for a huge assortment of just about every conceivable Korean food product available (fresh, frozen, and packaged), along with some Japanese items. There's a small, popular lunch counter that serves soups, rice and noodle dishes, and a variety of pickled vegetable side dishes. You'll also find a "salad bar" with an extensive assortment of *kimchi*, fish, and seaweed. These are labeled in English and Korean for easy identification.

LATIN AMERICAN

El Mercado Food Mart
Lakeview
3767 North Southport Avenue
(773) 477-5020

Located in the trendy Lakeview neighborhood next to their Argentine steak house, Tango Sur, El Mercado carries a wide array of products from Argentina, Brazil, Ecuador, and Peru, as well as a good selection of South American meat.

La Unica Food Mart
East Rogers Park
1515 West Devon Avenue
(773) 274-7788

In the ethnically diverse neighborhood of Devon Avenue, La Unica stocks a large assortment of food products from Spain, Central America, South America, and the Caribbean. Fresh meats, produce, and frozen products including tropical fruit pulp are available. There is a small café featuring Latin American foods.

MEXICAN

Chicago possesses a number of Latin American grocery chains and independent grocers that specialize in typical Mexican ingredients, usually with better selection, prices, and quality than at your local supermarket.

Some basic staples found at Mexican grocery stores include fresh, and if your timing is right, still-warm corn and flour tortillas; spices, seasonings and pastes; fresh and dried peppers, including guajillo, ancho, and arbol; dried corn husks for tamales; a variety of cheeses and *crema*; a colorful array of tropical produce, and much more. Most grocers feature an in-house butcher, where one can find an astounding variety of meat, typically of high quality. Some of the delicacies you'll find yourself waiting in line for include skirt steaks, *arrachera*, chorizo, pig's feet, or pork head. Despite the possibility of a language barrier, the butcher can recommend what meat works best in different applications. Most larger stores will also have *carnitas*, an entire pig that has been fried to perfect tenderness, so you can choose just about any part you want, skin and all.

If looking at all the food on the shelves stirs up an appetite, some stores also have food counters serving very good and simple dishes, such as tacos, *tortas* (sandwiches), skirt steak, and often *menudo* (tripe stew) on the weekend.

Carniceria Guanajuato
Noble Square
1438 North Ashland Avenue
(773) 384-4567

Carniceria Jimenez
Logan Square
3850 West Fullerton
(773) 278-6769
Humboldt Park
4204 West North Avenue
(773) 486-5805
Logan Square
2140 North Western Avenue
(773) 235-0999

Fiesta Market
Albany Park
3925 West Lawrence Avenue
(773) 478-2882

La Justicia
Pilsen
3435 and 3644 West 26th Street
(773) 521-1593 or 277-8120

POLISH

Andy's Deli and Mikolajczyk Sausage
Jefferson Park
5440 North Milwaukee Avenue
(773) 631-7304

Mikolajczyk Sausage has been supplying Chicagoans with their home-made sausage and deli meats since 1918, beginning at its Wicker Park/Division Street location. Andy Kolasa purchased the business, and in addition to the deli in Avondale (3055 North Milwaukee Avenue), just opened his latest expanded venture—a combination deli, supermarket, café, and take-out store—at 5440 North Milwaukee Avenue. All the pre-pared entrées are available for consumption on the premises at one of the café tables in the store, and they rival the food at any full-service restau-rant. The deli is well stocked with homemade soups, salads, and fresh baked breads and pastries, in addition to fresh meat, dozens of deli meats, and imported cheeses.

Other Locations
1721 West Division Street, Chicago (Wicker Park); (773) 394-3376
3055 North Milwaukee Avenue, Chicago (Avondale);
    (773) 486-8160

Note: Also worth a visit is **Sweet World Pastry,** right next door at 5460 North Milwaukee Avenue; (773) 792-5566.

Gilmart
Archer Heights
5050 South Archer Avenue
(773) 585-5514

Shop to the sounds of Polish highlander music emanating from the PA system. A deli counter and small cafeteria-style restaurant occupy one corner of the store.

Joe and Frank's Homemade Sausage
Garfield Ridge
7147 West Archer Avenue
(773) 586-0026
8720 South Ridgeland
Burbank
(708) 599-3800

A full-service Polish grocery store with a large bakery and delicatessen/meat counter. Try one of the whipped-cream-filled waffle tubes—they're delicious.

Kasia's Deli
Ukrainian Village
2101 West Chicago Avenue
(773) 486-7500

Kasia Bober and her family consistently win Chicago's best *pierogi* contest; their mushroom *pierogi* are delectable. Many hot entries are available daily for take-out; catering is exemplary.

Montrose Deli
Portage Park
5411 West Montrose Avenue
(773) 725-6123
and
Cicero Deli
Craigin
3206 North Cicero Avenue
(773) 777-1615

Both the Montrose and Cicero delis offer a wide selection of baked goods, fresh meat, homemade deli items, and imported goods. Frozen *pierogi* and *uszka* (filled dumplings) are available to cook at home; call ahead for piping hot *nalesniki* (similar to crêpes) or *pierogi* made to order.

Wally's Market
Avondale
3256 North Milwaukee Avenue
(773) 202-1784
Dunning
6601 West Irving Park Road
(773) 427-1616

Wally Mulica's two stores bake their own breads and have an amazing variety of ready-to-eat salads and soups; a full meat counter/deli; and imported fruit, candy, teas, and salads.

SCANDINAVIAN

Erickson's Delicatessen
Andersonville
5250 North Clark Street
(773) 561-5634

Swedes and other aficionados of Scandinavian cuisine come here for brown beans, cheese, crispbread, flatbread, preserves, cookies, chocolates, and seafood. Owner Ann-Mari Nilsson sells anything you'd want for an old-fashioned smorgasbord. That might include pickled herring, Viking mustard, or King Oscar label fish balls. This is the only shop around where you can find fresh lingonberries, the Nordic answer to the wild cranberry. Erickson's will ship anything from its extensive inventory anywhere in the United States. Feel free to ask questions about unfamiliar foodstuffs at this friendly, mom-and-daughter shop established in 1925.

SOUTHEAST ASIAN

Tainam Food Market   *(Thai)*
Uptown
4925-J North Broadway
(773) 275-5666

Tainam Food Market is a wonderful resource for a wide choice of fresh fish, including live crabs, and an enormous selection of fresh vegetables. Looking for durian, gingerroot, coconuts, *yaca* root, or ginkgo nuts?

Tainam Food Market is a great resource for Thai fish, vegetables, canned goods, and noodles. Whatever it may lack in American tidiness, it makes up for in a big way by offering a fabulous and fresh selection.

Thai Grocery, Inc. *(Thai)*
Uptown
5014-16 North Broadway
(773) 561-5345

Thai Grocery, Inc., is more like a Thai convenience store than a grocery store. It is perfect for picking up Thai canned goods and snacks like Mr. Squid, crispy and fun baked squid. It also has a small curry counter in the back and a small sampling of fresh vegetables. Thai Grocery, Inc., sells Thai periodicals and even Thai Global Network Satellite TV!

MULTIETHNIC

Five Continents International Club
Archer Heights
4000 West 40th Street
(773) 927-0100

The International Club is a somewhat grungy, cavernous store that carries a wide variety of ethnic foods, primarily Asian (Japanese, Chinese, Thai, and Korean), Hispanic, and Filipino, but other cuisines, such as Polish, are also represented. It's fun to peruse the entire wall of ramen and other noodles, or the five-pound bags of dried black mushrooms and tea. While the aisles are helpfully marked, interesting juxtapositions abound, such as the shelf featuring Manzanilla olives next to West African palm oil. The store has a full service meat and seafood department, and also carries some more unusual cuts of meat and offal. A fresh produce section and an expansive freezer section make this one-stop shopping for your ethnic culinary adventures.

PRODUCE MARKETS

Andy's Fruit Ranch
Albany Park
4725 North Kedzie Avenue
(773) 583-2322

As its name suggests, Andy's is *the* place to go for fresh produce. Heavy on fruits that grow primarily in tropical climates, such as mamey and guava, if it's in season anywhere in the world, you can find it here. Groceries, canned goods, and a nice meat department round out the store's offerings.

Market Place on Clark Street
Uptown
4610 North Clark Street
(773) 506-1120

This extremely clean market offers some of the best values around. The amazingly low prices run the gamut of products, including the excellent and varied produce; the assortment of fresh chiles is particularly good.

Mayflower Food Company
Chinatown
2104 South Archer Avenue
(312) 326-7440 or 326-7450

Of the many produce markets in Chicago's Chinatown, Mayflower receives consistent praise for its outstanding produce in a setting that is cleaner than some of its competitors. An excellent source for Chinese greens of any type.

SPICES & HERBS

Penzey's Spices
1138 West Lake Street
Oak Park
(708) 848-7772
235 South Washington Street
Naperville
(630) 355-7677
www.penzeys.com
(800) 741-7787

Bill Penzey is the brother of the owner of the Spice House, but the businesses are actually competitors. Penzey's philosophy is to provide the highest-grade product by keeping most of his spices in whole form, thus retaining the most essential oils. To maintain maximum freshness spices are ground only when they are ordered.

With some 250 spices and about 40 custom blends, you are sure to find what you're looking for here. Shipping varies from what the Penzey's Web site calls "slow," which means seven to fourteen days, all the way up to next-day air. Their products are available via catalog or Web site, or visit

one of their seventeen locations nationwide. For all you Chicagoans, here's where to get your spices locally.

The Spice House
Old Town
1512 North Wells Street
(312) 274-0378

This family business, now in its forty-seventh year, has three stores, all specializing in what they claim to be "the highest-quality, hand-selected and hand-prepared spices and herbs."

The greatest thing about The Spice House is that the human element is still a large part of their craft and appeal. While proprietors Tom and Patty Erd import all their spices from countries where the individual spice is known to have the highest quality and flavor, the real treat is the hand sifting and mixing of the spices they do after you've made your selection.

In addition to pure spices the owners have created several unique spice blends with colorful names that play on Chicago landmarks and history. For example, the Back of the Yards blend recalls a large, now-defunct cattle stockyard located just south of downtown Chicago. As you might have guessed, this spice is excellent with red meat.

Other Locations
1941 Central Street, Evanston; (847) 328-3711
101 North Old World Third Street, Milwaukee, Wisconsin;
(414) 272-0977

FARMERS' MARKETS

All across the United States interest in farmers' markets has exploded as more and more people strive to make a personal connection to their food. In the Midwest our main growing season tends to run from late May through late October. Almost in defiance of this brief period, the market at the Cooking and Hospitality Institute of Chicago (CHIC), 361 West Chestnut Street, operates year-round on Sundays from 8:00 A.M. to 1:00 P.M., providing a sales venue for farmers who use hoop houses for extending the season and/or have good cold storage for root vegetables.

Chicago Green City Market
Lincoln Park, north of LaSalle Street, along the path between
  1750 North Clark and Stockton Drive
www.chicagogreencitymarket.org
Wednesdays

Mayor Richard M. Daley has the dream of making Chicago "America's Greenest City." To that end, he has introduced some innovative programs and environmental success stories such as Green Roofs—a rooftop garden project that promotes urban agriculture.

In a similar vein, in 1999 Abby Mandel and a team of prominent Chicago chefs such as Sarah Stegner and Rick Bayless founded Chicago's Green City Market. The market was created in response to the growing desire among the public for a place where one could buy a diverse selection of organic and sustainably grown foods in season. The Green City Market is the city's only market focused on sustainable production methods, and its painstaking attention to quality has been rewarded with ever-growing crowds. A committee of chefs and farmers screens vendors to determine that growing practices conform to strict criteria, and a good number of the vendors are certified organic or transitional, including Homegrown Wisconsin, a cooperative of twenty-five mostly organic farms surrounding Madison, Wisconsin. The farmers of Homegrown Wisconsin have expanded into the Chicago market by means of a simple business solution: a truck. Now instead of each grower making the four-hour drive to Chicago every week, they consolidate their orders and hire one driver to deliver them all. Check out restaurants that serve Homegrown Wisconsin food at www.homegrownwisconsin.com.

Over the years Green City has become a center of midweek socialization as well. It's not only a place where regular folk can buy the same food that is destined for tables at Blackbird and North Pond Café; you can get a cooking lesson as well at the weekly chef demonstration, and you can sometimes spot the top chefs arriving with their own trucks to cart away their custom-grown salad mix. And shoppers can listen to live music and enjoy a French-style crêpe made to order using market ingredients like

fresh raspberries from Blue Skies Farm, herbs from Smits Farm, and cheese, including from Judy Schad, who brings in her Capriole goat cheese from Indiana once a month.

CITY OF CHICAGO FARMERS' MARKETS

The Mayor's Office of Special Events operates an extensive network of farmers' markets downtown as well as in neighborhoods throughout the city. All through the season, downtown commuters can be spotted on the bus or El, loaded down with bags of fresh vegetables and a bouquet of peonies or hydrangeas peeking out. And just as popular are the various neighborhood markets that dot the city.

The city markets allow for cooperative agreements, which mean that farmers can bring in products grown outside the Midwest in partnership with farms in other areas of the country. The city is determined to help shoppers know where their food comes from by enforcing the rule that requires all food to be labeled with its point of origin. So look for farms that grow their own food so that you can enjoy the most flavorful local vegetables and fruits.

DOWNTOWN MARKETS

Daley Plaza
Washington and Dearborn (100 North–50 West)
On Daley Plaza
Thursdays

Federal Plaza
Adams and Dearborn (230 South–50 West)
On Federal Plaza
Tuesdays

The Park at Jackson and Wacker
311 South Wacker (311 South–350 West)
On the park at Jackson and Wacker
Thursdays

Prudential Plaza
Lake and Beaubien Court (200 North–150 East)
On Prudential Building Plaza
Thursdays

WEEKLY MARKETS

Sundays

Beverly
95th and Longwood (9500 South–1821 West)
City parking lot, southeast corner

Garfield Park
Washington and Central Park (300 North–3600 West)
In Garfield Park, north of the conservatory

Roscoe Village
Belmont and Wolcott (3200 North–1900 West)
Friedrich Ludwig Jahn play lot

Wicker Park and Bucktown
Wicker Park and Damen (1500 North–1800 West)
In Wicker Park

Tuesdays

Lincoln Square
Lincoln/Leland/Western (4700 North–2400 West)
City parking lot

Museum of Contemporary Art/Streeterville
Chicago and Mies van der Rohe Way (800 North–220 East)
MCA Plaza
10:00 A.M.–6:00 P.M.

Wednesdays

Auburn/Englewood/Gresham
63rd and Halsted (6300 South–740 West)
On the plaza at the corner of 63rd and Halsted

Gately/Pullman
111th and Cottage Grove (11100 South–800 East)
In Arcade Park

Lawndale
Grenshaw and Homan (1100 South–3400 West)
Community Bank of Lawndale parking lot

South Shore
70th and Jeffery (7000 South–2000 East)
South Shore Bank parking lot

Thursdays

Dunning—Eli's/Wright College
Montrose and Forest Preserve Avenue (4400 North–6701 West)
Eli's Cheesecake Company parking lot

Hyde Park
52nd Place and Harper (5200 South–1500 East)
On the cul-de-sac at Harper Court

Saturdays

Austin
Madison and Central (0 North/South–5600 West)
Emmet Math, Science & Technology Academy parking lot

Edgewater
Thorndale and Broadway (5800 North–1200 West)
Broadway Armory parking lot

Lincoln Park
Armitage and Orchard (2000 North–700 West)
Lincoln Park High School parking lot

Morgan Park
92nd and Ashland (9200 South–1600 West)
Shiloh M.B. Church parking lot

Near North
Division and Dearborn (1200 North–50 West)
On Division between State and Clark

North Center
Belle Plaine/Damen/Lincoln (4100 North–2000 West)
North Center Town Square

North Halsted
Grace/Broadway/Halsted (3750 North–800 West)
Faith Tabernacle Church parking lot

Rogers Park
Howard and Marshfield (7600 North–1632 West)
Gale Academy Elementary School parking lot
10:00 A.M.–2:00 P.M.

South Loop
18th and Wabash (1800 South–45 East)
St. Agnes Health Care Center parking lot

MONTHLY MARKETS

Ashburn
82nd and Kedzie (8200 South–3200 West)
Brown's Chicken parking lot
Wednesdays

Edison/Norwood Park
Oshkosh and Northwest Highway (6150 North–7800 West)
Parking lot next to Edison Park Field House
Wednesdays

Galewood/Montclare
Cortland and Newland (1850 North–6934 West)
Sayre Language Academy parking lot
Sundays

Lincoln Park Zoo
2001 North Stockton (2001 North–100 West)
Farm in the zoo
Sundays

West Lawn
65th and Pulaski (6500 South–4000 West)
Republic Bank parking lot
Sundays

OTHER CITY MARKETS

City Farm
Clybourn Avenue at Division Street
info@resourcecenterchicago.org

When tomato season finally hits, in-the-know food enthusiasts stop by City Farm's farm stand to score the same heirloom varieties that show up on tables at The Ritz-Carlton and Frontera Grill. City Farm is an extension of the Resource Center, a not-for-profit organization that picks up kitchen trimmings and plate scrapings from restaurants and turns them into compost. It uses that compost to grow organic vegetables on formerly vacant lots, first at the 70th Street location and now on the Clybourn site near the Cabrini Green housing project. The land is on loan from the city until it's ready for development; then the farm will pick up its compost and move it to another nearby site. In the meantime some of the best restaurants serve the thirty-plus varieties of tomatoes, as well as other vegetables grown on the farm. Slow Food supports City Farm through regular fund-raising dinners at the site, surrounded by the abundance of the farm and a spectacular view of the skyline.

Kawo Kabiyesi Farm
Austin
219 North Kenneth Avenue (200 North–4400 West)
(773) 921-1055
Wednesdays 9:00 A.M.–2:00 P.M.

The name of the farm, a praise name for an African thunder deity who infuses plants with the power to heal, comes from the Yoruba tribal nation in Nigeria. The weekly farm stand is one of several organic operations spearheaded by LaDonna Redmond, whose efforts stemmed from her son's life-threatening allergies. When Redmond made the connection between her son's allergies and the food he ate, she launched what has become something of an organic empire. A resident of the Austin neighborhood on the West Side, she could feed her family every sort of fast food but no organic vegetables. So she worked with the city to launch the Austin Black Farmers' Market, operated as part of the city network of markets. Now she leads the Kawo Kabiyesi Farm and also spearheads the farming of eighteen acres in Kankakee. Her premise is simple: Because city-dwelling middle- and lower-income African-Americans tend to spend a lot on fresh food, due mostly to the lack of grocery store competition in their neighborhoods, why not have fresh food that's organic and locally grown?

SUBURBAN FARMERS' MARKETS

Evanston Farmers' Market

Downtown Evanston at University and Oak avenues
(847) 866-2936
www.cityofevanston.org/government/citymanager/
   farmersmarket.html
Saturdays

The Evanston market has a long history of featuring sustainably produced foods. Henry Brockman, whose Henry's Farm (www.henrysfarm.com) has been a mainstay at the Evanston Farmers Market for two decades, is an example of how biodiversity can work. On an intimate five acres, Henry grows enough tomatoes, corn, and other vegetables to feed about five hundred families. And sustainability runs in Henry's family. When sister Terra Brockman saw land near the family's farm falling to development, she took action. Armed with a personal loan and a strategy Terra bought a parcel of land, set up a not-for-profit organization, and established The Land Connection (www.thelandconnection.org) to help train novice organic growers and encourage small-scale farming in central Illinois. The Land Connection's annual summer solstice celebration features tours of area farms, as well as pilot programs like raising shaggy Highland cattle and organic free-range chickens that live in a mobile coop. The day is topped off by a potluck supper and storytelling.

At the Evanston market, more than thirty vendors sell fresh vegetables, fruits, flowers, and bread. Free parking is available in the Maple Avenue parking garage.

Oak Park Farmers' Market

Downtown Oak Park, at 460 Lake Street at Elmwood in Pilgrim
   Congregational Church parking lot
www.vil.oak-park.il.us/farmersmarket
Saturdays

An Oak Park fixture since 1976, the Oak Park market features almost thirty vendors, live bluegrass music, and weekly bake sales that benefit local organizations. Their Web site includes a crop calendar to help shoppers anticipate the season's bounty.

Prairie Crossing

851 Harris Road
Grayslake
(847) 548-4030

www.prairiecrossing.com
Wednesdays and Saturdays

Prairie Crossing, an innovative conservation community in north suburban Grayslake, boasts a ninety-acre organic farm at the heart of the site. Like many farms, Prairie Crossing operates a Community Supported Agriculture (CSA) program, and also offers a membership program where farm members exchange funds at the beginning of the season for credits to be redeemed throughout the growing season at their own pace rather than each week. The farm market is open on Wednesday and Saturday mornings throughout the season, but visitors can leave cash in an honor box at other times.

OTHER SUBURBAN MARKETS

Local chambers of commerce or village halls can provide opening and closing dates, as well as times of operation.

Antioch
900 Skidmore Drive
Fridays

Arlington Heights
Near North School Park on Eastman Street between Arlington
    Heights Road and Evergreen Street
Saturdays

Aurora
Aurora Transportation Center, 233 North Broadway
Saturdays

Barrington
South Cook Street and Lake Cook Road
Thursdays

Bartlett
Bartlett Plaza, Main Street and Devon Avenue
Fridays

Crystal Lake
Depot Park, Woodstock and Williams streets
Saturdays

Deerfield
Commuter parking lot at northwest corner of Deerfield Road and
Robert York Avenue
Saturdays

DeKalb
Palmer Court, downtown between 2nd and 3rd streets
Thursdays

Des Plaines
Library Plaza, 1501 Elinwood Avenue
Saturdays

Downers Grove
Train station, 1000 Burlington Street
Saturdays

East Dundee
Dundee Township Tourist Center, 319 North River Street
Saturdays

Elk Grove Village
In the Pavilion parking lot at the corner of Biesterfield and
Wellington roads
Wednesdays

Elmhurst
York Road and Vallette Street behind the Knights of Columbus
Hall
Wednesdays

Forest Park
French Market at Elgin Avenue and Madison Street
Saturdays

Frankfort
City parking lot next to Breidert's Green, Kansas, and Oak streets
Saturdays

Geneva
French Market in Metra parking lot at northwest corner of South
and 4th streets
Sundays

Glen Ellyn
Main Street parking lot, between Duane Street and Hillside Avenue
Fridays

Glencoe
Village Court, one block west of Green Bay Road and one block
 south of Park Avenue
Saturdays

Glenview
Metra station parking lot on Lehigh Road, just north of Glenview
 Road
Saturdays

Grayslake
Center Street at Slusser Street
Wednesdays

Gurnee
Viking Park, just east of Old Grand Avenue and O'Plaine Road
Fridays

Highland Park
Ravinia Farmers Market at Dean Avenue between St. John's and
 Roger Williams avenues
Wednesdays

Highwood
Everts Park on Highwood Avenue
Saturdays

Hinsdale
Garfield Street parking lot, between Garfield Street and First
 Avenue
Mondays

Joliet
Van Buren and Chicago streets
Fridays

Kankakee
Downtown at Merchant Street and Schuyler Avenue
Saturdays

La Grange
Village Hall parking lot, 53 South La Grange Road
Thursdays

Lake Bluff
Village Green, near Scranton Avenue and Sheridan Road
Fridays

Libertyville
Church Street, between Milwaukee and Brainerd avenues
Thursdays

Lincolnshire
Downtown Lincolnshire Village Green North, at northeast corner
 of Milwaukee Avenue and Old Half Day Road
Fridays

Lisle
College Square Shopping Center, College Road and Green Trails
 Drive
Saturdays

Lombard
French Market, in the parking lot next to 105 West St. Charles
 Road
Saturdays

Midlothian
147th Street and Springfield Avenue
Fridays

Mokena
French Market, at southeast corner of Wolf Road and Front
 Street
Saturdays

Mt. Prospect
Metra station parking lot, Northwest Highway and Main Street
Sundays

Naperville
Parking lot of 5th Avenue Station, 200 East 5th Avenue
Saturdays

Oak Lawn
Yourell Drive, between Cook and 52nd avenues
Wednesdays

Palatine
Parking lot of train station at Wood and Smith streets
Saturdays

Palos Heights
119th Street and Harlem Avenue
Wednesdays

Palos Park
Parking lot of Palos Park Presbyterian Community Church, 12312
　　South 88th Avenue
Fridays

Park Forest
Near Village Hall at Indianwood and Orchard Drives
Saturdays

Park Ridge
Prairie and Garden Streets
Saturdays

Plainfield
Plainfield Library parking lot, 705 North Illinois Street
Saturdays

Schaumburg
Athenaeum Museum parking lot, Town Square, 190 South Roselle
　　Road
Fridays

Skokie
Next to Village Hall, 5129 Oakton Street
Sundays

St. Charles
Lincoln Park, on Main Street between 4th and 5th streets
Fridays

Tinley Park
Metra station at 173rd Street and Oak Park Avenue
Saturdays

Villa Park
French Market, by the gazebo on Park Boulevard at Ardmore
   Avenue
Sundays

Wheaton
Cross Street, between Seminary and Wesley streets
Thursdays

Wheaton
French Market, Main and Liberty streets
Saturdays

Wilmette
Metra parking lot downtown
Saturdays

Winfield
Prairie Trail Center, on southwest corner of County Farm and
   Geneva roads
Wednesdays

Woodstock
Downtown square at the Old Court House Arts Center
Thursdays and Saturdays

Worth
Parking lot of Prospect Federal Savings Bank, 11139 South Harlem
   Avenue
Wednesdays

Yorkville
Town Square Park at Illinois Highway 47 and Main Street
Saturdays

FISH & SEAFOOD MARKETS

Burhop's Seafood
1413 Waukegan Road
Glenview
(847) 901-4014
14 North Grant Square
Hinsdale
(630) 887-4700

Albert Burhop opened his seafood business downtown at State and Grand in 1926 and began a tradition of providing the best-quality fish and seafood to Chicago's top restaurants and to retail customers. Since then the family tree has spread throughout the Chicago area, continuing the business Albert started more than seventy-five years ago. Albert's son, Vern, followed in his father's footsteps and expanded the wholesale side of the business. The Burhop family opened its first suburban retail market in 1973 in Wilmette, and Vern's sons, Jim and Jeff, took over several years later. In 1991 the Wilmette market was purchased by new owners, who have retained the Burhops' name but operate their market independently. Jeff Burhop now owns and operates retail seafood markets in Hinsdale and Glenview. The Burhop name remains synonymous with quality, service, and the freshest fish and seafood available in Chicago.

Related Listing
Burhop's Seafood, 1515 Sheridan Road (Plaza del Lago),
  Wilmette; (847) 256-6400

Collins Caviar
West Loop Gate
925 West Jackson Boulevard
(800) 226-0342
www.collinscaviar.com

At a time when imported caviar is threatened with extinction from over-harvesting, illegal trade, and water pollution, domestic caviar provides an environmentally sustainable alternative. Collins is dedicated to responsible stewardship of marine resources, and they have been at the forefront of the development of domestic caviar in the United States.

Sevruga, osetra, beluga—the world-renowned caviars from the Caspian Sea have nothing on the caviars of the Midwest. Carolyn Collins and her daughter Rachel produce freshwater salmon, hackleback sturgeon, whitefish, bowfin, and paddlefish caviars that come from the waters of the Great Lakes and their tributaries. Their caviar is fresh and clean, with a natural flavor. Collins Caviar has been in business for twenty years, after Carolyn perfected the process of salt-curing fish roe in her kitchen.

Chicagoans have been enjoying Collins Caviar for years at local restaurants, tasting events, and promotions. Now a mail-order operation makes their products available nationwide. The caviar line has expanded to include smoked caviars, caviar crème spreads, and specialty caviars infused with chile peppers, vodka, wasabi, and mango, among other distinctive flavors. The Collinses believe that caviar is not just an indulgence, and they encourage the use of caviar in everyday cooking.

DiCola's Seafood
Morgan Park
10754 South Western Avenue
(773) 238-7071

The DiCola family has operated its seafood business on Chicago's South Side since 1933. Behind its counters DiCola's retail store sports a blue wall full of fresh and frozen fish and seafood. They make their own seafood chowder and gumbo, crab cakes, and side dishes. Take-out fish and seafood dinners are popular.

 ## Dirk's Fish & Gourmet Shop
Lincoln Park
2070 North Clybourn Avenue
(773) 404-3475

Dirk Fucik, who worked at Burhop's for years, now has his own seafood shop in the Clybourn Corridor. In addition to the freshest fish and seafood, Dirk's carries homemade fish soups, stocks, salads, and marinades. The staff is friendly and helpful, offering to fillet or debone your selections. There are cooking demonstrations on Saturday afternoons and, weather permitting, Fucik can be found grilling fish in the parking lot. Dirk's Web site (www.dirksfish.com) contains recipes, links to other fish-related sites, "fish stories," and a chart with recommended cooking methods and marinades for every species of seafood.

The Fish Guy Market
Albany Park
4423 North Elston Avenue
(773) 283-7400

Bill Dugan is the Fish Guy, who sells wholesale fish and seafood to many Chicago-area restaurants. The Fish Guy also maintains a retail shop in the front of its Albany Park location, a few minutes east of the Kennedy

Expressway at the Montrose Avenue exit. Look for the huge game fish above the door. The shop carries a variety of quality fish and seafood. Call ahead if you need a large whole fish or something out of the ordinary; most likely The Fish Guy can get it for you. The Fish Guy Market produces its own seafood salads, crab cakes, fish stocks, sushi, and fried fish by the pound. Local chefs appear for cooking demonstrations and special chef dinners.

Fisherman's Choice
South Chicago
8918 South Commercial Avenue
(773) 734-8320

Fisherman's Choice carries a good selection of fresh and frozen fish and seafood. Fresh catfish are swimming in the in-store pool. Homemade *ceviche* is also available. You can eat in at the small counter, where fried fish, soups, and seafood tacos are served. Spanish is the predominant language spoken here.

Hagen's Fish Market
Portage Park
5635 West Montrose Avenue
(773) 283-1944

A family business since 1946, this Portage Park neighborhood fish market specializes in smoked fish. Hagen's operates a smoking service; bring in your fresh catch and they will smoke it for you. In addition to smoked fish (the smoked shrimp makes a great appetizer), Hagen's carries a full range of fresh, frozen, and fried fish, with recipes free for the taking.

ICE CREAM

Margie's
West Bucktown
1960 North Western Avenue
(773) 384-1035

Take a step back in time when you enter this family-owned icon, but a step back to an authentic experience rather than an overpolished reproduction. Visitors will overlook the vinyl booths patched with clear packing tape in favor of absorbing the decor that ranges from vintage dolls, fresh-made chocolates, sauces for sale, and a collection of Beatles memorabilia; seems the Fab Four enjoyed hot fudge sundaes at Margie's after a Comiskey Park concert in the 1960s. Margie's son Peter Poulos is the third generation to reign over the counter of this neighborhood treasure that's been around since 1921.

Classic sundaes come in shell-shaped bowls with generous scoops of house-made ice cream, sauces on the side for precision pouring, and wafer cookies peeking out the top. Turtles are a big theme here. The turtle sundae, with kettle-fresh fudge and caramel, is the biggest seller, and the menus lists the World's Largest Terrapin, with a whopping fifteen scoops of vanilla. The menu also includes diner items like chicken noodle soup and grilled cheese sandwiches, but serious ice cream enthusiasts will go straight to the banana splits, sodas, and shakes in order to do justice to the offerings.

Massa
7434 West North Avenue
Elmwood Park
(708) 583-1111

A real find in Elmwood Park, this gelateria has some of the best creamy Italian indulgences in the area. The fact that everyone there speaks with an Italian accent only enhances the experience. Gelatos and sorbets are made fresh daily using heavy cream, bases, and flavorings imported from Italy. Italian classics like hazelnut, spumoni, and *fruta di bosco* (wild berry) combine creamy richness with flavors that pop. More than fifty flavors are rotated throughout the seasons, and regular visits to taste what's new are well worth the trip. The fresh strawberries in the strawberry gelato were clearly picked in season—red all the way through and bursting with fresh flavor. One creative spin guaranteed to appeal to kids is Spaghetti and Meatballs, a vanilla gelato run though a spaghetti press, topped with fresh strawberry "pomodoro" sauce, sprinkled with grated coconut "cheese," and topped with chocolate ice cream "meatballs."

Massa is brightly lit with faux-finish walls and an outdoor café for warm-weather lingering. A selection of grilled panini, individual pizzas, and hot entrées make this a great place for lunch or dinner on the run. And a full coffee bar features locally roasted Caffe Fratelli Lollino brand coffee.

Miami Flavors
Humbolt Park
2504 West Division Street
(773) 227-2337

This Latin American and Caribbean ice cream shop stands only steps from the giant flag gateway that marks this proudly Puerto Rican neighborhood. Owner and chef Robert Bouyer is a Miami native and a graduate of Kendall Culinary College. He specializes in hard-to-find tropical flavors of homemade ice cream such as avocado, tamarind, guava, pumpkin, tomato, banana rum, and honeydew melon. Ice cream is sold by the scoop or used to create specialty sundaes like the Caribbean Carnival (rum raisin ice cream with fried ripe plantains, shredded coconut, dried mango, and pineapple).

On the shop's brightly colored walls hang photographs and paintings depicting the landscapes and people of Latin America and the Caribbean. Local artists' works are displayed and for sale, and the shop also hosts occasional poetry readings. The comfy couch by the window offers a perfect spot for perusing the Caribbean cookbooks on hand or for a game of chess while sampling the ice cream.

Homemade pies, cakes, cobblers, and cookies are available as well, along with fresh fruit smoothies, tamales, pan pizza, deli sandwiches, and *café bustelo* (traditional Puerto Rican coffee). One wall features sweets and toys from different countries, which change monthly. October's offerings might come from Brazil, November's from Puerto Rico, December's from Colombia, and so on.

Oberweis Dairy
9 East Dundee Road
Arlington Heights
(847) 368-9060

The dairy empire began with milk delivery by horse cart for this seventy-five-year-old business headquartered in North Aurora, Illinois. Still owned by the Oberweis family, the company ventured into ice cream fifty years ago, though they continue to deliver milk to the doorsteps of Chicago-area residents even today.

Walk into any Oberweis location and you're in the classic ice cream shop, complete with a red-and-white-striped awning. Even the sundaes are steeped in tradition, making it difficult to choose between Hot Fudge

Brownie, Rocky Road, or Tin Roof with chocolate sauce and fresh-roasted Spanish peanuts. There's something for everyone here, and those interested in a more contemporary, adventurous beverage can try out the Moo Coolers like Cowabunga Cappuccino or Pina Cowlada. Kid-size sundaes and shakes are perfect for the younger set, or adults who want a smaller indulgence.

Other Locations
For a list of all Oberweis Dairy's Chicago-area locations, go to
   www.oberweisdairy.com/alllocations.asp

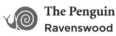

The Penguin
Ravenswood
2723 West Lawrence Avenue
(773) 271-4924

It would be easy to drive right past the nondescript location without knowing that this is a don't-miss ice cream treasure. What the Penguin lacks in ambience it makes up for in hospitality and great taste. Owner José Curci, born in Argentina to Italian parents, learned the art of ice cream in the Buenos Aires family shop operated by his in-laws. He brought his expertise, and his family, to the States in 2000.

The gelato-style ice cream is made in-house—favorites are *sabayon*, made with Marsala wine, and three variations on *dulce de leche*. As if this indulgence weren't enough, Curci embellishes the almond-chocolate and other flavors with nuts that are caramelized in butter and sugar before being stirred into the ice cream. Curci's Italian father takes charge of the pizza oven, creating authentic thin-crust pizza, calzones, and empanadas. And if you can't make it over to Lawrence Avenue, you can have your ice cream and pizza delivered for an in-home fix.

Petersen's
1100 West Chicago Avenue
Oak Park
(708) 386-6131

A childhood favorite of generations of Oak Parkers, Petersen's evokes memories of treats after dance lessons and Little League games. Founded by Danish immigrant Hans Petersen in 1919, it moved to its current location in 1931 and is now owned by Daryl Bartelson, who added home-made candies to the mix. The old-fashioned ice cream is made exclusively to Petersen's specifications by House of Flavors in Ludington, Michigan. Flavors also stick to tradition, like strawberry, mint chocolate chip, and black walnut, along with that increasingly elusive flavor, rainbow sherbet.

The adjoining restaurant serves a substantial breakfast as well as lunch and dinner featuring more old-fashioned favorites like meat loaf and soup made from scratch. The on-site bakery makes all of its own breads, cakes, and pies, in case you have to entice the unusual person whose dessert of choice is not ice cream.

Village Creamery
4558 Oakton Avenue
Skokie
(847) 982-1720

Bring an appetite and a sense of adventure to this northern suburban ice cream shop. Just sampling all of the flavors available on any given day—thirty-five of them—can take some time, and deciding on a single selection can make a visitor decide to skip dinner in favor of more indulgence.

Village Creamery was launched in 2001 by Filipino immigrants Lito and Ann Valeroso and son Rod, who frequently mans the counter and chats enthusiastically about creative ingredient combos like Morning Blend (vanilla ice cream with granola and raisins) or Flaming Chocolate Crunch (a hot-pepper chocolate with crunchy soy nuts). Recipes are inspired by Ann's grandparents, who owned a bakery in the Philippines. They probably did not serve Morning Blend or Flaming Chocolate Crunch, but they did know how to whip up a creamy extravagance.

All of the ice creams—a whopping 109 flavors in their repertoire, and counting—are made at the Niles location with milk from Elgin Dairy. The real finds are Filipino-inspired flavors like *ube* (purple yams), *macapuno* (young coconut pieces in a coconut-flake ice cream), and red bean, which is actually a popular Japanese flavor. All in all, Village Creamery is the best of many worlds, combining the exotic with good old American-inspired flavors. For instance, one flavor is vanilla with raspberry ribbon and cashews. The name? Baseball Nut.

Other Location
8000 Waukegan, Niles; (847) 965-9805

NOTABLE

Bittersweet
Lakeview
1114 West Belmont Avenue
(773) 929-1100

Pastry chef and dessert doyenne Judy Contino added made-fresh-daily ice cream to her offerings several years ago. The seven ice cream and sorbet flavors rotate, including classics like espresso and mint chocolate chip, with the occasional seasonal extravagance like Strawberry Balsamic. Ice cream maker Celeste Zeccola grows herbs on her porch for the lemon verbena ice cream.

Evanston Creamery
1301 Chicago Avenue
Evanston
(847) 328-3113

Situated right up the street from an area classic, the Blind Faith Café, the Evanston Creamery boasts of their house-made waffle cones in chocolate and cinnamon flavors and their extensive selection of custom ice cream cakes. The ice cream is made by Chocolate Shoppe Ice Cream in Madison, Wisconsin, which can also be found at the Chocolate Shoppe at 5337 West Devon in Chicago; (773) 763-9778. Look for the Door County Cherry variety, made when cherries are in season.

Gayety's Chocolates and Ice Cream Company
3306 Ridge Road
Lansing
(708) 418-0062

Another classic ice cream and candy shop. All seven flavors of ice cream have been house made since 1920. Out-of-towners can get a chocolate fix by mail.

Hartigan's Ice Cream Shoppe
2909 Central Street
Evanston
(847) 491-1232

The focus is on fun at Hartigan's, where patrons can join both a birthday club and the "I Love Ice Cream in the Dead of Winter" club. Twenty-two-year ice cream veteran Terry Hartigan partnered with Cedar Crest Dairy in Cedarburg, Wisconsin, in 1996, after extensive blind tasting. Of the forty-eight flavors he scoops, his favorite is Mackinaw Island Fudge.

Homer's Restaurant and Ice Cream
1237 Green Bay Road
Wilmette
(847) 251-0477

Since 1935 Homer's has been serving the North Shore some of the creamiest ice cream in town. All the ice creams are still made on the premises and Homer's has achieved the perfect balance of a specially formulated 14 percent butterfat and low overrun (air) that leads to really great-tasting ice cream.

Homer's Restaurant is styled after an old-fashioned ice cream parlor and is by far one of the most child-friendly spots in the North Shore. Not only do they serve ice cream, but they have a full counter menu with sandwiches, soups, and salads. You can purchase hand-packed ice cream for take-out, and they even ship their ice creams anywhere in the country for those who really are missing a bit of home. One story has it that there is a gentleman who has been coming here weekly for more than thirty years to get his hot fudge sundae fix.

Mario & Gino's
Roscoe Village
2057 West Roscoe Street
(773) 529-8664
Closed in winter

An intimate neighborhood favorite for gelato ranging from pistachio to tiramisu, as well as sorbets like Grapefruit-Campari.

Sukhadia's Sweets
West Rogers Park
2559 West Devon Avenue
(773) 338-5400

This Indian sweet shop in the heart of Devon Avenue gets milk from Fox Valley Farm to stir up tried-and-true standards like butter pecan, but more adventurous patrons might opt for Lychee or Saffron-Pistachio. The recipes, created by owner Jayant Sukhadia, are based on the 120-year-old Indian tradition of reducing the milk to thicken it.

Tom and Wendee's Italian Ice
Lincoln Park
1136 West Armitage Avenue
(773) 327-2885
Closed in winter

A magnet for the crowd that wants to balance health and indulgence, all of the homemade Italian ices use all-natural fruit juices and are entirely fat free. Choose from the three chocolate ices, or select combos like orange-tangerine and banana-strawberry.

MADE IN CHICAGO

Next time you're at the grocery store, look for some of these Chicago hometown favorites.

Baked Goods

Bays English Muffins

In 1933 George W. Bay opened a bakery in Chicago's downtown Loop district. He sold English muffins with orange marmalade, using the original recipe his English grandmother brought to this country in the 1800s. Sold by the dozen in brown paper bags, the muffins were hand delivered to bakeries, restaurants, hotels, and private clubs. Today Bays continues to carry on the family tradition—operating as a family business and adhering to the authentic, original recipe using only cane sugar, Minnesota spring wheat and whole milk, Wisconsin AA butter, and potato flour.

Eli's Cheesecake

This company makes more than ten thousand cheesecakes and other baked goods daily, using more than four million pounds of cream cheese, five hundred thousand pounds of eggs, and more than one million pounds of sugar per year. The family-owned company has been in the restaurant business for fifty years. The cheesecakes, which contain no preservatives and are kosher (except for two varieties), are sold in all fifty states and parts of Europe and Asia.

Gonnella Baking Company

Thirty-plus family members still work for Gonnella, which consistently ranks as one of the nation's top hundred bakeries. Though they now turn out 1.5 million pounds of products per week, the company strives to produce the same true hearth-baked breads Alessandro Gonnella baked in his small, wood-burning oven when he founded the company in 1886.

Candy

Ferrara Pan Candy

It puckers your mouth to even think about their goodies: They make Lemonheads (and their spawn, Appleheads, Cherryheads, etc.), Red Hots, Jaw Breakers, and Boston Baked Beans. The ninety-year-old company is still operated by descendants of its founders.

Tootsie Roll Industries

Founded in 1896, the company produces more than sixty million Tootsie Rolls per day, and is the world's largest lollipop supplier. The round piece of chewy, chocolaty candy still looks and tastes just like the first Tootsie

Roll, made more than 107 years ago. Leo Hirshfield, the Austrian immigrant who first made the candies, named them after his five-year-old daughter, whose nickname was Tootsie.

Meats

Hans All Natural

Known for their chicken sausage in tasty flavors such as spinach-feta, artichoke-kalamata, apple, and andouille, they use organic ingredients and only chicken raised using low-stress, environmentally responsible growing practices. Their beef and pork products are made without nitrites or nitrates, MSG, or antibiotics, and are raised on sustainable family-owned farms with no artificial growth stimulants or hormones.

Vienna Beef

Two young immigrants brought their hot dog sandwich—a pure beef frankfurter in a steamed bun with yellow mustard, bright green relish, chopped onion, tomato wedges, a kosher pickle spear, "sport" peppers, and a dash of celery salt—from Austria-Hungary to the Chicago World's Fair and Columbian Exposition in 1893, and started an empire. In Chicago more than 80 percent of the 1,800-plus hot dog vendors feature Vienna Beef products, including those at White Sox, Cubs, Bulls, and Blackhawks games. Today this family-run business sells its products to Mexico, Europe, and the Pacific Rim.

MEAT, POULTRY & GAME

Despite its proximity to Lake Michigan, Chicago is a meat town. Once famously (or infamously) known as the "Great bovine city of the world," "Porkopolis," and "Hog butcher to the world," Chicago's image has always been tied to meat. With the Union Stock Yards capable of holding some twenty thousand cattle and seventy-five thousand hogs at their prime, Chicago was the country's main meat supplier. In those days every neighborhood had its own butcher or two.

Today, unfortunately, the neighborhood butcher is rare, almost a novelty. Most people opt for the convenience of buying their meat at the supermarket where, sadly, the quality is not always what you expect and the cuts of meat are often not what you want. Typically there is no real butcher in these stores to complain to (in many stores the meat comes in precut) or make special requests of, so you are stuck musing how to alter your dinner plans with the weak selection before you. To their credit, some of the chains have recently realized this and have shown attempts to make their meat departments more butcher shop like.

Fortunately, Chicago has held on to some of its classic butchers and their traditions. If you truly relish a nice porterhouse steak, a succulent leg of lamb, some wonderful smoked bacon, or a plump roasting chicken, then make an effort to get to know your local butcher; you want to be on a first-name basis. Real butchers are out there, and the products they sell are usually far superior to the fare crudely wrapped in plastic and stacked in the fluorescent cold case at the chain grocer's.

Below is a list of some of the better meat markets in town. Certainly there are many other worthy neighborhood meat markets that we haven't listed—try exploring Argyle Street, Devon Avenue, Chinatown, or Pilsen for some great ethnic markets. Many cuts of meat you'll find there may be different from what you are used to, and not all of them will carry a USDA label, but you are bound to discover a great value and learn something new while you're at it.

Al's Market
1165 Wilmette Avenue
Wilmette
(847) 256-0070
Closed Sunday

Walking into Al's Market is a bit like stepping back in time, to an era when butcher shops were common in every neighborhood. Several large, heavy butcher blocks stand behind the cases and old meat posters dot the walls. The store was started by Al Spera in 1960, and is run today by his son Joe, who continues to hang his own beef and keep the hand-cut service alive. Meats are Prime and top-of-the-line Choice and are purchased mainly from local independent suppliers. Two big draws are the prime rib and the dry-aged beef, which Spera selects, hangs, ages, bones, and cuts himself. He also ages his lamb. Other popular items include pork, veal, and poultry, which is delivered fresh and kept on ice. The freezer case stocks organic beef, a variety of other poultry and game birds, and miscellaneous selections. In the summer pig roasts are a specialty.

Big Apple Market
Lincoln Park
2345 North Clark Street
(773) 871-2916

In the back of this small Lincoln Park independent grocery you'll find a first-rate independent butcher (they lease the space from the store). They have a special room for dry-aging your meat. Knowledgeable, friendly service and excellent meats will keep you coming back.

Bornhofen Meat Market
Edgewater
6155 North Broadway Street
(773) 764-0714

A classic neighborhood full-service butcher that has been purveying gorgeous Prime meats and Grade A pork and poultry since 1920. Dave and Bob are two fantastic young butchers who operate as if they were working back in the old country: "We always remember the names of our customers, who are sometimes the third and fourth generation." The butchers at Bornhofen have great meats, friendly service, and a genuine concern for how you are going to prepare that superb flank steak you just bought.

Casey's Market
915 Burlington Street
Western Springs
(708) 246-0380
Closed Sunday

Casey's is a bustling meat market that has become a fixture of the community. Now run by the second generation of Caseys, David and Dan, the store offers a full line of choice meats, and a prompt, friendly, and large staff of butchers who are helpful and obliging. Casey's also offers a myriad of oven-ready and prepared foods, including top-selling stuffed chicken breasts and marinated items.

Other Locations

Casey's Foods, 124 West Gartner Road (Naperville Plaza),
   Naperville; (630) 369-1686
Mike's Meat Market, 9 East Park Boulevard, Villa Park;
   (630) 832-1720

Chicago Live Poultry
West Rogers Park
6421 North Western Avenue
(773) 381-1000

If you want really fresh chicken, duck, quail, turkey, or rabbit this is the
place to go. You can walk in to the back room filled with cages of chatter-
ing chickens and point to the dinner you desire. In a matter of minutes
you'll be going home with some extremely fresh meat (and if you're not
squeamish you can watch the entire process). Don't worry: The animals
are not raised in the store; they are shipped in from farms in Michigan.

Columbus Meat Market
West Loop Gate
906 West Randolph Street
(312) 829-2480

This wholesale market is open to the public. They don't pretend to keep a
pretty shop or to be customer-service minded; it's a no-frills small storefront with a lightly stocked cold case. It's what they have in their *back*
coolers that you want: excellent quality beef, pork, and poultry. You don't

go into Columbus to browse; you go in knowing what you want to buy, and chances are pretty darn good they'll have it.

Gepperth's Meat Market
Lincoln Park
1964 North Halsted Street
(773) 549-3883

There is always a friendly atmosphere in this small classic meat market, where the butchers seem to know many of their customers by name. Their customers are loyal and return week after week: a sign of quality meats and top-notch service. They can dry-age whole loins of beef if you ask them.

Halsted Packing House
West Town
445 North Halsted Street
(312) 421-5147

Halsted Packing House is a fresh-kill butcher. Except for beef, their pork, lamb, and goat are slaughtered on the premises, guaranteeing you some exceptionally fresh meat. Since they work with the whole animal carcass, they specialize in custom cuts of meat.

Harrison's Poultry Farm Inc.
1201 Waukegan Road
Glenview
(847) 724-0132

This North Shore full-service poultry market provides superb all-natural, free-range chickens and eggs at very reasonable prices. The also carry duck, Cornish game hen, turkey, and rabbit. The service is excellent.

Jerry and John's Quality Meats
3706 Dempster Street
Skokie
(847) 677-9360

A small full-service butcher that aims to please, and please they do. Their cases are well stocked with Choice and Prime meats.

Joe's Market Inc.
Ravenswood
4452 North Western Avenue
(773) 478-5443

In this small, unassuming shop you will find some of the best homemade salamis and sausages in the city. Joe does several kinds of salamis, mostly in the Eastern European tradition, both fresh and cured. Hanging behind the counter is a grand offering of unique smoked sausages—sweet or spicy—and in the cold case are fresh sausages, like German-style veal brats and wonderful all-beef hot dogs. Joe also does excellent bacon and other smoked meats. Be brave and try some of the headcheese; Joe will let you taste it before you buy it. You'll be glad you did.

Paulina Market
Lakeview
3501 North Lincoln Avenue
(773) 248-6272

The largest full-service retail butcher in Chicago, Paulina Market was founded by Sigmund Lekan in the former Germantown area. It's since moved, but its selection of sausages and smoked meats is still heavily German. The smokehouse is visible through large windows behind the counter, and the aroma upon entry leaves no doubt where the work is done.

They stock a complete selection of meats: beef, pork, lamb, veal, and chicken. It's easy to get carried away here; everything looks delicious. You name it and Paulina likely has it, including some excellent homemade salamis, veal bratwursts, and smoked pork tenderloins (these make for superb sandwiches). Be prepared to wait, since the place is always bustling. You won't mind, however, as this might be the best-smelling place on earth.

PASTRIES & BAKED GOODS

Bittersweet Bakery
Lakeview
1114 West Belmont Avenue
(773) 929-1100

Bittersweet, located in the Lakeview neighborhood, is a bright, sunny bakery reminiscent of a French patisserie. It has been providing Chicago with the highest-quality cakes, tarts, pastries, cookies, and holiday treats for more than ten years. Bittersweet also makes its own chocolate candies, ice cream, and gelato. Stop in for coffee and a brioche for breakfast, or a light lunch of soup, quiche, or a sandwich. When you need a dessert to impress your dinner guests, Bittersweet is the place to go. The daily pastry specials, or perhaps a seasonal fruit pie, are displayed on top of the counter. Pastry chef and owner Judy Contino personally assists patrons in the design of cakes for special occasions.

Bombon Bakery
Pilsen
1508 West 18th Street
(312) 733-7788

Pastry chefs/owners Luis Perea and Laura Cid-Pfeiffer, both formerly of Mexico City and the Frontera Grill restaurant family, combine European techniques with traditional Mexican specialties to create unique interpretations of old favorites. Their *tres leches* cake, in several flavors, is an example of their ability to transform what can sometimes be a rich, heavy cake into a light, elegant dessert.

The bakery sells individual French pastries, children's birthday cakes, *conchas* (sweet buns), and other traditional Mexican sweets. During the Day of the Dead celebration in early November, the bakery makes personalized molded sugar skulls and sets up an altar to honor deceased family members, encouraging customers to leave a memento of their loved ones at the altar. The bakery is located in the vibrant Pilsen neighborhood, the heart of Chicago's Mexican community.

Deerfield's Bakery
813 North Waukegan Road
Deerfield
(847) 945-0068

In 1886, Adam Schmitt opened his first bakery in Germany and earned the title of Master Baker. His descendants have operated Deerfield's Bakery since 1911, although the bakery has moved over the years from Chicago's North Side and suburbs to the current Deerfield location.

Deerfield's is a full-service bakery, but it is the cakes that stand out—they are simply works of art! A wall of coolers holds various creations available for any occasion and every taste. The buttercream frosting, a secret recipe, melts in your mouth without overpowering the cake, which is light and moist. Chocolate mousse cakes lined with ladyfingers are tempting. Even Deerfield's cupcakes, decorated in three sizes, are miniature works of art.

With more than seven hundred cookie-cutter shapes, sugar cookies decorated as ballerina slippers, soccer balls, or various animals and insects are always behind the counter to delight children. In the center of the bakery are self-service tables and shelves full of that day's bagels, croissants, challah bread, kuchen, danish, coffee cakes, strudels, muffins, and fruit pies. Tradition and a commitment to excellence are what make Deerfield's one of the best bakeries in the Chicago area.

Lutz Continental Café and Pastry Shop
Ravenswood
2458 West Montrose Avenue
(773) 478-7785

Step into Lutz Continental Café and Pastry Shop and you'll feel as if you are on a visit to Germany, which is where the Lutz family began its bakery business in the eighteenth century. Several generations later, in 1948 the Lutz Pastry Shop opened in Chicago, and it continues to operate in an expanded space at the same location. Lutz is famous for their traditional German several-layer tortes, individual pastries, strudels, and butter cookies. Lutz tortes can be ordered in sizes to feed up to a hundred people!

There are no shortcuts to quality at Lutz. They use only the freshest ingredients, resulting in cakes that are light and not too rich. They create fruits, animals, and figurines out of marzipan; they make their own hand-dipped truffles and ice cream (for their ice cream cakes); and they even have their own blend of coffee. Their sheet cakes and wedding cakes are all personally designed.

Christmas is a special time at Lutz, with the family's own recipe for *Christ Stollen*, dating back to 1790. There is *baumkuchen*, (the "King of cakes"), gingerbread houses, Christmas tortes, and Yule logs. The marzipan is shaped into Santas, angels, and snowmen.

While the pastry shop occupies the front room, beyond the bakery counters Lutz Continental Café serves light lunch and dinner in a European-style dining room. Customers are free to choose a slice of pastry at the bakery counter and have it served in the café or in the outdoor garden in the summer. Lutz Continental Café is the perfect spot for romantic couples, ladies who lunch, or generations of families to experience a little piece of Germany without ever leaving Chicago.

San Juan Bakery
Humbolt Park
3437 West North Avenue
(773) 395-0099

San Juan Bakery specializes in Puerto Rican desserts as well as sandwiches. At the bakery counter, they offer bread and rolls baked on the premises. Their pastries are accented by grated coconut cream, pineapple purée, and guava paste. They have large coconut macaroons. Their *pastelillo con guava* is a layered puff pastry with a layer of guava paste dusted with powdered sugar. *Coconut con queso de guava* is a flaky pastry with a bottom layer filled with coconut cream, a center layer with sweetened cream cheese, and a guava-filled layer on top. Their *tres leches* cake is from a Colombian recipe. They also offer desserts such as chocolate éclairs and sponge cakes with whipped cream and decorated with glazed peaches. In addition, they sell single- and multiple-serving trays of *tembleque* (coconut pudding), three kinds of flan, bread pudding, and rice pudding with raisins.

San Juan Bakery daily roasts legs of pork for use in sandwiches. Unlike the newly popular Cubano sandwich, their *pernil* sandwich is not pressed, but is a bullet-shaped roll stuffed with shredded pork and topped with garlic mayonnaise, lettuce, and tomato. The bakery has seating, so you can enjoy your cup of coffee, sandwich, or pastry right here.

The Swedish Bakery
Andersonville
5348 North Clark Street
(773) 561-8919

The Swedish Bakery recently celebrated its seventy-fifth anniversary in 2003 in the Swedish neighborhood of Andersonville. Their coffee cakes include traditional cardamom braids, flaky fruit *kringlers*, Danish almond rings, *morskaka* (a round, raisin-filled plain dough), and *julekaka* (a cardamom-spiced, buttery cake flavored with citron, fruits, and raisins). Handmade Swedish butter cookies come in a variety of flavors and shapes. The Swedish Bakery's heart-shaped spicy ginger cookies (*pepparkakor*) are available during the holidays, as well as *pfeffernuesse* (spice cookies), Swedish pastries such as *toska* (a shortdough crust with a dense almond cake finished with a caramelized almond glaze), and *marzariner* almond tarts that will tempt even those counting calories. Swedish *limpa* breads, tea rolls known as *bullar*, and cinnamon breads are also available. Wedding cakes are made in the European tradition, with white marzipan, fruit glaze, and fondant available to finish off the cake. Many people consider The Swedish Bakery to be the best bakery in Chicago, and its loyal customers flock there on weekends. Don't let the crowd discourage you—take a number; the line moves quickly.

Vanille
Lincoln Park
2229 North Clybourn Avenue
(773) 868-4574

Husband and wife Dimitri and Keli Fayard recently opened their upscale patisserie in the Clybourn Corridor, making French pastries, petit fours, and macaroons, personally designed wedding cakes, handmade chocolates, and breakfast sweets. Dimitri and Keli have brought their training and experience at such respected establishments as Payard Patisserie and Bistro in New York and the Bellagio Hotel in Las Vegas to Chicago to create a chic bakery with several tables for enjoying their pastries with a cup of coffee. Sugar and chocolate showpieces, usually created only for pastry competitions, can be ordered.

Dimitri was on the silver-medal-winning team at the 2003 National Pastry Championship. His prize-winning dessert, Entremet Vanille, is featured at the bakery: a light coconut cake with white chocolate mousse, vanilla sable, fruit coulis, and vanilla cream. Or try Manjari, a chocolate biscuit under a dome of chocolate cream and chocolate mousse. Everything at Vanille is of the highest quality. This French patisserie is a welcome addition to Chicago's bakeries.

Vienna Pastry Shop
Portage Park
5411 West Addison Street
(773) 685-4166

Master Baker and pastry chef Gerhard Kaes, a member of the Vienna Pastry Guild, and his family have been providing baked goods to Chicago for more than thirty years in this brightly lit bakery in the Portage Park neighborhood. No need to travel to Vienna—the shop offers more than thirty different Viennese pastries and twenty-six classic tortes and cakes. Counters and shelves from wall to wall are stocked full of French pastries, cakes, fruit pies, strudels, doughnuts, coffee cakes, and cookies, as well as daily specials—all of the same high quality. Several tables provide a place to enjoy a slice of pastry with coffee served on a silver tray, *mit schlag* (with whipped cream), as in Vienna. The Vienna Pastry Shop also sells imported candies, coffees, teas, and preserves.

NOTABLE

Central Continental Bakery
101 South Main Street
Mt. Prospect
(847) 870-9500

Four generations of the Czerniak family have provided Chicagoans with traditional Polish and Slavic pastries, as well as French and Viennese pastries. In addition to the European delicacies, every inch of this small bakery is filled with sweet breads, strudels, cookies, coffee cakes, doughnuts, and sweet rolls. People travel to this northwest suburban location from all over Chicagoland for Central Continental's specialty cakes.

Dinkel's
Lakeview
3329 North Lincoln Avenue
(773) 281-7300

Joseph Dinkel, of Dinkelsbuehl, Germany, opened his Chicago bakery on Lincoln Avenue in 1922. The Dinkel family continues to produce German pastries using the same original recipes. Delicious strudels, butter cookies, coffee cakes, fresh breads and rolls, and birthday cakes fill this large bakery. Their *stollen*, which comes in several varieties, is packed for shipping at Christmastime and mailed to devoted customers around the world.

Ferrara Bakery
Little Italy
2210 West Taylor Street
(312) 666-2200

Three generations of the Ferrara family have provided Chicagoans with Italian pastries since 1908. Ferrara's uses only imported spices and no artificial flavorings or preservatives. Ferrara's is famous for its Cannoli Cake, a yellow layer cake soaked in rum with alternating fillings of strawberry, Italian custard, and ricotta creme, all frosted with whipped cream. You can enjoy a slice of Cannoli Cake or any one of Ferrara's assortment of Italian cookies, pastries, and biscotti, along with an espresso or cappuccino, at one of the tables in this historic bakery, which is located on the western edge of the Italian neighborhood on Taylor Street.

Gerhard's Elegant European Desserts

720 North Western Avenue (in Market Square)
Lake Forest
(847) 234-0023

Gerhard's provides traditional European pastries and fabulous decorated cakes to the North Shore, using only the freshest ingredients. (Gerhard's even makes its own granola!) Austrian Linzer torte is one of Gerhard's specialties, as are the European *friandises* (tea cookies). Gerhard's signature cake is his chocolate *marjolaine*, although the dark chocolate mousse cake and the caramel *feuilletine* are also popular favorites. Wedding cakes are custom designed and showcase Gerhard's European training and artistry.

Hellas Pastry Shop

Ravenswood
2627 West Lawrence Avenue
(773) 271-7500

Gus and Toula Spanos provide freshly made, traditional Greek pastries, such as *kouranbiethes* (almond shortbread cookies), *kataifi* (shredded wheat rolls), baklava, and specialty cakes at their shop in the Ravenswood neighborhood.

Kirschbaum's Bakery

825 Burlington Avenue
Western Springs
(708) 246-2894

Kirschbaum's Bakery has been serving the western suburbs for fifty years. Their cakes are among the best anywhere, incredibly light and moist. Kirschbaum's makes traditional bakery products too: doughnuts, danish, coffee cakes, cookies, and cupcakes. They also package miniature pastries and muffins for those who only want to indulge a little.

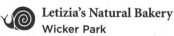

Letizia's Natural Bakery

Wicker Park
2144 West Division Street
(773) 342-1011

Letizia Sorano, a retired teacher from Rome, presides over her bakery/espresso bar/gelateria/café. Sorano uses no bleached flours, artificial flavors, preservatives, or hydrogenated oils in her pastries. Cakes are the specialty of the house, although Sorano also makes muffins, scones, and biscotti, and serves pizza and panini. The interior is homey, with tables for eating, reading the newspaper, catching up with the neighbors, or connecting to the Internet. Weather permitting, the outdoor garden behind the bakery and the sidewalk café in front of the café provide two flower-filled options in which to enjoy your selections. Sorano wants her bakery to be "a place where people can get together, relax, put their feet up . . . while enjoying a great pastry."

Oak Mill Bakery
8012 North Milwaukee Avenue
Niles
(847) 318-6400

Bogna Solak and her crew have established themselves as the Chicago area's best Polish bakery, making everything from fancy tortes and pastries to *paczki* and *babki*. Visit the main location in Niles to sample everything, or check out the stellar selection at either one of the Chicago retail locations.

Other Locations
5635 West Belmont Avenue, Chicago (Belmont Central);
    (773) 237-5799
5747 South Harlem Avenue, Chicago (Garfield Ridge);
    (773) 788-9800

Pasieka Bakery
Avondale
3056 North Milwaukee Avenue
(773) 278-5190

An excellent Polish bakery. Try their *makowiec* (poppy-seed cake), *szarlotka* (apple cake), and their crusty round rye bread.

Pticek & Son Bakery
Garfield Ridge
5523 South Narragansett
(773) 585-5500

Pticek & Son provides traditional Polish/Bohemian/Croatian pastries to the Garfield Ridge neighborhood on the Southwest Side, and the family has been doing so for more than sixty years. This small bakery is filled to capacity on a typical Saturday morning. Sculptured cakes are their specialty; Pticek's will transform your pictures or photos into a computer-

generated three-dimensional model for creation. Not only are Pticek's cakes visually stunning, but they are moist and flavorful.

Everything at Pticek's is outstanding. Their strudels have the flakiest pastry, and their *kolackys* (little sweet pastries with a dollop of fruit, nut, or poppyseed filling) are light, with the proper hint of cheese in the dough. On Fat Tuesday before Lent, they sell approximately a thousand traditional Polish *paczkis* (puffed doughnuts filled with jelly or custard and dusted with powdered sugar). Service and quality are their priorities.

Roeser's Bakery
Humboldt Park
3216 West North Avenue
(773) 489-6900

Four generations of the Roeser family have served the Humboldt Park neighborhood since 1911. A wide variety of specialty cakes are available, as well as coffee cakes, doughnuts, and cookies. The quality and freshness of Roeser's cakes and other baked goods is beyond comparison. Roeser's has successfully weathered the socioeconomic changes that have forced other local bakeries to close their doors. And they have introduced tropical flavors and decorations for their now predominantly Hispanic customers. In an innovative nod to modern technology, Roeser's entertains customers with a television monitor focused on the action in the back of the bakery—you can watch cookies being piped onto baking sheets or cakes being decorated while you wait. Roeser's is a true Chicago treasure.

Sweet Thang
Wicker Park
1921 West North Avenue
(773) 772-4166

French pastries, fruit tarts, cookies, brownies—you name it, Sweet Thang makes it delicious. Pastry chef/owner Bernard Runo studied culinary arts in Paris before opening his bakery in the Wicker Park neighborhood. His mission is "bringing pastry to the masses." Specialty cakes include Black Forest cake, *Sachertorte*, chocolate mousse cakes, and nontraditional mousse flavors like peanut butter, cappuccino, and coconut-pineapple. There are tables for you to enjoy your pastry selections with a cup of coffee.

A Taste of Heaven
Andersonville
1701 West Foster Avenue
(773) 989-0151

A Taste of Heaven is a friendly, homey café in the Andersonville neighborhood, but the desserts are the real stars in this establishment. Their cakes, cookies, muffins, brownies, and other delectables are truly a taste of heaven. Most items are individually portioned; you can buy just a slice of one of their specialty cakes or order up to half a sheet to feed a crowd. A Taste of Heaven also serves breakfast, lunch, and dinner. This is a great place to stop for sweets or a light meal.

Vesecky's Bakery
6634 Cermak Road
Berwyn
(708) 788-4144

Vesecky's Bakery has been producing Czech and Bohemian pastries for seventy-plus years. Senior citizens and immigrant families who appreciate the craftsmanship of the Old World traditions flock to Vesecky's. Apple, cheese, and poppy-seed strudels; Bohemian rye bread; and *vanocka*, a braided buttery loaf of raisin-stuffed dough with slivered almonds on top, are just a few of the favorites from Vesecky's.

WINE & BEER RETAILERS

Bennett Wine
West Loop Gate
802 West Washington Avenue
(312) 274-0488

Are you overwhelmed by warehouse-sized wine stores? Then check out Bennett Wine, a tiny, brand-new boutique wine shop. Although its location is new, the owner has lots of experience; she ran a very successful wine store in Lincoln Park for eighteen years. She is charming and helpful, and has a very discriminating palate, stocking only forty or fifty different wine labels, all priced under $30. The store also has a special tasting bar in the back.

Binny's
Lakeview
3000 North Clark Street
(773) 935-9403

Although Binny's has numerous venues in the Chicagoland area, this Lakeview branch is notable for its location in the Ivanhoe Castle and Catacombs. Although there is no moat or drawbridge to navigate, you will find a very large store. The Catacombs, which once housed a Prohibition-era speakeasy, now house climate-controlled wine-storage lockers that provide safety from light and heat, as well as from Elliot Ness.

Convito Italiano
1515 Sheridan Road
Wilmette
(847) 251-3654

It's worth the drive north up Sheridan Road to Convito Italiano, winding your way past a mind-boggling array of mansions and luxury homes. They have been serving Chicago's North Shore with a fine selection of Italian wines for more than twenty years.

Fine Wine Brokers
Lincoln Square
4621 North Lincoln Avenue
(773) 989-8166

If you find yourself far north of downtown, stop by this shop in the historic Lincoln Square neighborhood. Don't be intimidated by the gruff owner smoking furtively behind the counter; his eyes will light up when you ask for something other than a California chardonnay.

The House of Glunz
Old Town
1206 North Wells Street
(312) 642-3000

A fourth-generation business and Chicago's oldest wine merchant, the House of Glunz was established in 1888 by Louis Glunz. Continuing the beer-and-wine business of his family in Westphalia, Germany, Glunz opened up his shop in the Old Town neighborhood, and that original site is still the home of the House of Glunz.

Most wine shops like to think they are ahead of the curve in finding the next great wine-producing region. While California was making a name for itself around the world in the 1970s, the House of Glunz staff had already been touting California wines for decades, initially deeming them "pretty good" almost a hundred years ago.

During Prohibition the House of Glunz was able to stay afloat by selling sacramental and "medicinal" wines, as well as selling the hardware for home winemaking. Customers at this time often called on Louis Glunz Jr. for his experience and expertise in winemaking. Once Prohibition was repealed, the first barrels of beer to roll back into Chicago were brought in courtesy of the House of Glunz.

If you get a chance to peruse the photos in the store, you will see that the Glunz family did not just import the finished bottled product. Like the French *négociants*, the Glunz family often imported port and sherry by the barrel and then blended and bottled it right in the cellar.

Today the House of Glunz remains a landmark, carrying an abundance of great and off-the-beaten-path wine selections. Three of the best wines I have ever had the pleasure of drinking were purchased there; two were less than $50 (a Côte Rotie and a Coulée de Serrant) and one was less than $15 (a Condrieu Moelleux).

Howard's Wine Cellar
Lakeview
1244 West Belmont Avenue
(773) 248-3766

Step down into this tiny wine cellar/seller (though the shop is larger than it first appears) and you'll be greeted by owner Bob Kovacs, mostly likely with an open bottle or two for you to sample. He'll happily and enthusiastically help you choose just the right bottle for dinner or a gift. Selection is small but well chosen, and you'll enjoy a chat with a passionate wine lover.

Other Location
Wine Seller, 227 South Third Street, Geneva; (630) 232-2130

John Hart Fine Wine, Ltd.
Old Town
363 West Erie Street
(312) 482-9996

John Hart specializes in the sale of fine and rare wines. If you have a collection of rare and pricey wines you would like to unload, they will appraise and/or purchase your wine.

Kuhn's Deli
749 West Golf Road
Des Plaines
(847) 640-0222

Serving the greater Chicago area since 1929, Kuhn's is your one-stop shop for fruit brandies and other traditional German beverages. They also have a great selection of imported and house-made German food items.

Randolph Wine Cellars
West Loop Gate
1415 West Randolph Street
(312) 942-1212

This self-proclaimed "secret wine shop" is just west of the hot Randolph Street dining area, and well worth discovering. Their spacious store offers a selection of wines from winemakers that "put the money in the bottle" rather than spending it on expensive marketing campaigns. Next door to the shop is The Tasting Room (see p. 266), where you can enjoy a selection of wines—whether by tasting portion, flights, glasses, or bottle—as well as a great selection of cheeses and small plates.

Sam's Wines and Spirits
Goose Island
1720 North Marcey Street
(312) 664-4394

Sam's is a massive warehouse of wine, beer, and distilled spirits from all over the world. As you wander awestruck up and down the aisles, the knowledgeable staff is there to guide you to what you are looking for or offer some surprising selections. Although the cavernous building lacks charm, the incredible selection makes it hard to leave without stocking up; make sure you go with a friend who has a truck and a strong back to carry those cases.

Schaefer's
9965 Gross Point Road
Skokie
(847) 673-5711

Schaefer's is one of the North Shore's finest wine stores, with a relatively small but distinctive collection. It also features a good variety of gourmet cheeses.

Taste
Wicker Park
1922 West North Avenue
(773) 276-8000

A hip Wicker Park wine shop that proudly advertises JUICY WINES/STINKY CHEESES on their sign. Inside you will find a wide variety of ready-to-drink wines at reasonable prices. Wines are organized from lightest to fullest bodied; the kitschy descriptions above the wine shelves provide further assistance. And as the name implies, this is a great place to taste many juicy wines and sample stinky cheeses while mingling with the indie-rock-loving staff.

Whole Foods Market
River North
30 West Huron Street
(312) 932-9600

Amid the organic produce and New Age holistic therapies, you will find a decent selection of imported and microbrewed beers and hard ciders from around the globe. A small but broad-reaching and thoughtfully assembled collection of wines rounds out this national chain's spirits offering.

Other Locations
3300 North Ashland Avenue, Chicago (Lakeview);
   (773) 244-4200
1000 West North Avenue, Chicago (Lincoln Park);
   (312) 587-0648

NEIGHBORHOOD & SUBURB INDEX

NEIGHBORHOODS

SUBURBS

ALPHABETICAL INDEX

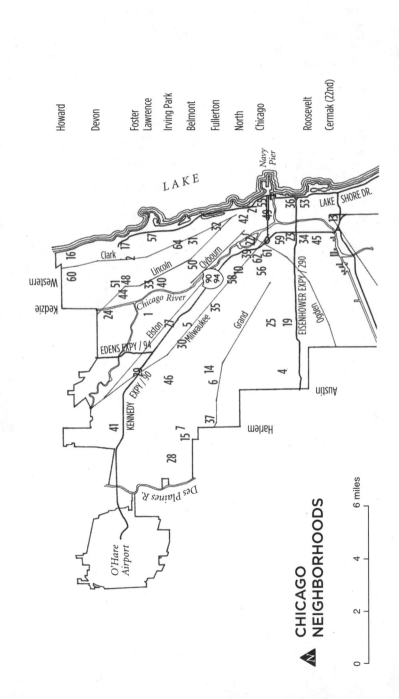

Howard

Devon

Foster
Lawrence
Irving Park
Belmont
Fullerton
North
Chicago

Roosevelt
Cermak (22nd)

LAKE

Navy
Pier

LAKE SHORE DR.

**CHICAGO
NEIGHBORHOODS**

N

0   2   4   6 miles

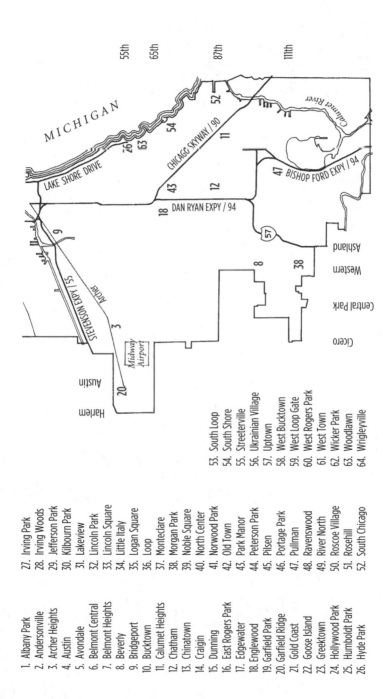

1. Albany Park
2. Andersonville
3. Archer Heights
4. Austin
5. Avondale
6. Belmont Central
7. Belmont Heights
8. Beverly
9. Bridgeport
10. Bucktown
11. Calumet Heights
12. Chatham
13. Chinatown
14. Craigin
15. Dunning
16. East Rogers Park
17. Edgewater
18. Englewood
19. Garfield Park
20. Garfield Ridge
21. Gold Coast
22. Goose Island
23. Greektown
24. Hollywood Park
25. Humboldt Park
26. Hyde Park

27. Irving Park
28. Irving Woods
29. Jefferson Park
30. Kilbourn Park
31. Lakeview
32. Lincoln Park
33. Lincoln Square
34. Little Italy
35. Logan Square
36. Loop
37. Monteclare
38. Morgan Park
39. Noble Square
40. North Center
41. Norwood Park
42. Old Town
43. Park Manor
44. Peterson Park
45. Pilsen
46. Portage Park
47. Pullman
48. Ravenswood
49. River North
50. Roscoe Village
51. Rosehill
52. South Chicago

53. South Loop
54. South Shore
55. Streeterville
56. Ukrainian Village
57. Uptown
58. West Bucktown
59. West Loop Gate
60. West Rogers Park
61. West Town
62. Wicker Park
63. Woodlawn
64. Wrigleyville

◤ CHICAGO SUBURBS

1. Arlington Heights
2. Bellwood
3. Berwyn
4. Blue Island
5. Bolingbrook
6. Buffalo Grove
7. Burbank
8. Burr Ridge
9. Cicero
10. Deerfield
11. Des Plaines
12. Downers Grove
13. Elmwood Park
14. Evanston
15. Evergreen Park
16. Forest Park
17. Galewood
18. Geneva
19. Glen Ellyn
20. Glencoe
21. Glenview
22. Harwood Heights
23. Highland Park
24. Highwood
25. Hinsdale
26. Homewood

LAKE

EDENS EXPY.

TRI-STATE TOLL-WAY

NORTH WEST TOLL-WAY

O'Hare
Airport

94

294

90

53

290

120

31

90

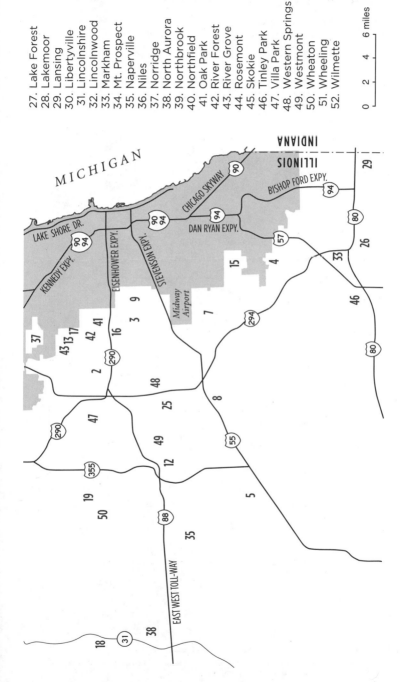

27. Lake Forest
28. Lakemoor
29. Lansing
30. Libertyville
31. Lincolnshire
32. Lincolnwood
33. Markham
34. Mt. Prospect
35. Naperville
36. Niles
37. Norridge
38. North Aurora
39. Northbrook
40. Northfield
41. Oak Park
42. River Forest
43. River Grove
44. Rosemont
45. Skokie
46. Tinley Park
47. Villa Park
48. Western Springs
49. Westmont
50. Wheaton
51. Wheeling
52. Wilmette

0   2   4   6 miles

MICHIGAN

INDIANA
ILLINOIS

LAKE SHORE DR.
KENNEDY EXPY.
EISENHOWER EXPY.
STEVENSON EXPY.
CHICAGO SKYWAY
DAN RYAN EXPY.
BISHOP FORD EXPY.
EAST WEST TOLL-WAY

Midway Airport

WE INVITE YOU TO JOIN OUR TABLE AND BECOME A MEMBER OF SLOW FOOD USA

As a Slow Food member, you'll become an active participant in a growing network of individuals dedicated to improving food in this country.

A one-year membership entitles you to:
- A personal membership card
- Four issues of the international magazine, *Slow*
- Four issues of *the Snail*
- Invitations to attend all local, regional, national, and international events
- Discounts on all Slow Food publications and merchandise

To become a member, please visit us online at www.slowfoodusa.org. You can also sign up by faxing this completed form to 212-966-8652.

Telephone: 212-965-5640
E-mail: info@slowfoodusa.org

Membership type:
- ❑ Individual - $60
- ❑ Couple - $75
- ❑ Student - $30 (does not include *Slow*)

This is a:
- ❑ New Membership
- ❑ Renewal
- ❑ Gift

Is there a particular convivium you would like to join?

❑ Yes, place me in the _____ convivium.

❑ No, place me in the convivium closest to me.

Last name(s) _____

First name(s) _____

Organization (if applicable) _____

Occupation _____

Street Address _____

City _____ State _____ ZIP code _____

Daytime telephone _____ Evening telephone _____

Fax _____ E-mail _____

Please send me *Slow* in:
❑ English ❑ Italian ❑ German ❑ French ❑ Japanese

I would like to make an additional donation to Slow Food USA to support its many projects in the amount of $ _____.

I would like to make an additional donation to the International Slow Food Foundation for Biodiversity to support its efforts in the Third World in the amount of $ _____.

Method of Payment:

❑ Check ❑ Visa ❑ American Express ❑ Mastercard

|__|__|__|__|__|__|__|__|__|__|__|__|__|__|__|__| Exp. Date |__|__|__|__|

Total Amount $ _____

Cardholder name _____

Signature _____

Slow Food USA® is tax-exempt under section 501 (c)3 of the Internal Revenue Code. All donations are tax deductible, except for $15 allocated to publications.

MUSCAT LOVE

MUSCAT is the name for a family of grapes with a perfume like flowers and ripe fruit. They are eaten as fresh fruit or dried into raisins or made into dessert wines. The most common Muscat varieties are the *Muscat of Alexandria* and the *Muscat Blanc (Muscat Canelli)*. Some other Muscat varieties, which are made into wine, are: *Muscat Ottonel, Moscato Giallo*, and the *Moscato Rosa*.

QUADY WINERY in Madera, California pioneered making dessert wines from the unusual *Orange Muscat (Moscato fior d'Arancio)* and *Black Muscat (Muscat Hamburg)* varieties. The first wine from the *Orange Muscat*

was named **Essensia** because it was felt that it contained the essence (an orange-apricot aroma and flavor) of the grape. **Elysium** (from the Greek word for Heaven) made from the *Black Muscat* has an aroma of roses. **Essensia** and **Elysium** are best drunk after dinner with or instead of dessert and (especially **Elysium**) with cheese.

ELECTRA (Orange Muscat) and RED ELECTRA (Black Muscat) were named after the electric like feeling on the end

of the tongue caused by a small amount of carbon dioxide gas, a remnant of the cold slow fermentation. Quady refers to these wines as **Picnic Wines**. They have only 4-5% alcohol and a soft feeling in the mouth.

~~~~~~~~~~~~~~~

Quady Winery is a proud member of the
Madera, California Slow Food Convivium
Quady Winery, P. O. Box 728, Madera, California 93639
559 673-8060   www.quadywinery.com.

THE LONG ISLAND CONVIVIUM
www.slowfoodlongisland.org

Salutes "America's Breadbasket" on the publication of The Slow Food Chicago Restaurant Guide!

Congratulations from your Partners in the Slow Food Movement:

The East End of Long Island, America's First Breadbasket

The Great Peconic Bay, one of America's premier seafood producing regions and home of the Slow Food Ark-Protected Peconic Bay Scallop

The Long Island Wine Country

And these proud supporters of Slow Food principles:

Amagansett Wines & Spirits, *Amagansett, NY*
www.amagansettwine.com

The American Hotel, *Sag Harbor, NY*
www.theamericanhotel.com

Bedell Cellars, *Cutchogue, NY*
www.bedellcellars.com

Channing Daughters Winery, *Bridgehampton, NY*
www.channingdaughters.com

Dairyland USA, *Bronx, NY*
www.dairylandusa.com

Le Clos Therese, *Aquebogue, NY*
www.lctwinery.com

The Lenz Winery, *Peconic, NY*
www.lenzwine.com

Paumanok Vineyards, *Aquebogue, NY*
www.paumanok.com

Wolffer Estate, *Sagaponack, NY*
www.wolffer.com

For a map with all member locations go to:
www.slowfoodlongisland.org

AMAGANSETT
WINE & SPIRITS

Comtesse
Thérèse

THE AMERICAN HOTEL

LENZ

NORTH FORK · LONG ISLAND

BEDELL
CELLARS

PAUMANOK
Vineyards

North Fork of Long Island

Wölffer Estate
Vineyard and Stable

CHANNING
DAUGHTERS

Dairyland
The Chefs' Warehouse ®